DATE		

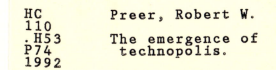

THE EMERGENCE OF TECHNOPOLIS

The Emergence of Technopolis
KNOWLEDGE-INTENSIVE TECHNOLOGIES AND REGIONAL DEVELOPMENT

Robert W. Preer

PRAEGER

New York
Westport, Connecticut
London

Library of Congress Cataloging-in-Publication Data

Preer, Robert W.
 The emergence of technopolis : knowledge-intensive technologies
and regional development / Robert W. Preer.
  p. cm.
 Includes bibliographical references and index.
 ISBN 0-275-94090-X (alk. paper)
 1. High technology industries—United States—Location.
2. Information technology—United States. 3. United States—
Economic conditions—1981- —Regional disparities. I. Title.
HC110.H53P74 1992
338.6'042—dc20 91-30616

British Library Cataloguing in Publication Data is available.

Library of Congress Catalog Card Number: 91-30616
ISBN: 0-275-94090-X

First published in 1992

Praeger Publishers, One Madison Avenue, New York, NY 10010
An imprint of Greenwood Publishing Group, Inc.

Printed in the United States of America

∞™

The paper used in this book complies with the
Permanent Paper Standard issued by the National
Information Standards Organization (Z39.48-1984).

10 9 8 7 6 5 4 3 2 1

TO ADELE

Contents

Preface

The extraordinary advances in information technology and related fields in the latter half of the twentieth century have brought sudden and far-reaching changes to societies throughout the world. The technological revolution not only has created new products such as fax machines, digital watches and notebook-sized computers, it also has changed the way we do things—how we manufacture cars, make music, learn foreign languages, and write books, to name a few. All of society's complex systems, from transportation to medicine to education to defense, have been altered in fundamental ways.

One of the processes that has changed—and the one that is the focus of this book—is regional economic development. A few decades ago, economists could feel comfortable stating that the determinants of growth were land, labor, capital, and a few other miscellaneous factors. Today, a consensus is emerging that the most important factor of production in advanced industrial societies is knowledge. The regions in which knowledge is created and then transformed into commercial products and processes are the ones prospering in this new competitive environment.

Beyond this general point, though, little can be said with certainty. Global geographic restructuring is far from over. In the 1960s and 1970s, regions that had been the geographic centers of the previous industrial revolution collapsed and new high technology districts emerged. In the late 1980s and early 1990s, some high-technology regions experienced sharp declines. As the technological revolution unfolds, further shifts in the fortunes of regions no doubt lie ahead.

Writing a book on such a dynamic topic is a perilous undertaking. One must stay abreast of rapidly changing events, while avoiding getting caught up in the drama of the moment. This book underwent numerous revisions as the deadline for publication approached. I have tried to maintain a sense of historical perspective while making the work as up-to-date as possible. The passage of time and progress of events will reveal whether the conclusions here are valid.

I am deeply grateful to Ishwer C. Ojha of Boston University, who encouraged me to undertake this project. His wisdom and guidance were invaluable from beginning to end. I am also indebted to Terry MacDougall, who provided valuable insights and encouraged me to expand the original study into a book. Many others at Boston University—faculty, students, and staff—provided support and helpful advice in the course of this project.

During part of the time I was researching this book, I worked for former Massachusetts state Senator William B. Golden. His leadership and vision were a source of inspiration. Many others with whom I worked in state government, from both the legislature and the administration, provided valuable information and insights. Long-time friend and colleague Patricia Nealon reviewed part of the manuscript and made important suggestions.

I cannot begin to express my appreciation to my wife, Adele Foy. She provided support of all kinds—emotional, editorial, technical, and financial. My early research led me in a number of very different directions, and she helped me pull things together into a coherent form. She read the manuscript with the eye of a professional copy editor, which she happens to be. Writing this book was a long, stressful, and often isolating process, and without her understanding and encouragement it would not have been possible.

About the time I began working on this project in earnest, my son, Sam, was born, and my daughter, Lily, turned two. They provided me with a good excuse to retreat from the out-of-home work force long enough to write this book. Although they often were unhappy and confused when I had to closet myself in my study for long periods, their capacity to forgive was limitless.

Chapter 1

Introduction

Progress does not follow a straight line; the future is not a mere projection
of trends in the present. Rather, it is revolutionary. . . . It overturns the
conventional wisdom of the present, which often conceals or ignores the
clues to the future.

An Wang, *Lessons*, p. 2.

PUBLIC POLICY AND THE TECHNOPOLIS

By the early 1970s, something important clearly was happening in Santa
Clara County in Northern California. The fledgling semiconductor industry had taken off, and almost overnight the local economy and landscape
had been transformed. Fields that only a few years earlier had grown fruit
trees sprouted prosperous high-technology businesses. Silicon Valley, as
a local journalist labeled it, had become a land of enormous wealth, a fact
readily apparent in its white-hot real estate market and trademark upscale
lifestyle.

On the other side of the continent, an even more remarkable transition
was getting under way. The stagnant industrial region of Eastern
Massachusetts was on the verge of rebirth. Most of the mainstays of the
state's economy—textiles, machine tools, and other traditional manufacturers—had either gone out of business or moved away. But a number of
small companies, most of which were involved in computers, began to
appear on the highway that circled Boston. The Route 128 high-technology firms, some of them housed in renovated mills, would drive the

Massachusetts economy from a 12 percent unemployment rate in 1975—one and a half times the national average—to virtually full employment in less than a decade. The state's governor would cite the "Massachusetts miracle" as the basis for his run for the U.S. presidency in 1988.

The emergence of Silicon Valley and Route 128 represented a new kind of regional economic development. The geography of older industrial complexes had been determined largely by the availability of disciplined labor and proximity to raw materials, energy supplies, and markets. The source of growth in Silicon Valley and Route 128, however, was knowledge. Organized research had created new knowledge, which was then turned into commercial products. These products quickly found large global markets. New industries sprang up overnight. Because the new products were applied in virtually all economic sectors, the industries of Route 128 and Silicon Valley became the core industries of the national and global economies. The new high-technology regions eventually acquired a name: technopolis.[1]

The Silicon Valley and Route 128 success stories captured the attention of the world. Their attraction was enhanced by their emergence against a backdrop of sharp economic decline in much of the rest of the developed world. Particularly hard hit during the 1960s and 1970s were the once-prosperous industrial regions and large cities of Europe and North America. The great U.S. manufacturing belt became known as the Rust Belt for its deteriorating factories. Once powerful industrial labor unions in these regions were devastated. New York City nearly went bankrupt. Punctuating the distress of these areas were the oil shocks and recessions of the 1970s and the deep recession of the early 1980s.

The technopolis, however, seemed to promise fast and propulsive growth, which would be barely disturbed by national and global economic downturns (Thompson 1987, 1988; Mead and Ramsay 1985). It produced high-paying jobs. Further, the industries of the technopolis seemed not to have the damaging environmental side-effects of traditional manufacturing, such as high energy consumption and pollution.[2] To make the prospects even more enticing, high technology was not bound to the immobile production factors that had anchored older industries.

Policy makers from Tokyo to Paris to Philadelphia hurriedly developed strategies they hoped would duplicate the experiences of Silicon Valley and Route 128. Since the technopolis was a different kind of economic development, different kinds of economic development strategies were needed. In the late 1970s and early 1980s, a new generation of regional development policies emerged simultaneously throughout the world. Instead of trying to attract industry by promising low taxes, relaxed regulation, and cheap labor and land, policy makers developed small-business incubators, venture capital funds and science parks. Investments in university science departments replaced "smokestack chasing."

No one has calculated how much money has been spent on technopolis policies, but it is surely in the tens of billions of dollars. In 1984, the U.S. Congressional Office of Technology Assessment identified more than 150 high-technology initiatives by state government alone (Office of Technology Assessment 1984). Britain embarked on the construction of more than two dozen science parks (Sunman 1987; Lowe 1985). Japan began implementing a multibillion dollar, twenty-year program to build research cities throughout the country (Tatsuno 1986; Masser 1990). The quest to create the technopolis even engaged some policy makers in the Third World (Fong 1986; Jingyuan et al. 1988).

What have been the effects of these policies? New Silicon Valleys obviously have not sprouted all over the world, but have more subtle changes in regional economies occurred as a result of these policies? Have some policies performed better than others? Why did technopolis policies function the way that they did?

This study attempts to answer these questions. It approaches the task from several directions. First, it presents a comparative survey and analysis of global technopolis policies (Chapter 2). This policy overview is needed before the analysis can move on to the more complex questions of how and why policies have functioned. Second, a theoretical model is advanced to explain how a technopolis forms (Chapter 3). Using this model and empirical evidence from a number of secondary sources, conclusions are drawn about the effectiveness of various technopolis policies (Chapter 4). To illustrate and test the model, case studies are then presented of the Route 128 and Silicon Valley technopolises and the role of policy in their development (Chapters 5 and 6). Finally, lessons are drawn from the preceding analysis and suggestions offered for the most effective directions in which policy could proceed (Chapter 7).

In the past decade, a significant theoretical literature has emerged on high-technology regional development.[3] This literature has focused on the process of high-technology development and why it has located where it has. Many studies also have been published during this time describing particular high-technology regions.[4] A smaller number of studies have identified and evaluated technopolis policies (Miller and Côté 1987; Smilor, Kozmetsky, and Gibson 1988a; Allen and Levine 1986). However, there have been few attempts to link policy with both theory and empirical research. Accomplishing this task is the principal goal of this work.

SPATIAL IMPACT OF THE INFORMATION TECHNOLOGY REVOLUTION

A recurrent theme and fundamental assumption of this analysis is that the world is now experiencing a great technological revolution that is as profound and far-reaching as the industrial revolution or the neolithic revolution. During the industrial revolution, machine power replaced muscle power. In the information/knowledge revolution, machine power replaces human mental and sensory capabilities. The technological advances that are driving this great change are occurring, for the most part, in convergent information technologies: microelectronics, computers, software, advanced telecommunications and electronic equipment. Advances in one area of information technology often produce synergistic progress in the others (Arnold and Guy 1986). These changes have dramatically increased the speed at which information is transmitted and processed.

The technological revolution has had a major impact on the economic realm. Manufacturing has been transformed. The application of advanced information technology has made possible flexible manufacturing systems, just-in-time, and other productivity enhancing processes. The result has been a dramatic shrinking of manufacturing employment, accompanied by an expansion of productive capacity. (The same phenomenon occurred earlier with the mechanization of agriculture.) At the same time, services for both businesses and individuals have expanded significantly. As information handling becomes increasingly the main activity in both manufacturing and services, the distinction between the two sectors is becoming blurred.

The technological revolution has been to this point an information revolution, in the sense that most of the advances have resulted from the automation of simple information processing (Brotchie, Hall, and Newton 1987). The second stage of the technological transformation will be a knowledge revolution, in which human reasoning and expert knowledge are automated. This involves the development of artificial intelligence, which is slowly and painstakingly finding uses in a variety of areas. The widespread application of artificial intelligence will have far-reaching consequences about which one can only speculate.

Although the geography of the information technology revolution is still unfolding, rapid shifts already have occurred. Information technologies have facilitated the dispersal of production, which previously was concentrated in a few central locations in advanced countries, to national and world peripheries. At the same time, new technology has made possible the centralization of control in ever-larger transnational corporations.

Another fundamental shift in economic geography has been the decline of regions based on the technologies of the industrial revolution and the rise of regions based on the technologies of the information or knowledge revolution. The collapse of the older industrial areas and the emergence of the technopolis were part of the same process—the shift in the technological bases of modern economies. The technopolis emerged when and where it did because of this technological revolution.

REGIONAL SPECIALIZATION AND THE
SHIFTING FORTUNES OF THE TECHNOPOLIS

Technopolises, in various stages of development, are found all over the developed world.[5] They are diverse in composition and appearance. Technopolises tend to have characteristic styles, which reflect a unique set of community values (Scott 1988c). Each has its own distinctive educational, cultural, and business institutions. Most importantly, each technopolis has a core technology or set of technologies. This specialized nature of technopolises explains the differences among high-technology regions in responding to global economic and technological change.

The specialized industries of technopolises have in common a reliance on advanced scientific and engineering knowledge (Scott and Storper 1987). Within that framework, however, they are many and varied. The most important ones are semiconductors (hence the countless Silicon Valleys, Gulches, Glens, and so on) and computers. Others are biotechnology, software, aerospace, defense systems, electronic equipment, advanced materials, and pharmaceuticals. The core industry of Route 128 is minicomputers. For Minneapolis-St. Paul, it is supercomputers; for Silicon Valley, semiconductors and microcomputers; for Orange County, aerospace and electronics; for Salt Lake City, biotechnology; and for Research Triangle, microelectronics.

Precisely why particular technologies cluster is not well understood. Innovations often occur in more than one location at about the same time; largely because of different environmental conditions, however, commercial exploitation flourishes in a much smaller number of places.[6] Powerful agglomeration advantages develop in the specialized technopolis. Supplier and service firms arise to serve the growing industry. In many instances, firms that represent downstream markets join the cluster. A specialized labor market forms, which reinforces the growth of the industry (which, in turn, attracts more specialized labor). Local educational and research institutions collaborate with industry to develop programs to meet the needs of the industry. Universities thus develop national and international reputations for excellence in the specialized field of the regional industry.

In mature technopolises, diversification of the industrial base occurs. This is a natural consequence of the agglomeration process and linkages among certain technologies. In Silicon Valley, semiconductors led to video games, which led to computers, which led to software. The large technical labor force attracts other industries that demand skills similar to those needed by the core industry. In some instances, service industries that arose to meet the demands of local industry find export markets and become an independent source of growth for the technopolis. Universities and other research institutions sometimes broaden their areas of specialization and generate growth in new fields.

Nevertheless, a reliance on one or a handful of core technologies is strong even in the older technopolises. This specialization heightens the sensitivity of the technopolis to outside forces. Although the highs are very high, the lows also are very low. An industry slump or national economic downturn can send a once-soaring high-technology region into a tailspin. A technopolis that depends on defense spending for research and development funding or procurement is vulnerable to cuts or shifts in military budgets. Rapid contraction in a core industry of a technopolis can have a dramatic effect on supplier and service industries, and the entire region can slide into recession.

The most striking contemporary example of this is the decline in the Route 128 technopolis in the late 1980s and early 1990s (Putka 1989; Gold 1989). Although Route 128 is one of the strongest and most diversified technopolises in the world, it still relies heavily on minicomputers. In the late 1980s, minicomputers became caught in a squeeze between powerful mainframes and networked desktop computers. The entire industry went into a slump that battered the largest and most important high-technology companies in Massachusetts. Digital Equipment Corporation, the company that founded the minicomputer industry and for years Massachusetts' largest private employer, laid off thousands of workers in its facilities in Massachusetts and around the world. Prime Computer, which was acquired by a Wall Street investment firm after fighting off a hostile takeover bid by a New York financier, laid off 2,500 employees in 1990 alone. The large Boston-based computer division of Honeywell Inc., which was acquired by the French-based Bull HN Information Systems, shed thousands of jobs in Massachusetts in a series of layoffs. The most dramatic reversals probably were those of Wang Laboratories, one of the first and brightest success stories of Route 128, and Data General, the high flying company made famous by Tracy

Kidder's Pulitzer Prize-winning *Soul of a New Machine.* In the late 1980s, Wang lost hundreds of millions of dollars and eliminated 10,000 jobs—nearly a third of its work force worldwide—amid recurring rumors that the faltering company would be snapped up and stripped of its assets in a takeover. Legendary founder An Wang died of cancer in 1990, a year after his son Frederick Wang resigned as president after failing to revive the firm. Data General, once the fastest growing company in the computer industry, closed plants, sold assets, and slashed its work force from a high of 17,700 in 1985 to 9,500 in 1990. The board of directors fired Edson D. de Castro, the technical and entrepreneurial genius who founded and built the company, replacing him with a financial specialist who had had no experience in the computer industry before joining the firm. By early 1991, an estimated 14,000 employees in the minicomputer industry in Massachusetts had lost their jobs.

The sudden downturn in minicomputers coincided with a slump in Boston's financial services, another core industry of the regional economy. Suddenly the bottom seemed to fall out beneath the real estate, construction, and banking industries, all of which had expanded rapidly and, many now believe, recklessly in the early and mid-1980s. The collapse of a number of small banks was followed by the failure of one of the largest financial institutions in the region, the Bank of New England, which was taken over and sold by the Federal Deposit Insurance Corporation. By April 1991, the unemployment rate had climbed to just under 10 percent. A national recession in the early 1990s crippled the region's prospects for a quick recovery, and the specialized nature of the technopolis intensified the impact of the recession. The customers of Massachusetts' high-technology products are mainly other producers (Dorfman 1982). As businesses elsewhere began to struggle, becoming less reliable customers, Route 128 firms lacked consumer markets to cushion the fall. In contrast, some of Silicon Valley's industries—microcomputers, in particular—do serve consumer markets. Thus Silicon Valley has been less severely affected than Route 128 by national economic downturns.

Route 128 is a large, vital technopolis that, despite its weaknesses, possesses the resources to recover from its slump. Diversification has occurred, although many of the smaller industries and technologies—software, biotechnology, supercomputers, instruments, environmental services, materials, and others—have yet to achieve the prominence of minicomputers. Also, despite their woes, the minicomputer companies have not vanished. Most have restructured their work forces and product lines. And while further shake-outs are likely, mid-sized computer makers will remain an important component of the regional economy for some time to come. Seen from the heights of the "miracle" years of the mid-1980s, Massachusetts' situation in the 1990s appeared bleak indeed, but compared with most resource-based economies and traditional manufacturing regions, Massachusetts' predicament was neither desperate nor unique. Even the troubled real estate industry saw nothing like the collapse that occurred in the oil-producing areas of the Southwest in the 1980s. In the volatile external environment of the late twentieth century, the Route 128 experience demonstrates the dangers that lie ahead for all regions, especially those that possess a weaker and less diversified industrial base.

HIGH TECHNOLOGY AND POLICY

Technological progress is neither predetermined nor inevitable. The interaction of economic, political, and social institutions shapes the pace and direction of technological change (Michalski 1989). The importance of government in technology development has been heightened during the course of the information/knowledge revolution. After World War II, governments began to influence technology development through education policies, support for research and development, macroeconomic management, trade policy, and defense policy (Rosenberg 1982). During the industrial revolution, governments provided early markets for some products, and they also built much of the necessary infrastructure. However, the central role of government in the economy and the commitment of vast public resources for technology development are unique to this new industrial age.

Public policies also have shaped the global geography of high-technology industry. The electronics industries that arose during and after World War II were centered in the United States because of massive expenditures of government money for research and development and procurement (Hall and Preston 1988). Similarly, Japanese postwar industrial policy directed that country's reemergence as an industrial power and as a leader in high-technology products and processes (Johnson 1982).

Although the challenge of fostering high-technology development at the regional level is new for government, it is nonetheless important. National as well as regional economies depend on the innovation that occurs in high-technology regions (Florida and Kenney 1990a, 1990b). The communities, regions, and nations that grow and develop in this new era will be those that have taken an active part in the process and discovered ways to turn technological change to their advantage.

NOTES

1. Tatsuno (1986) credits the mayor of the Japanese city of Kurume with coining the term in the 1970s. Smilor, Kozmetsky, and Gibson (1988b) were the first to offer a precise definition: "the modern city-state linking technology and economic development" (p. xvii).

2. This, like many of the overly optimistic assumptions about high-technology development, has proven to be false; witness, for example, contaminated water supplies and increased cancers associated with the production of electronic components.

3. For surveys, see Thompson 1989; Malecki 1989; Rees 1989; Malecki and Nijkamp 1988; Clark 1988; Daniels 1988; and Malecki 1983.

4. Silicon Valley was the most examined (Rogers and Larsen 1984; Malone 1985; Hanson 1982), but major studies also were published on Britain's M-4 corridor west of London (Hall et al. 1987; Breheny and McQuaid 1987), North Carolina's Research Triangle (Whittington 1985a), and Route 128 (Lampe 1988). One national survey and analysis of high-technology regions in the United States was conducted (Markusen, Hall, and Glasmeier 1986), although it is now outdated. A number of other studies exist on the location of high-technology industries within nations, including Canada (Britton 1987), France (Pottier 1987), and Japan (Nishioka and Takeuchi 1987).

5. No comprehensive listing of technopolises worldwide exists. Tatsuno (1986) identifies forty technopolises in the United States, while Rogers and Larsen (1984) list twelve (see Appendix A). Both of these compilations are impressionistic and do not use rigorous or operational definitions of a technopolis. Among the regions commonly identified as technopolises outside the United States are London's M-4 corridor, Munich/Silicon Bavaria, Scotland's Silicon Glen, Southern Ontario in Canada, and France's Scientific City and Sophia-Antipolis.

6. The most obvious example is that of semiconductors, which were invented almost simultaneously in laboratories in Dallas, Phoenix, and Santa Clara County, California. Largely because its environment was so favorable for innovation, Silicon Valley became the center of the industry.

Chapter 2

Technopolis Policies

In the past decade, policies designed to create technopolises have prolif-erated. Governments, universities, businesses, and various private groups have pursued a broad range of strategies. They have built science parks, set up business incubators, invested in research universities, established venture capital funds, and formed all manner of public-private partnerships. The technopolis has become the "economic holy grail" of development planners: "industrial renaissance through high-technology job creation" (Hall 1985, p. vii).

Technopolis policies are a global phenomenon. They have emerged in places as diverse as the American Midwest, the French Riviera, central Scotland, and the newly industrializing countries of East Asia.

This chapter examines these policies in a comparative framework. First, the origins of these policies are identified. The study proceeds by describing the policies themselves in some detail. Next, the manner in which different societies have used technopolis policies is described. A comparative analysis of the main features of technopolis policies is then presented.

ORIGINS OF TECHNOPOLIS POLICIES

The technopolis policies of today have their antecedents in policies de-veloped by a handful of innovators in the United States in the early post-World War II years. Silicon Valley, the home of the first modern tech-nopolis, was also where the first modern technopolis policy was developed. Frederick Terman, a Stanford University professor now known as the "godfather of Silicon Valley," created the first university science park in the world. In 1948, he leased portions of land owned by Stanford to graduate students and faculty who were setting up high-technology businesses. The firms in the park were to become the core of the early explosive growth of Silicon Valley.

Another pioneer was Ralph Flanders, a president of the Federal Reserve Bank of Boston and a U.S. senator. Flanders saw the need to revitalize the New England economy by boosting entrepreneurship (Jacobs 1969). In 1946, he founded American Research and Development, a venture capital firm that was the first lender to bankroll Boston's emerging high-technology firms. Boston's conservative bankers then were afraid of investing in the region's new science-based firms. American Research and Development and its followers provided the capital that would fuel New England's economic revival.

Also in the vanguard of technopolis policies was Governor Luther Hodges of North Carolina. In the 1950s, Hodges began laying the groundwork that would lead to the construction of Research Triangle Park, which would become the largest planned science park in the United States. The 6,700-acre park is home to more than fifty private and government research facilities. If Hodges had not moved to upgrade North Carolina's three major universities (Duke University, North Carolina University, and North Carolina State University) the development that occurred at Research Triangle could very well have located elsewhere (Whittington 1985b).

High-technology development policies spread in the United States in the 1960s and early 1970s. In 1967, twenty-three colleges and universities founded University City Science Center in Philadelphia. Two years later, the research center became the home of the country's first small-business incubator. By 1985, University City Science Center housed eighty organizations employing more than 5,000 people.

The ideas behind these U.S. programs made their way to Europe in the late 1960s. Pierre Laffitte, former director of the Ecole des Mines in Paris, one of France's top educational institutions, created the *technopole* concept after a visit to Silicon Valley. He was a leader in the founding in 1969 of Sophia-Antipolis, which would become the largest science park in Europe. In 1970, Cambridge University established Cambridge Science Park, which has become the largest and most successful science park in Britain and part of a major regional high-technology cluster. Japan began planning its first unofficial technopolis, Tsukuba Science City, in 1963. Originally designed to relieve urban congestion in Tokyo,

Tsukuba has grown to a city of 150,000 and is home to a major university and many government research institutes. By 1980, when Tsukuba was completed, the government had spent $5.5 billion on the development.

In the 1980s, technopolis policies snowballed. The U.S. Congressional Office of Technology Assessment identified 153 state government high-technology initiatives in 1984 (Office of Technology Assessment 1984). In 1986, the National Governors' Association estimated that states had spent $450 million on high-technology development (National Governors' Association 1986). A 1971 survey found eighty-one science parks in the United States; a decade later, their numbers had nearly doubled (Minshall 1984). The Minnesota Office of Science and Technology in 1988 counted forty-four state technology programs nationwide that spent a combined $550 million a year (D. Brown 1989).

In Europe, a similar surge in technopolis policies occurred. In the 1970s, Britain had only three science parks. By 1985, ten more were established, seven were under construction, and eight were in the advanced planning stages (Sunman 1987). In 1980, Germany had no science parks; in 1985, it had eighteen (Williams 1987).

STRATEGIES

Technopolis policies range in scale from the formation of an informal task force to the construction of entirely new cities. The policies sometimes start out small and grow large. In many cases they have evolved into something very different from their original concept. They are often part of a larger policy milieu that includes programs dealing with issues of regional equality, international competitiveness, environmental protection, and national defense.

Science Parks

In the early 1980s, George Low, president of Rensselaer Polytechnic Institute (RPI), concluded that New York's capital region could no longer be sustained by the big industrial firms that had dominated the regional economy during the first half of the century. These firms, which had been central to the growth of RPI, had either moved or gone out of business. Low decided that high technology held the most promise for RPI and the region.

In 1981, the institute invested several million dollars of its endowment in the development of Rensselaer Technology Park. RPI owned 100 acres of pasture and woodland five miles south of the campus that would become the park site. The school built the infrastructure and leased lots to businesses. Firms built their own facilities under strict guidelines set down by RPI. On its own, the school built several multitenant buildings, which are leased on a short-term basis. The park now has thirty-four businesses, which employ 350 people (Abetti, Le Maistre, and Wacholder 1988).

The history of Rensselaer Technology Park illustrates many of the features of science parks as technopolis strategies. The central role of the university, support from key government and civic leaders, infrastructure development, a rural setting, and strict controls on the use of land all have been characteristics of science parks around the world.

There is no accepted set of definitions that distinguishes a science park from a research park or a technology park or knowledge center. In practice, the terms are used interchangeably (Macdonald 1987a; Sunman 1987). In France they are called *technopoles*; in Germany, innovation centers and technology centers; in Belgium, research parks; and in the Netherlands and Britain, science parks. The precise number of science parks in the world or in specific countries is difficult to assess because the figures grew so rapidly during the 1980s. In 1989, the journal *Site Selection* counted 426 science parks worldwide, with 230 in the United States, 49 in Britain, 43 in France, 23 in Canada, and 14 in Australia (Conway 1989).

Science parks are often collaborative efforts involving universities and local governments. In Europe, local governments have initiated most science parks, although universities play an important role (Sunman 1987; *OECD Observer* 1987). At the very least, most science parks are built in close proximity to universities. Some science parks have been established as commercial, for-profit developments.

University connections are considered important to the success of science parks because of the flow of personnel and ideas between the two institutions. The goal of many science parks is to provide a setting in which ideas developed in the university can be translated into commercial products. University students provide a labor pool for companies in the park. Even when the ties between the university and the science park are weak, the presence of the university—especially if it is an institution with a reputation for excellence—will draw companies because of the associated prestige.

Not all science parks are linked to a university, however. France's Sophia-Antipolis, the largest science park in Europe, has no university affiliation or ties to an existing industrial base (Laffitte 1988). The park started out as essentially a non-profit real estate operation, initiated by a public-private partnership, that sold its desirable location on the French Riviera to multinational firms seeking sites for their research facilities. Eventually the park became an attraction in its own right.

Science parks are typically governed by a board made up of representatives of the public and private sector organizers. The board usually turns over the day-to-day operation of the park to a professional management team.

Many science parks offer significant financial incentives to prospective tenants. These range from the provision of basic infrastructure and maintenance to elaborate packages of grants and loans. For example, Taiwan's Hsinchu Science-based Park gives businesses a five-year exemption from tax and rental payments, low-interest loans, research grants, business assistance, and an exemption from tariffs on imported components for products designed for export (Johnstone 1988).

Developers of science parks also give considerable attention to the physical environment. Patterned after the first parks at Stanford and Research Triangle, science parks today tend to be low-density developments set in wooded locations with modern buildings and many amenities. Arizona State University's recently built park has tennis courts, jogging paths, equestrian trails, ramadas, picnic areas, and a heliport (Wigand 1988).

Most science parks prohibit manufacturing activities, preferring to confine them to areas beyond the perimeter of the park. Research Triangle Park allows assembly but prohibits manufacturing. Several of the big firms with research facilities in Research Triangle have set up manufacturing operations outside the park's boundaries (Welter 1988). The restrictions on manufacturing often are relaxed to increase the tenants in a park (Minshall 1984; Macdonald 1987b). Parks often will accept medium-technology firms when high-technology companies cannot be found. There are probably only several hundred free-standing research and development centers in the United States, so the possibility of filling an entire science park with them is remote (Minshall 1984).

Some science parks specialize in specific technologies. Biotechnology is the focus of San Antonio's Texas Research Park; microelectronics is the theme at Research Triangle (Smilor, Kozmetsky, and Gibson 1988c; Whittington 1985b). However, given the competition for tenants, few parks can be selective about whom they allow in.

Marketing is an important part of the operation of science parks (Ryans and Shanklin 1988). Developers of science parks do extensive recruitment efforts, including advertising and personal visits. Recruitment drives for science parks are often part of local government and chamber of commerce business promotion schemes.

University Investments

An almost universal technopolis strategy is investment in university research. These investments are carried out largely by governments, although private firms and coalitions of interests do contribute resources to upgrade university facilities. The largest share of government investments comes from the national level. For example, Cambridge University's engineering and scientific departments have benefited from millions of dollars in national government funds intended to improve the university's research capabilities (Saxenian 1988; Segal 1988).

As a regional technology development strategy, local and regional governments have increased their contributions to universities. During the 1970s, the Texas state government poured millions of dollars of the new revenue from the oil boom into its public university system. These investments helped to create the Austin/San Antonio high-tech corridor (Smilor, Kozmetsky, and Gibson 1988c). In 1981, California spent most of a $21 million state appropriation, which was intended to reinvigorate the state's electronics industry, on state universities. Prefectural governments in Japan are investing in universities as part of the technopolis program. Similar investments have occurred in states throughout the United States and in regional governments around the world.

A more dramatic approach that emerged in the 1980s to investing in universities is the establishment of new research institutes. State government and the leading high-technology firms in Minnesota created the Center for Microelectronics and Information Sciences at the University of Minnesota. Arizona spent $54 million building four new research centers for Arizona State's engineering and science programs. New York state government contributed a $30 million interest-free loan for RPI's Center for Industrial Innovation, which also was supported by local industries.

In 1980, Governor James B. Hunt of North Carolina committed $1 million of the state's emergency fund to found the Microelectronics Center of North Carolina. A year later, he won legislative approval of a $24.4 million appropriation for the project. Two years later, the state spent another $18 million on the center. Some analysts believe that the center, which initially focused on building a skilled labor force for the region, played an important role in enticing General Electric to locate a microelectronics facility in North Carolina (Whittington 1985b).

Capital Assistance

The absence of sufficient capital is often seen as a barrier to the formation and growth of new high-technology firms (Oakey, Rothwell, and Cooper 1988). High-technology enterprises tend to be highly risky because they involve new products or processes. Traditional sources of capital are reluctant to invest in these enterprises. Further, high-risk venture capital is not available in many locations (Engstrom 1987). Venture capitalists have tended to invest in businesses that are nearby because of the need for frequent on-site visits, especially during the early stages of a company's development. Even when venture capital is available, its cost may be prohibitive (Allen and Levine 1986). Consequently, the establishment of capital assistance programs has been a commonly used technopolis strategy.

These funds often are components of other technopolis strategies, such as innovation centers, business incubators, and science parks. Capital assistance is available for firms in establishments as diverse as the Ben Franklin Partnership in Pennsylvania and the Hsinchu Science-based Park in Taiwan. Capital assistance funds are established for the most part by governments and universities seeking to stimulate high-technology development in their regions. As in the case of private venture-capital funds, the lender assumes part ownership of the firm. Most funds also require a portion of the new firm's capital requirements to be supplied by private sources. Profits are usually plowed back into the fund for investment in other enterprises.

American states and universities have pioneered the creation of venture capital funds (Livingston 1989; Office of Technology Assessment 1984; Engstrom 1987). One of the first such programs was the Connecticut Product Development Corporation. Through this quasi-public corporation, the state has established a fund that provides up to 60 percent of the cost of developing new products. The state then receives royalties from the sale of the products. New York State uses state-administered pension funds to finance high-technology start-ups. Maine offered tax breaks to banks and companies that invested in a $2 million fund to provide venture capital to high-risk firms.

Venture capital funds also are a part of Japan's technopolis program (Tatsuno 1986). Prefectural governments, working with local businesses, are setting up funds to stimulate entrepreneurship and to promote the application of new technologies in established industries. The Japanese technopolises are also setting up funds to provide low-interest loans to innovative firms.

Small-Business Incubators

One of the more widespread technopolis policies to emerge in the 1980s is the small-business incubator, also known as venture center or innovation center (Giese 1987; Allen and Levine 1986; Carroll 1986). These facilities are designed to assist creative entrepreneurs by providing them with a nurturing environment in the early stages of their businesses.

A typical small-business incubator offers below-market rents for office and laboratory space. It provides a common switchboard, reception area, copy and facsimile machines, and clerical help. Many incubators provide business assistance to entrepreneurs, who may have little management experience. Technical assistance also is commonly available through an affiliated university.

Incubators have been established as business development instruments by governments, universities, and private groups. Some have been set up as for-profit operations by real estate developers, although these are rare. Incubators have spread throughout the United States and Europe, with much of the growth occurring in the past ten years. In 1989, an estimated 330 existed in the United States (B. Brown 1989).

The mission of an incubator—at least those run by government, universities, and non-profit groups—is fulfilled when its tenants leave. Incubators are often affiliated with nearby science parks, and firms that survive the start-up phase frequently move to the park.

Infrastructure

Governments historically have built the infrastructure needed for economic development. The roads, bridges, ports, canals, and water and sewer systems constructed during the past two centuries made possible the development that has occurred throughout the world. As the advanced countries shift to a new industrial era, it is surprising that so little attention has been given to the infrastructure that will be needed. In part this is because much of the infrastructure vital to high-technology development is "invisible"—primarily telecommunications networks, the need for which is less obvious than more noticeable infrastructure requirements. Also, in the United States the telecommunications infrastructure has traditionally been provided by private firms. Technopolis strategies also have tended to overlook the infrastructure requirements common to any economic development: housing, roads, airports, and trains.

The Japanese have been the most concerned about the infrastructure needed for high-technology development, and the technopolis program has elaborate infrastructure plans built into it (Tatsuno 1986, 1988; Glasmeier 1988). The technopolises are required by law to have access to a major airport or a bullet train. The Ministry of International Trade and Industry (MITI) also requires the technopolis sites to provide housing, schools, and recreational facilities. Telecommunications systems are being rebuilt and upgraded. Tsukuba Science City represents a major investment in infrastructure of approximately $5.5 billion over two decades. Transportation and communication systems, housing, research institutes, schools, and many urban amenities have been built at Tsukuba (Tatsuno 1986; Onda 1988). Osaka also is trying to build a new infrastructure to support the regional economy (Morita and Hiraoka 1988). Among the projects under way are a new international airport in Osaka Bay; the Naniwa Necklace, a new rail line that will circle the city; and Technoport Osaka, a chain of artificial islands that will become a new business and recreational center.

Science parks in Europe and the United States provide infrastructure within their boundaries. Most include roads, sewers, water, some buildings, and various amenities, from jogging tracks to day-care centers. Of course, infrastructure development occurs regularly in communities all over the world, usually in response to particular needs or pressures and not as part of a plan to restructure the economy or promote technology development. In some of the more mature technopolises, awareness is growing of the importance of infrastructure to high-technology development. Boston is planning a technology center to be located above the tracks of South Station, the city's major rail station for the East Coast corridor, and within close proximity to Logan Airport (Sciacca 1989). The city and the state of Massachusetts have made major improvements to the transportation network, including renovation of the train station and the rapid transit line to which it is linked, and the introduction of water transport, and more improvements are planned.

Another infrastructure issue is the development of information infrastructures through public policy (Wilson and Teske 1990; Gillespie and Williams 1988; Schmandt, Williams, and Wilson 1989; Berger et al. 1989; Coopers & Lybrand 1987; Hepworth and Waterson 1988). Governments are reexamining telecommunications policies, particularly in the United States, where the prime function of government in telecommunications has been regulation. Some states have tried to upgrade their telecommunications systems to promote economic competitiveness. As a technopolis strategy, however, the development of information infrastructure is only just emerging.

Public-Private Partnerships

If one characteristic distinguishes modern technopolis policies, it is the establishment of new relationships among institutions and individuals (Office of Technology Assessment 1984; Smilor, Kozmetsky, and Gibson 1988b; Allen and Levine 1986; Miller and Côté 1987). With few exceptions, technopolis initiatives are the product of cooperative efforts of two or more previously divergent interests. Business, government, and universities fashion technopolis policies jointly. Sometimes labor is included in the coalition. Groups that had long viewed each other as adversaries or that had functioned in isolation from each other are collaborating. Public-private partnerships were instrumental in the development of the major planned technopolises: Research Triangle, Sophia-Antipolis and the Austin/San Antonio Corridor.

Another aspect of the partnership phenomenon is cooperation among industrial competitors. In the United States, this can be seen most clearly in the establishment of the Semiconductor Manufacturing Technology Institute, a prototype manufacturing center established in Austin, Texas, by a consortium of sixteen major U.S. semiconductor firms. It also can be seen on a smaller scale in Silicon Valley, where high-technology firms are pooling precommercialization research and development efforts (Saxenian 1990; Larsen and Rogers 1988). Elsewhere, large businesses that are unable to generate innovation internally have supported the development of small businesses by offering venture capital and business assistance (Office of Technology Assessment 1984).

Different levels of government also cooperate in the development of technopolis policies. In Japan, MITI and several other national agencies are working together with the prefectural governments to build the technopolises. State, local, and national governments in the United States have worked together to foster regional development.

Recruitment

Recruitment of firms or government facilities to a community or region is not generally thought of as a high-technology development initiative. Luring companies with sales pitches and financial incentives is more akin to the "smokestack chasing" that characterized the "old" economic development. Nevertheless, recruitment of high-technology firms has become so prevalent, even at some of the most highly regarded technopolises, that it merits mention.

Research Triangle Park is filled largely with government research institutes and branch plants of multinationals that were recruited to the site.

Sophia-Antipolis began as a real-estate operation. More recently, the managers of Sophia-Antipolis have tried to lure innovative small firms (Fairburn 1988). Hsinchu Science-based Park in Taiwan tries to entice companies with a smorgasbord of tax breaks and subsidies. State government officials in the United States routinely travel the country trying to raid other states with recruitment drives.

One of the most celebrated high-technology recruitment episodes was the competition for the research headquarters of the semiconductor industry's Microelectronics and Computer Technology Corporation (MCC) in the early 1980s. A number of states and communities—including Research Triangle, San Diego, Phoenix, and Texas—became locked in a bidding war for the facility. Texas finally won with an offer that included subsidized mortgages for MCC employees, job placement for employee spouses, and free use of a Lear jet.

Recruitment strategies are used most often by less advantaged areas, which have no significant high-technology base on which to build. Leaders in these areas reason that if a large outside facility can be recruited, the area could begin to acquire the agglomeration advantages that can lead to sustained economic growth.

Quality of Life

Developers of existing and would-be technopolises are increasingly paying attention to quality-of-life issues. Some of the mature technopolises seem to be choking on their own success. The high cost of housing in Silicon Valley and the Boston area limits the ability of the regions to attract and retain key personnel needed by high-technology firms (Grove 1987; Malone 1989). Munich, one of the largest high-technology centers in Europe, and London's M-4 corridor are experiencing similar problems (Schares 1988; Hall et al. 1987).

Japan has made the provision of amenities an important part of its technopolis program. Innovative leaders in U.S. states have developed wide-ranging environmental protection, housing, and quality-of-life programs as strategies to encourage economic development (Osborne 1988).

Other Policies

A number of other technopolis policies that do not fall into any of the above categories have been used. Training programs designed to prepare workers for new high-technology jobs are common initiatives of governments, universities, and private groups. Most training programs that can be considered technopolis policies develop technical or business skills.

Investments in primary and secondary education are another technopolis strategy. Many communities have concluded that the entire educational infrastructure, and not just the engineering departments of major universities, must be upgraded if high-technology development is to succeed. Human capital development is a concern of all businesses, not just those in high technology.

Another technopolis initiative worthy of mention is the creation of task forces or working groups. These are the vehicles by which most technopolis strategies get started. Typically, a group of leaders from government, business, and academia will get together, commission a study, and issue recommendations. In this way, the public-private partnership is created that leads to the more tangible steps designed to foster high-technology development.

INTERNATIONAL TECHNOPOLIS POLICIES: AN OVERVIEW

Japan

Japan has probably the most ambitious technopolis plans, at least on the drawing board (Masser 1990; Edgington 1989; Tatsuno 1986, 1988; Fujita 1988; Poe 1986; Toda 1987). The Japanese technopolis program includes not only science parks, capital and technical assistance, research centers and government-university-industry partnerships—the standard fare of U.S. and European technopolis policies—but also elaborate arrangements for new infrastructure, including housing, rail and air transportation, and information networks. The plan envisions a series of prosperous new science cities dotting the country, away from the established industrial and population centers. The industrial base of most of these cities would be the so-called sunrise industries and technologies of the twenty-first century: biotechnology, software, computers, fine ceramics, new materials, advanced electronics, mechatronics, and robotics.

The technopolis program, conceived by the Ministry of International Trade and Industry in the early 1980s, is part of a broader Japanese plan to shift from its present industrial structure to one based on advanced technology (Ken-ichi Imai 1986; Glasmeier 1988; Tyson and Zysman 1989). The Japanese government is using a range of developmental strategies to effect this move: tax incentives, subsidies, procurement, promotion of industry collaboration, and protection of the domestic market. Although the technopolis program relies heavily on local governments for planning and funding, the program is a component of centrally directed industrial policy.

The Japanese technopolis proposal emerged from a MITI study group in 1982. When the program was announced, a stampede occurred of prefectures offering to become host sites for a technopolis. MITI originally planned to select five to seven locations out of nineteen applicants. However, the pressure from the prefectures was so great that MITI was forced to accept all nineteen. By the end of the 1980s, twenty-five technopolis sites had been designated.

According to MITI's guidelines, the technopolis sites must be close to a bullet train or airport and a parent city of at least 200,000. A technopolis must have a mix of industrial sites, academic institutions, and housing. It must upgrade its physical and information infrastructures. MITI has required the prefectures to provide most of the funding and the detailed planning through cooperative efforts with local businesses and higher education institutions.

Since 1985, the regions have been actively building the technopolis infrastructure: new highways, university complexes, research parks, airports, and information networks. Construction costs are expected to reach $200 million annually for each technopolis (Tatsuno 1986). Some of the prefectures have set up technical assistance centers for businesses. Subsidies and other incentives are being offered to companies that invest in the technopolis sites.

The technopolis plans attempt to build on existing industrial strengths in each of the regions. Rather than replace old industries with new ones, the Japanese technopolis strategies propose to upgrade the technological level of existing industries. The original 1990 target date for completion of the technopolises has been pushed back, in some cases by a decade. Raising the funds locally for such ambitious projects has proven more difficult than anticipated. Nevertheless, planners of the technopolises contend that the projects are long-term efforts that cannot be judged this early in their development.

A forerunner of the technopolis program is Tsukuba Science City, a planned community built in the 1960s thirty-five miles northeast of Tokyo. Tsukuba is home to forty-six government research institutes, a major university, thirty private research and development laboratories, and newly developed housing and transportation. Tsukuba was designed originally to relieve the congestion in metropolitan Tokyo. More recently, Tsukuba has been seen as part of the country's broader technology development strategy, akin to the technopolis plan. However, Tsukuba Science City differs from the technopolis plan in several important respects (Tatsuno 1986). Tsukuba was developed with a large construction budget supplied by the national government, which the technopolises do not have. Private industry played a relatively minor role in Tsukuba, while industry is supposed to play a large part in the technopolises. Tsukuba's emphasis is on basic research, while the technopolises are to focus on applied research.

Japan's technopolis policies are not confined to the formal technopolis program. In communities and regions throughout the country, leaders are carrying out efforts to promote economic development through high technology. These undertakings include assistance to firms, infrastructure development, and public-private partnerships. An example is the comprehensive regional infrastructure development activity in Osaka. Local planners there are developing a new regional airport, science city, business parks, rail line and multiuse "technoport" on outlying islands (Morita and Hiraoka 1988).

The New Media Community initiative and the Intelligent Cities program, which were launched in the mid-1980s, are centrally directed technopolis policies that emphasize development of information infrastructure (Masser 1990). Under the New Media Community program, various cities are designated for accelerated development of advanced media technologies, such as two-way cable television and satellite broadcasting. Similarly, the Intelligent Cities program designates communities for construction of fiber optics networks and other advanced telecommunications infrastructure.

United States

Technopolis policies are abundant in the United States, where they originated. Although federal government policies do affect regional technology development, the United States has no coherent national technology development policy encompassing states and regions. Most regional high-technology development initiatives have come from state and local governments.

State government, in particular, has been active in developing technopolis policies and new economic development strategies (Burton 1989; Fusi 1989; Osborne 1988; Fosler 1988; Eisinger 1988; Premus 1988; Atkinson 1988; Rees and Bradley 1988; Schmandt and Wilson 1987). Leadership has come from innovative governors, such as Richard Thornburgh of Pennsylvania, William Clinton of Arkansas, Thomas Keane of New Jersey, Jerry Brown of California, Mario Cuomo of New

York, and Michael Dukakis of Massachusetts. In some states, such as California, Florida, and Ohio, legislatures have been in the forefront.

State governments have developed training and education programs to create a high-technology work force. They have financed university research and promoted university-business technology transfer through the establishment of new research centers or centers of excellence. States have created a range of financial incentives for high-technology business, from tax breaks to direct investments in firms. Other support programs of state governments include export assistance, incubator facilities, science parks, and public-private partnerships.

In some parts of the United States, local governments have taken the lead in technopolis policies. In San Antonio, Mayor Henry Cisneros was active in targeting biotechnology development (Smilor, Kozmetsky, and Gibson 1988c). Mayor Raymond Flynn of Boston is trying to create several mini-technopolises modeled after the Japanese technopolis program (Sciacca 1989).

Universities also have pursued high-technology development strategies. Stanford University's role in the development of Silicon Valley has long been recognized. University City Science Center in Philadelphia was built by a consortium of higher education institutions. Universities have developed incubators, venture capital funds, training programs, and science parks.

Individual businesses and business groups in the United States also have undertaken technopolis policies. In the 1980s, education became a focus of U.S. business as firms and business groups developed a broad range of initiatives, from providing aid to elementary and high schools to offering grants to colleges and universities. Some large firms have supplied capital and technical assistance to start-up firms, which can provide technological innovation needed by the big firm. Also, the siting decisions of some large U.S. firms can be considered technopolis strategies such as Digital Equipment Corporation's establishment of a plant in the blighted Roxbury section of Boston.

Europe

Europe has many and varied technopolis policies. They range in size from small innovation centers in Germany to France's technology cities or *technopoles*. European technopolis strategies aim to nurture new or existing firms and attract footloose multinationals (Oakey, Rothwell, and Cooper 1988).

Local and regional governments have been the leading instigators of technopolis policies in Europe with varying degrees of involvement from universities, central governments, and businesses (Sunman 1987). The recent focus on regionally based, high-technology development—with the nurturing of small business as a top priority—contrasts with the European development strategies of the 1960s, which tried to build large, "national champion" companies in key industries.

Britain has been the pioneer of European technopolis policies. High-technology development has been a major priority of British governments since the mid-1960s. The central government has fostered technology development through funding of university and government research, defense spending, and its ownership of transportation and communication industries (Nelson 1984). Although the British government has backed regional high-technology policies, most of the financial support for them has come from regional or local public bodies, such as the Scottish Development Agency or the English Estates. The most common projects are innovation centers and science parks. Universities have played a lesser role. Twelve universities have established science parks, with Cambridge, Heriot Watt, and Ashton the most successful. Since 1981, British governments and universities have invested a total of £150 million in high technology centers (Saxenian 1988).

In France, government has historically played a more activist role in industry and technology policy. National strategies include subsidies, procurement, tariffs, and nationalization of industries. The principal high-technology strategy in France is the *technopole* concept, which is an expanded version of a British or American science park. Almost all regional governments in France have established *technopoles*. The best-known *technopole* is Sophia-Antipolis, a science city on the Riviera. Opening in 1973 with only five companies, it now has more than 500 establishments and housing for 5,000 people. Sophia-Antipolis is home to many of the largest high-technology companies in the world, including Digital Equipment Corporation, Dow Chemical, Rockwell International, and Wellcome Pharmaceuticals. Although the multinationals are the heart of Sophia-Antipolis, the development has started to spawn some start-up companies.

Germany has developed many regional high-technology development policies, although they tend to be on a smaller scale than those in Britain or France. They are carried out for the most part by local governments with support from the national government (Giese 1987). A 1965 federal law that establishes regional economic equality as a national goal has been an important force promoting technopolis policies. Local German governments and universities have been active in setting up programs to support new or existing firms. A network of technology transfer centers for small businesses has been established. Incubators, known as venture centers, have been established, as have science parks. Investments in education also are part of the strategies. The cornerstone of Germany's technology development policy remains its historical support for excellence in technical and scientific education.

Sweden's technopolis strategies are, for the most part, centered around its universities (Nijkamp and Mouwen 1987; Sweeney 1987). "Competence centers" and other technology transfer agencies have been established at universities to assist small firms in applying new technologies. These centers serve as intermediaries between university researchers and small businesses.

Science parks of varying sizes have been established in the Netherlands (Nijkamp and Mouwen 1987; Sunman 1987). The larger parks are designed to lure branch plants of multinationals or other large firms, while the smaller parks are designed to attract small high-technology firms or start-ups. The smaller parks offer an array of technical assistance programs. Microelectronics centers have been established at the technical universities in Delft, Twente, and Eindhoven in the Netherlands and in Flanders in Belgium. Local and regional governments, as well as local business groups, have developed many smaller-scale high-technology programs in both countries.

Newly Industrializing Countries

In the 1980s, some newly industrializing countries (NICs) and other less developed nations eyed technopolis strategies as possible avenues toward overcoming technological dependency. Technopolis policies provide an ingredient in what these countries hope will be a means of leapfrogging past the advanced countries in the key industries of the twenty-first century.

The most common technopolis strategy used in the NICs is the science park. Korea has Daeduk Science City; Taiwan, Hsinchu Science Park; and Singapore, Singapore Science Park. Even Hong Kong's laissez-faire government is reserving land in its two industrial parks for high-technology development and is considering building a new science park.

The Hsinchu Science-based Industrial Park is, according to the *Far Eastern Economic Review*, "a deliberate attempt to create a Taiwanese version of Silicon Valley" (Johnstone 1988, p. 70). Hsinchu is about forty miles from Taipei and is near Tsunghua and Chiaotung universities.

One of the government's principal motives in building the facility was to entice back to Taiwan expatriate high-technology entrepreneurs who would otherwise establish new companies in other countries (Darlin 1990; Watanabe 1989). The park, which opened in 1980, is home to seventy-three companies, mostly in the fields of computers, semiconductors, and telecommunications. The Taiwanese government has spent $200 million on the park. It purchased the land from farmers and built housing and "standard" factories for prospective tenants. The government also provides substantial incentives for firms that locate there. The government's long-range plan for Hsinchu is to build a science city for 70,000 people at a cost of more than $1 billion.

Singapore Science Park, which opened in 1984, is not as large as Hsinchu, but in a sense, it is more ambitious (Hock 1988; *Asian Finance* 1988). It focuses on industrial research, while Hsinchu is production-oriented. The park has thirty-nine companies engaged in research in a variety of new technologies, including medical diagnostics, chemicals, electronic components, biotechnology, and computers. Firms that locate in the park receive a range of incentives. The park is next to the National University of Singapore and is run by a board of representatives from industry, government, and academia.

Hong Kong has traditionally shunned any intervention in the market economy. However, as the country's leaders have recognized the need to shift from labor-intensive to knowledge-intensive industry, government has taken a more activist role. The principal industrial development activity of the government has been the establishment of the industrial "estates" or parks (Goldstein 1988). The parks, at Tai Po and Yuen Long, have drawn an odd assortment of companies since they were established in the late 1970s. The government has set aside the remaining available land at Tai Po for high-technology development, and consideration is being given to building a new science park.

Science parks are not the only technopolis policies being pursued by the NICs. Many that hope to leap-frog ahead of the advanced countries are establishing research centers and investing in technical universities. They also are assisting entrepreneurs and improving training and basic education. Some NICs have struck deals with multinational corporations in an attempt to develop indigenous technological capacity.

CONCLUSION

Technopolis policies, which had their origins in the immediate post-World War II years in the United States, have multiplied during the past decade in advanced industrial societies. Newly industrializing countries also are experimenting with them. Technopolis policies are viewed by their architects as the means of achieving regional economic development through the commercialization of new technologies.

What is most striking about technopolis policies is their uniformity. Science parks in Britain are not much different from those in the United States, which resemble those in Singapore and Japan. Sometimes the names change—an "innovation centre" in Europe and a "small business incubator" in the United States—but the institution is basically the same. Even the mix of policies being applied varies little from country to country.

The reason for these similarities is simple: They all are based on the same understanding of the process by which Silicon Valley and, to a lesser extent, Route 128, developed. Outsiders have probed the two great American regional success stories for the secrets that unlock the door to high-technology development. For years, busloads of foreign visitors toured Silicon Valley (Tatsuno 1986; Macdonald 1987b). They returned home and, using a form of reverse engineering, arrived at the same conclusion: The formula for creating a technopolis is a world-class university, an affiliated science park where research can be commercialized, an ample supply of venture capital, a pleasant physical environment, and a stimulating social milieu. Thus, a rather superficial analysis was all that preceded the development of many of these policies. Most policies were designed simply to replicate the conditions that had existed in Silicon Valley and Route 128. No economic or development theory guided regional planners in the way that supply-side or Keynesian economics had directed national economic policy makers.

Development economist John Friedman once wrote, "Planners who would interfere in regional development must understand the process by which it is generated" (1966, p. 20). The next chapter attempts to build that understanding by constructing a theoretical model of how the technopolis develops.

Chapter 3

The Technopolis and
Regional Development Theory:
A Framework for Analysis

This chapter builds a theoretical model for understanding the emergence of the technopolis. This framework is limited in scope. It does not try to account for all of the shifts in regional geography that have happened in the world during the past forty years. It does not attempt to explain the more general process of technological innovation. The orientation of the model is toward policy. What it lacks in theoretical elegance it seeks to compensate for with its applicability to practical regional planning.

The chapter is divided into three parts. The first examines the theoretical literature of regional development. During the past century, geographers, economists, sociologists, urban planners, political scientists, and other social scientists have developed explanations of why economic activity locates where it does. A review of this literature provides direction in building an understanding of the development of the technopolis. The second section turns to the dramatic changes in regional geography that have occurred since World War II. This section argues that established regional development theories have been unable to account for this global geographic restructuring.

The third section presents the theoretical framework that will be used in the rest of the book to explain the dynamics of the technopolis. This framework is an amalgamation of a number of different perspectives and lines of inquiry. It is influenced by the growth pole theory of François Perroux (1950, 1955, 1961, 1973) and by the concept of innovative environments, developed recently by a number of European and U.S. theorists (Malecki and Nijkamp 1988; Aydalot and Keeble 1988; Aydalot 1988; Andersson 1985). The model suggests there are two important conditions necessary for the development of a technopolis: the presence of a knowledge or growth center and the existence of an environment that supports innovation. The implications of the model for regional development policy will be discussed in subsequent chapters.

REGIONAL DEVELOPMENT PERSPECTIVES

No paradigms or overarching theories dominate regional development literature. What exists is a collection of theoretical perspectives, most of them limited in scope, some complementary and some competing, and together spanning a number of disciplines (Malecki 1983; Rees and Stafford 1984; Thompson 1989).

Although some early literature exists on the location of agriculture (von Thünen 1966), major research on the location of economic activity did not begin until after the industrial revolution. Regional development theory has been concerned mainly with the manufacturing industries that arose during and after the industrial revolution. Manufacturing before that era tended to take place in dispersed cottage industries (Hekman and Strong 1981; Oakey 1984). The nineteenth century produced the great industrial cities of Europe and North America, prompting theorists in the emerging social sciences to set forth broad explanations of why industries developed where they did.

German economist Alfred Weber established the field of industrial location with the publication of his *Theory of the Location of Industry* in 1909.[1] This work prompted a wave of research by European and U.S. authors in the first half of the twentieth century. Interest in industrial location and regional economic development waned after World War II, when the industrialized countries were preoccupied with rebuilding shattered national economies. Later, as problems of regional inequality received public attention in advanced countries, theoretical and applied research increased. In the 1980s, dramatic swings in regional economies stimulated renewed interest in regional development theory.

Because it cuts across a number of traditional academic disciplines, regional development literature is difficult to categorize. Most of the research can be traced to one of two scholarly traditions: neoclassical economics and political economy. The former stresses the importance of markets in determining industrial location; the latter emphasizes the role of the dynamics of global capitalism. Within the political economy framework are several distinct research areas, including product life cycles, long waves of development and growth poles, as well as various neo-Marxist and dependency perspectives.

Neoclassical Frameworks

Weber (1929) theorized that firms and industries located to optimize their access to raw materials, labor, and markets. He envisioned a triangle, with the relative importance of these factors, along with transportation costs, determining where within the triangle economic activity would occur. Firms would seek locations that offered the lowest costs. Industrial location was thus set by an equilibrium of market forces. In the tradition of classical economics, Weber constructed a mathematical model, which assumed a flat plane, an even spatial distribution of population, complete knowledge by both producers and consumers, and perfect competition. Agglomeration and "deglomeration" (the disadvantages of agglomeration) factors were included as secondary influences.

Lösch (1954), Christaller (1966), and Hoover (1948) expanded Weber's model, incorporating the notion of a hierarchy of urban centers that serve surrounding areas. These theoretical formulations explained the number, size, and distribution of urban areas. More recent neoclassical studies have argued that the propensity of market forces to seek an equilibrium creates a tendency toward regional equality (Wheaton 1979; Weinstein and Firestein 1978). To the extent that labor and capital are mobile, they will shift from one region to another, seeking the most favorable conditions, according to this view. The up-and-down fortunes of regions in the United States in the post-World War II years are often cited as evidence. According to this perspective, regional convergence is the process by which growth is transmitted throughout the system (Rees and Stafford 1984).

Another outgrowth of the neoclassical tradition is trade theory, which is an adaptation of the notion of international comparative advantage (Courchene and Melvin 1988). In short, trade theory applies the concepts of comparative advantage and specialization to regions. According to this perspective, the process by which regions specialize and trade with other regions generates growth for the whole system. This theory has been applied by policy makers, for whom it represents a less costly approach than most alternative regional development strategies (Higgins and Savoie 1988). Concentrating on a region's strengths is easier than attempting a major industrial restructuring.

A common manifestation of the neoclassical approach is the "business climate" study, sometimes issued by government agencies, popular business publications, chambers of commerce, and other business organizations. Typically, a set of qualities attractive to business are defined (with distinctions rarely being made about the kinds of businesses being considered and how their needs might differ). Regions then are ranked by how well they supply these qualities. Surveys of business owners and managers are often included in these studies and are frequently used by government development agencies to define a region's strengths and weaknesses.

One of the most important contributions of neoclassical theory is its early recognition of agglomeration advantages. Although Weber believed that agglomeration played a role in industrial location, he saw advantages coming only from production economies of scale in clusters of plants. Lösch expanded the concept to include marketing advantages for firms in urban agglomerations. In the post-World War II years, a number of diverse studies demonstrated the richness of agglomeration economies (Hoover and Vernon 1959; Hall 1962; J. Martin 1966). Researchers identified complex webs of linkages among firms. Materials and information were found to flow among manufacturing concerns in ways that reinforced the competitive advantages of firms near one another.

The decline of traditional manufacturing centers in Western industrialized countries during the 1960s cast doubts on the validity of the concept of agglomeration advantages (Oakey 1984). Further, the new science-based industries, particularly in the expanding field of electronics, relied less on geographically fixed inputs and appeared generally more foot-loose. However, the rise of high-technology industrial clusters represented new evidence of the importance of agglomeration economies. These new industrial concentrations seemed to exhibit many of the characteristics of traditional industrial agglomerations, in particular the interrelationships among firms, information flows, and backward and forward linkages (Hall and Preston 1988; Hall 1985). However, some differences also were apparent. High-technology enterprises appeared to gain considerable advantage from the large pool of technical labor that arose around high-technology industrial agglomerations (Premus 1982). These firms also were unlike traditional manufacturing concerns in that proximity to raw materials and markets was relatively unimportant because of the small amount of physical materials required and the high value-to-weight ratio of the finished product. Nevertheless, the internal dynamism of the modern technopolis—created by information, labor, and product linkages among firms—strongly resembled the process at work in many nineteenth- and early twentieth-century industrial centers. Thus, the importance of agglomeration economies in regional economic development has been recognized by researchers from a broad range of schools, including the full spectrum of political economy, as well as the neoclassical tradition (Moomaw 1988; Miller and Côté 1987; Scott and Storper 1987; Oakey 1984).

Political Economy

A large and diverse body of regional development literature falls under the classification of political economy. Some of it traces its roots to Marx; other branches are outgrowths of dependency theory. Some of the political economy literature also springs from more mainstream academic traditions. What the work has in common is the central role ascribed to the dynamics of the capitalist world economy in determining the location of industry. The neoclassical perspective on the world economy perceives individual, single plant firms operating in open competition and responding to the law of supply and demand. Political economy stresses the role of large, multinational corporations, for whom the entire world is their space economy. Neoclassical theory sees the play of market forces creating a tendency toward regional equality. Political economy sees the same process producing inequality and domination.

Neo-Marxist Perspectives. Although Marx was little concerned with spatial aspects of capitalism, his notion of uneven development strongly influenced theorists and scholars who followed him. Marx believed that inequality accompanied the advance of capitalism and that uneven development was fundamental to the capitalist mode of production. Hobson (1938) and Lenin (1970) expanded Marx's ideas into theories of imperialism, which explained spatial patterns of development and underdevelopment on a global scale. However, it was not until after World War II that a Marxist perspective was brought to the issue of subnational, regional development.

Two of the most important neo-Marxist scholars, Doreen Massey (1984) and Stephen Hymer (1975), argue in their most influential works that a hierarchy of places has emerged as a result of the behavior of multinational corporations. The efforts of these global enterprises to maximize profits and to establish corporate control have created vast inequality. The center-periphery relationships that form on a global basis are replicated on a smaller scale within national and regional economies. In a comprehensive study of the global electronics industry, Morgan and Sayer (1988) focus on the interplay of economic, political, and social relationships in capitalism and their impact on uneven regional development. Also stressing social relations of production, Storper and Walker

(1989) try to move beyond an analysis of static uneven development to an explanation of the instability of regions in the world economy.

According to Castells (1985a, p. 28), regional dislocations are the consequences of global capitalist competition. He writes that regional restructuring is

an attempt to supersede the structural crisis of capitalism by continuously shifting the location of capital, labor, markets, production, distribution, and management to the most advantageous location for each economic unit. High technology plays a major role in such a process, both as a technological tool and as the core of new sectors of economic growth. (1985a, p. 28)

New information technologies, which are the principal instrument in this capitalist restructuring, have created a "space of flows," replacing the "space of places" (Castells 1989).

Contemporary neo-Marxist regional analysis has been influenced by the so-called French regulationist school (Aglietta 1976; Lipietz 1986). This literature argues that for each regime of capitalist production, there arises a new mode of social regulation. One of the more influential scholars to build on this tradition is geographer Allen J. Scott. In a series of books and articles he either authored or co-authored in the late 1980s, Scott constructed a model of "flexible accumulation" and "flexible production," which he says is becoming the next dominant phase of capitalist development (Scott 1988a, 1988b, 1988c; Scott and Storper 1987; Scott and Kwok 1989).

According to Scott, the regime of flexible accumulation—based on new management systems and flexible automation technologies—is replacing the Fordist mass production regime, which dominated from the 1920s until the late 1960s. The geographical consequences have been the rise of new industrial spaces that specialize in flexible production: Cambridge and the M-4 corridor in Britain, Sophia-Antipolis and Scientific City in France, the Third Italy region, central Portugal, northeastern Spain, and Silicon Valley, Orange County and other locations in the U.S. Sun Belt. Michael Piore and Charles Sabel (1984), in their study of the clothing and footwear industries of northern Italy, were the first to identify these flexible production centers. A characteristic of all of these regions is that relations between capital and labor are re-created so that there is an absence of the working class unionism and labor-oriented political machines. This provides the flexible work force needed by the new capitalist regime.

Using the same framework as Scott, Schoenberger (1986, 1988,

1989) foresees some unexpected geographical consequences of the new regime of accumulation. First, reagglomeration of industry may occur in older industrial regions, she argues, because of the disciplining effects of restructuring on industrial labor. Second, the industries that moved to the world periphery during the standardization phase of the product cycle may be inclined to remain there even after automation marginalizes the importance of cheap, routinized labor. The reason is that these countries are becoming more technologically sophisticated. These two tendencies obviously are contradictory. Schoenberger does not hazard a prediction of the outcome except to state that a new and disruptive phase of geographic restructuring is about to unfold.

Product Life Cycles. Product life-cycle perspectives hold that products, industries, and regions go through predictable stages of development—much like people—from birth to growth to maturity to old age. Life-cycle theory became recognized as an important explanation of regional development with the publication of Raymond Vernon's 1966 article in the *Quarterly Journal of Economics*. In the 1930s, a number of scholars had broken with neoclassical tradition and started to point the way to Vernon's product cycle formulation. Burns (1934) and Kuznets (1930) were the first economists to recognize that industries progressed in cycles. Schumpeter studied cyclical changes closely; he saw development as "the spontaneous and discontinuous changes in the channel of the circular flow" (1934).

Vernon, however, was the first to offer a complete theoretical framework and is recognized as the founder of product cycle theory (1966, 1979). In the first stage of the cycle, new industries emerge in the form of many small firms clustered in a few areas to communicate directly with customers and to gain other agglomeration advantages. In the second, or maturation, phase, standardization of the product starts to occur. Many early entrants drop out, leaving a few large firms to dominate. Firms relocate within developed countries to serve new markets and to take advantage of cheaper labor costs. In the final phase, standardization of the product is complete and production is shifted to less developed countries. Empirical research has validated aspects of the theory (Barkley 1988; Markusen, Hall, and Glasmeier 1986).

Markusen (1985) added the concept of a parallel profit cycle to Vernon's product cycle model. According to Markusen, early entrants to an industry reap huge profits. Then competition sets in, and profits sag. Oligopolies can temporarily lift profits in this middle phase. In the last stage, profits fall as markets become saturated. Companies then contract, and jobs are either eliminated or exported.

Another view of product cycles as they relate to regions envisions an additional stage evolving after standardization. According to this perspective, a new growth phase can be triggered by the concentration of standardized manufacturing industry (Norton and Rees 1979; Rees 1979; Rees and Stafford 1984; Steed 1986; Cooper 1985). Agglomeration effects come into play after manufacturing operations are established, and entrepreneurs are drawn to the area. The example most often cited by proponents of this view is the indigenous growth that occurred in the Sun Belt of the United States following the location of branch plants in the region.

Growth Poles. Economist François Perroux introduced the concept of growth poles in a 1955 French journal article (Perroux 1955). He argued that economic growth is generated by innovative firms, which are clustered together in propulsive industries. These poles spread growth to nearby "economic space." Like the other political economy theorists of his era, Perroux rejected the neoclassical position that market forces would distribute growth evenly throughout an economic system. He believed instead that growth was polarized: "Growth does not appear everywhere and all at once; it reveals itself in certain points or poles with different degrees of intensity; it spreads through diverse channels" (Perroux 1961).

Perroux's work was built on Schumpeter's concept of innovation. Schumpeter saw economic growth coming from entrepreneurship, which, in his usage, was synonymous with innovation (Schumpeter 1934). Underlying this phenomenon was the "social climate," which determined the level of innovation a society had. Neoclassical economists had recognized that entrepreneurship was important, but they had no way to incorporate it into their models. It loomed as a "meta-economic" factor, shaping the economy but not part of it. Schumpeter was thus the first economist to deal directly with innovation (Drucker 1985).

"Perroux took over the whole of the Schumpeterian system and put it into space," Higgins writes (1988, p. 40). The growth poles he described are clusters of Schumpeter's innovating enterprises. The important point added by Perroux was that these enterprises agglomerated at specific locations. Polarized growth meant that some areas that were not encompassed by the poles became either dominated by or dependent on them. Hirschman (1958) and Myrdal (1957) argued that growth poles siphoned off talent and resources from surrounding areas, leaving the hinterland with nothing but meager trickle-down benefits.

Perroux's concept of "economic space" was widely misunderstood. He termed it a "field of forces" that bore no relation to geographic or "banal" space. Growth poles generated growth in spaces that were sometimes far away from the pole, according to Perroux. In an early article that laid the groundwork for growth pole theory, he wrote: "The topographical zone of influence of Michelin in France is inscribed in a region, but its economic zone of influence, like that of all large firms, defies cartography" (Perroux 1950, p. 96).

However, many planners overlooked this point, as well as the perspectives of Hirschman and Myrdal, and assumed that the establishment of growth poles would revitalize surrounding depressed regions. The result was a multitude of failed policies in both industrialized and less developed countries. The initial appeal of growth pole theory to planners is easy enough to discern: It seemed to promise relatively fast and inexpensive results in depressed areas. After an initial investment in a growth pole, growth presumably would radiate outward and become self-sustaining, with no need for massive, long-term transfers of resources (Higgins and Savoie 1988). Further, some scholarly justification existed for the alteration of Perroux's concept of economic space (Darwent 1969; Boudeville 1976).

In the 1960s and 1970s, governments all over the world implemented regional development programs based either explicitly or implicitly on the growth pole concept. Growth poles were the guiding principle for regional planners in France, Belgium, and Italy (Higgins 1988). President Lyndon Johnson's Economic Development Administration (EDA) was modeled on the notion of growth poles (Hansen 1978). To receive aid from EDA, depressed areas had to designate "growth centers" to be the focus for regional development. In less developed countries in Africa, Asia, and Latin America, investments in urban centers were made in attempts to spread growth to the hinterlands.

These policies usually failed to create propulsive centers of industry. Higgins (1988) points out that the growth pole concept, applied to geographic space, is only likely to work in natural resource-based industries. In the increasingly common case of industries based on human resources, propulsive effects are unlikely to occur in the periphery unless the periphery happens to contain the same human resources as the center. In most places where it was tried, strong economic links between the growth poles and the targetted hinterlands did not exist.

Although growth pole theory fell into disfavor for a time, it is experiencing a revival in the form of technopolis research and policies being undertaken all over the world (Rees 1989). The science parks, *technopoles*, centers of excellence, and innovation centers described in Chapter 2 are modeled after the Silicon Valley and Route 128 phenomena. These two early technopolises behaved like Perrouxian growth poles, with development radiating outward from the propulsive industries and research institutes at their centers. In the 1970s, efforts were made to apply growth pole theory to concepts of technological change (Thomas 1975). Growth pole theory also has been of interest to scholars examining the development of concentrations of service industries (McKee 1987; Friedman, Hakim, and Weinblatt 1989).

Long Waves of Development. Another theoretical approach that has had an impact on regional development issues is Kondratieff's concept of cycles of economic growth (Kondratieff 1935). Kondratieff, a Soviet economist, observed that approximately every fifty years, a technological wave crests and is replaced by another. The first wave was based on the steam engine, textile manufacturing, and the processing of iron; the second on railroads and steel; and the third on chemicals, automobiles, and electrical devices. The latest wave, believed to be just getting under way, is based on electronics and other high-technology industries.

According to Kondratieff's theory, during the last half of the cycle, the growth industries of the most recent technological revolution appear to be prospering when, in fact, they are stagnating, feeding off no longer needed capital. Then, a crisis of some sort triggers a collapse of these industries. Prosperity does not return until new industries, based on new technologies, generate sufficient growth and employment to offset the consequences of the decline of the old industries.

Schumpeter (1982) popularized and expanded Kondratieff's concept, which was aspatial in its original form. Location researchers after World War II soon adapted the notion to regional development issues. Research found that centers of old technologies rarely spawned the next wave of innovation (Checkland 1975; Markusen 1985). Thus, placed in a spatial context, long-wave theory predicts the decline and stagnation of old industrial regions and the rise of industry in new locations. More recent research has merged neo-Marxist thought and long-wave theory (Booth 1987; Mager 1987; and Marshall 1987). This literature has tried to uncover the interrelationships between uneven development and long waves. Marshall argues that in Britain at least, the national long waves are not produced by global technological change but by social and political struggles in regions.

CRITIQUE OF THE LITERATURE

Global Restructuring

In the 1970s, the field of economic geography was cast into disarray.

Important economic, technological, social, and political changes, which had been under way for some time, became unmistakable and began to have global geographic consequences. Regional economies throughout the world experienced major restructuring. In light of these events, existing theories of regional development had to be reexamined. Before proceeding with the discussion of theory, an outline of the forces that caused the restructuring will be presented, followed by an overview of their geographic impacts.

The Information Technology Revolution. The most far-reaching change occurring in the second half of the twentieth century has been the revolution in information technologies. This shift in the technological basis of society is potentially as significant as the two previous great human revolutions: the industrial revolution of the eighteenth and nineteenth centuries and the neolithic revolution, in which humans developed agriculture. The knowledge revolution could be even more profound because the pace of change seems likely to accelerate, while in the previous human revolutions, there was a levelling-off period in which change subsided.

At the core of this technological revolution are the key inventions of the mid-twentieth century: the silicon chip, the digital computer, advanced telecommunications, and new electronic equipment. These technologies have been converging to the extent that differentiating among them is no longer useful (Arnold and Guy 1986; Gilder 1989). Changes in one technology have an almost immediate impact on the others. In the advanced countries, information technology has, in a matter of years, altered the complex systems of society: manufacturing, education, health care, social services, defense, transportation, and research. As computers become more powerful and versatile, approaching and surpassing the cognitive and physical capabilities of humans, more profound changes may occur. Also, breakthroughs in other fields, including materials, lasers, and biotechnology, promise to alter further the technological underpinnings of society (Finkelstein 1989).

One reason that the pace of change in the second half of the twentieth century has accelerated is that the process of invention has become more efficient. Before World War II, most of the important new products were developed by solitary inventors or tinkerers. In the era since then, organized research laboratories, most of them based in universities or contract research institutes, have produced most of the major inventions (Bell 1973). Vannevar Bush, whose career spanned both eras, described the new process of invention as being carried out "by teams of individuals in laboratories where it is not so much a spark of ingenuity that counts as it is a knowledge of physics and mechanics and painstaking work in development" (1970, p. 172).

Another force propelling the information technology revolution has been military spending. In the United States, Defense Department funding has fueled the scientific research that led to the major product innovations in the post-World War II years. Military funding shielded research and development from the short-term profit requirements common in private industry. During the Cold War, the Defense Department also was a reliable market for high-technology products. With the Cold War ending, it is uncertain whether military spending will continue to provide the impetus it has in the past to technological innovation.

The technological revolution has had a major impact on economics. New industries have arisen and old ones have been reshaped (Rubin and Huber 1986; Machlup 1962). The nature of work has changed for people in societies all over the world. Important new high-technology industries—computers, semiconductors, electronic equipment—have emerged almost overnight. High-technology companies grew from one-man shops to multimillion dollar, multinational giants in less than two decades. The growth rates of these firms was unprecedented. For example, from 1965 to 1977, the revenues and profits of Digital Equipment Corporation increased between 25 and 40 percent every year.

These industries also became the core industries of many countries, the way steel and automobiles once were, in that so many other industries depended on them. Information technologies reshaped traditional manufacturing, as well as many service industries, changing the rules of production and competition.

The Rise of Services. The revolution in information technologies facilitated a shift in the economies of advanced countries from the production of goods to the production of services. In less than a century, the developed countries have undergone a transition from industrial to postindustrial societies (Bell 1973). Although the transformation is incomplete and the shape of the postindustrial society (a term that merely describes what it is not) is still unknown, profound changes already have occurred.

In the United States, the turning point in the transition to post-industrialism occurred around 1950, when the number of workers employed in the production of goods was about the same as that employed in production of services. By 1980, approximately 70 percent worked in services and 30 percent in goods production. The shift has continued throughout the 1980s and 1990s, and many analysts predict that manufacturing will eventually go the way of agriculture, which has become extremely productive while employing less than 3 percent of the population.[2]

Underlying this transition are technological advances that have dramatically increased manufacturing productivity. New information-based automation technologies—numerical control, computer-integrated design, computer-integrated manufacturing, and others—have moved labor expenses in many industries to below 15 percent of total cost. These technologies also have given manufacturers greater flexibility in adapting to product cycle changes. Technological change is not the only factor in increasing manufacturing productivity; new management techniques, such as "just-in-time" and quality circles, have also played important roles.

A number of other forces came into play to contribute to the shift to a postindustrial society. Increased goods production prompted the creation of a broad range of services for producers, including accounting, data processing, and legal (Kirn 1987; OhUllacháin 1989). Producer services also proliferated because, for a number of reasons, producers have tended to unbundle their operations, or to contract out specialized services that companies in the past might have done in house (Drucker 1989; Kirn 1987; OhUllacháin 1989; Noyelle 1987). This has been referred to more broadly as the "vertical disintegration" of industries (Scott and Storper 1987; A. Scott 1988b).

The shift from manufacturing to services also was promoted by rising personal incomes in advanced societies. The proportion of demand for personal services increased in relation to that for goods. Another factor has been the rise of the welfare state, which has been a major provider both directly and indirectly of service employment (Clairmonte and Cavanagh 1986). Finally, the export of many manufacturing plants to low-wage countries hastened the shift to postindustrialism in the more advanced societies.

Services now employ approximately two-thirds of the labor force in advanced countries. They have become major exports for countries and regions. They are critical to the productivity of both manufacturing and other service firms. Although manufacturing and agriculture remain important in advanced societies, services have become the most critical area. Hall writes:

Implicit in this emphasis on the service base of urban economies is the notion that in advanced industrial countries the tertiary sector is now the real engine that drives economic advance. This idea is contrary to traditional ones, but it seems the only reasonable hypothesis corresponding to the known facts: in national economies where some two-thirds of all employment is now in the tertiary sector, this sector is constantly growing at the expense of the manufacturing sector. (1988, p. 125)

As mentioned above, the nature of the postindustrial society is unclear because the evolution is still occurring. Technological and institutional changes will continue to propel the process. One factor that will have a great impact in the near future is the development and increased application of flexible manufacturing technologies. These technologies will further diminish the importance of routine labor in the manufacturing process. The basis of competition in manufacturing will continue to shift from reducing costs to rapid development and delivery of new products. A second important force that will shape the postindustrial society is the use of automation and other productivity-enhancing measures in service industries (McCrackin 1985). Many of the new jobs that have been created in services, from data entry to accounting to food preparation, could become obsolete with future advances in expert systems, robotics, and other information technologies. Whether new jobs will be created to replace the ones lost is unknown. It remains to be seen what kind of jobs those might be and where they would be located. Contractions in service industries also could occur for other reasons, such as over-expansion or problems elsewhere in the world economy or in national economies.[3]

Globalization. Another major factor in the reordering of geography after World War II was the rise of the global economy. World trade has increased exponentially, and foreign investment also has expanded rapidly, especially since 1960. National boundaries no longer protect firms from competition. Most large growth companies must compete abroad and also face foreign competition in domestic markets. This change has been particularly dramatic in the United States. Approximately 25 percent of all goods produced in the United States were subject to foreign competition in 1965. Twenty years later, the figure was 75 percent (U.S. Congress 1984).

The globalization of national economies occurred for a number of reasons. First, the United States created and maintained an open world trading system, using its influence to discourage protectionism. Second, major progress in transportation, communications, and other technologies made dramatic increases in international commerce possible. Vernon has called these advances "the spectacular shrinkage of space" (Vernon 1977, p. 3). Computerization and computer networks have enabled businesses to coordinate production, marketing, and financial management across national borders.

A third factor was the growth of multinational corporations. Although multinationals had dealt in primary products for many years, it was not until the 1960s and 1970s that they took up manufacturing. Firms based in the United States and other industrialized countries began setting up manufacturing facilities in foreign countries to serve local markets. Other companies started manufacturing operations in foreign countries to export back to home markets or to markets in other countries. Some multinationals became global corporations, spreading their different stages of production around the world to gain comparative advantage at each stage.

Globalization has changed the landscape for competition for firms all over the world. For companies, regions, and countries, it has made for a more volatile environment. With staggering rapidity, events in one part of the world can affect conditions in another, with the multinational corporation serving as the conduit for change.

Social Consequences. The major technological and economic changes that have occurred since World War II have been accompanied by significant social changes. The knowledge revolution has not produced the violent upheavals and political movements that accompanied the industrial revolution of the eighteenth and nineteenth centuries. However, there have been significant shifts in occupations, the nature of work, income distribution, and family systems.

The rhythm of society is changing from the mechanically paced rhythm of manufacturing—the lengths of shifts, the spacing of holidays, the division of time into work and leisure—to the more flexible rhythms of a postindustrial society (Bell 1973). Workers now deal with information and not goods (Zuboff 1988; Stanback 1987; Flynn 1988). Creativity and technical competence have replaced discipline and physical strength as the most valued skills in the workplace.

Class relationships also have been altered. The decline of the industrial working class has meant a shrinking middle in advanced countries. This "hour-glass" effect has produced a polarization of society, with a high-paid technical and professional class at one end and unskilled service and unemployed workers at the other (Harrison and Bluestone 1988). Although many jobs in the service economy are high paying and high status, many more are low-paying, low-status positions. In the industrial age, employment usually meant a living wage. In the postindustrial economy, employment is not guaranteed to lift an individual or family out of poverty (Graham and Ross 1989). Indeed, underemployment has been associated more with successful economies than with stagnant ones, according to one study (Sheets, Nord, and Phelps 1987). This polarization has been particularly pronounced in the United States, which does not have redistributional policies effective enough to counter it (Harrison and Bluestone 1988).

Geographic Restructuring

The great changes outlined above—the revolution in information technologies, globalization, and the shift from manufacturing to services—have had major impacts on regions.[4] There have been large shifts of population and industry within countries, regions, and around the world. These dislocations have been costly in both human and financial terms (Markusen 1988). The "creative destruction" quality of capitalism identified by Schumpeter forty years ago is now being brought to bear on economic geography, as the economies of regions are destroyed and re-created at a rapid pace. The major geographic changes that have occurred so far in the advanced countries include:

- The decline of the traditional manufacturing belts in Europe and North America and the rise of new industrial regions in Sun Belts.
- The decline of cities and the growth of suburban and rural areas.
- The emergence of large cities as centers of corporate, producer, and personal services.
- The rise of the technopolis—propulsive regional centers of technological innovation.

In the 1950s, the most prosperous and innovative regions of Europe and North America were the manufacturing belts (Clark 1985). In the United States, the region encompassed the northeastern seaboard, the southern Great Lakes, and the Midwest. Iron and steel were the basic industries, anchored by the Appalachian coal fields, and centered in Pittsburgh, Youngstown, Duluth, Chicago, Detroit, Cleveland, and Buffalo. Secondary manufacturing—motor vehicle production being dominant—was located on the edges of the region, in Cincinnati, Milwaukee, and Detroit. The poorer economies of the South and West were based on primary products. In Europe, a similar pattern emerged, with the manufacturing belt running across the northwest portion of the continent, encompassing the Northwest and West Midlands of Britain, northern France, southern Holland, Belgium, the Ruhr area of Germany, northwest Italy, and southern Sweden. The economies of the southern part of Europe were largely agricultural.

A second major feature of industrial geography was the concentration of population and economic activity in large cities. In the United States at mid-century, 70 percent of the population lived in urban areas. Cities had grown rapidly in the first half of the century, driven by the growth of manufacturing and the population migration that accompanied the collapse of agricultural employment. The largest cities on the East Coast, from Boston to Washington, grew so big and so fast that they almost merged, becoming one great "megalopolis" (Gottman 1961).

The rapid plunge in the economic fortunes of the manufacturing belts and the cities has been well documented for both the United States (Bluestone and Harrison 1982; D. Clark 1985) and Europe (Massey 1984; Massey and Meegan 1982; Martin and Rowthorn 1986; Massey 1986). As factories closed in these areas, unemployment rose sharply and population began to fall. Suburban shopping malls replaced downtown shopping districts as centers of commerce. The hardest hit places in the United States were the core cities of the manufacturing belt: Detroit, Pittsburgh, Cleveland, and Buffalo (Markusen and Carlson 1989). In Britain, the story was much the same, with the large cities, the Northwest and West Midlands suffering high job and population loss.

Coinciding with the decline of the traditional manufacturing belts and large cities was the growth of new industrial regions. In the United States, population and industry grew rapidly in the South and West, with the greatest expansion occurring in California, Florida, and Texas. Within regions, non-metropolitan areas—especially the outer limits of commuter fields—grew significantly (Clark 1985). Similar patterns emerged in Europe. The new industrial regions were the south of England, the French Riviera, and Bavaria. Countries in the south of Europe—Spain, Italy, and Portugal—saw dramatic growth and became known as the European Sun Belt (Laffitte 1988). Suburbanization grew in Europe as it had in the United States (Hall 1988; Keeble and Wever 1986).

Rural areas in advanced countries also grew significantly, while moving further from their agrarian orientation. Many rural areas became centers of a variety of manufacturing activities and services (Bradshaw and Blakely 1982; Singlemann 1978). Some peripheral areas also began to attract high-technology industries (Oakey and Cooper 1989; Bar-El and Felsenstein 1989).[5]

The 1970s witnessed the rebirth of many previously decaying urban areas in the United States and Europe. This phenomenon was a geographical consequence of the larger shift from manufacturing to services in advanced societies. A diverse array of businesses, from fast-food restaurants to airlines, fall under the category of services. However, the most important and fastest growing segments of the service economy—corporate services—found it advantageous to locate in cities.[6]

The large, multiplant firms that became dominant after World War II needed a variety of specialized services, including accounting, legal, financial, insurance, management, public relations, and information processing. These became the urban growth industries of the 1970s and 1980s. The comparative advantages of cities in attracting these businesses are their central location and the intense concentration of people and information in urban environments (Stanback 1985; *OECD Observer* 1987). These agglomerations expand personal interactions and information exchanges, which are the competitive tools of the information age (Kasarda 1988).

The reagglomeration of cities prompted the formulation of the "world city" concept by a number of neo-Marxist scholars (Castells 1988; Friedman and Wolff 1982; Friedmann 1986). This model sprang from Hymer's observation that at the same time that multinational capital was decentralizing production, it was recentralizing control (Hymer 1975). The world cities became the headquarters of multinational capital. Relatively few in number, world cities were to be found almost exclusively in the advanced capitalist countries, according to this view. Friedmann writes: "Key cities throughout the world are used by global capital as 'basing points' in the spatial organization and articulation of production markets. The resulting linkages make it possible to arrange world cities into a complex spatial hierarchy" (1986, p. 71).

The world city hypothesis has not held up to scrutiny. Although a global hierarchy of spaces may indeed exist, the sharp distinctions in the status of urban centers have not been validated by empirical studies. Important service agglomerations are found in smaller regional and local urban centers as well as in some rural areas. The world city concept exaggerates the importance of the upper end of the urban hierarchy (OhUllacháin 1989).

Nevertheless, the renaissance that has occurred in major cities has been a remarkable turnaround (Frieden 1990; Frieden and Sagalyn 1989; Davelaar and Nijkamp 1989). Cities that had been economic disaster zones sprouted vibrant commercial and business districts less than a decade later. Depressed inner-city neighborhoods were transformed into high-priced residential areas desired by corporate professionals.

Despite this new service-based urban growth, the jobs that have been created have not yet compensated for the lost manufacturing positions from the previous industrial era. Neither is the match of skills to jobs very favorable for a large segment of urban populations. Most inner cities still contain a large underclass that does not have the skills to work in the corporate service economy (Hall 1989; Harrison and Bluestone 1988; Kasarda 1988). These individuals wind up either unemployed or in low-paying personal service jobs. In societies already becoming split between rich and poor, polarization is most pronounced in cities.

Another important feature of geographic restructuring has been the emergence of the technopolis, fast-growing agglomerations of high technology. At the core of these regions are propulsive industries—computers on Route 128, chips and computers in Silicon Valley, aerospace and electronics in Orange County—that make the technopolises behave like Perrouxian growth poles. These industries employ large numbers of people and usually are critical to the success of the larger economy, in the same way that automobiles and steel were in the previous industrial era. Technopolises have generally arisen in spaces away from the old manufacturing belt. In those exceptions (Route 128 being the most significant), the technopolis has been centered on the fringes of the old manufacturing center. The technopolis is the geographic center of the process of commercialization of new technologies (Smilor, Kozmetsky, and Gibson 1988b). Characteristics of these regions include the presence of major research institutions, public-private linkages, and a strong entrepreneurial environment. The technopolis is sustained by the creation of new and innovative firms. Accompanying the development of the technopolis has been the growth of a large pool of technical and scientific labor.

The role of military spending in regional restructuring has been the subject of considerable research and debate. Numerous studies have found correlations between regional economic growth and military spending in the United States (Markusen, Hall, and Glasmeier 1986; Malecki and Stark 1988; Markusen 1988; Crump 1989; Bolton 1980). Similar correlations have been discovered in Britain (Breheny 1988; Lovering 1988), France (Dyckman and Swyngedouw 1988), and West Germany (Kunzmann 1988). The argument can be made that the shift in regional fortunes in the United States after World War II simply followed the flow of military contracts.

Military spending clearly fueled the industrial growth in the Great Lakes states during the World War II years and the rebirth of the New England economy and the boom in California after the late 1960s. Military spending, whether it is research and development funding, equipment and weapons procurement, or location of installations, is a powerful stimulus to regional economies. However, the relationship between the two is more complex than simple cause and effect. The high technology resources of New England may have drawn defense spending to the region. The impact of military spending on regional restructuring can be understood only if it is placed within a larger framework of regional growth and development.

In concluding this discussion of regional restructuring, it is important to note that the process is still unfolding. The geographic patterns that have been described above could very well be altered significantly in the coming years and decades. The shape of the future is unknown, but some possible trends can be identified. Advances in information technology will, no doubt, continue to be a major influence (Brotchie, Hall, and Newton 1987; Hepworth 1987). New communication networks could have as important an impact on geography as the electricity and telephone networks did in an earlier era (Tarr and Dupuy 1988). Some have predicted that the diffusion of information technology will promote the dispersal of economic activity from central cities toward peripheral areas (Kutay 1988b; Brotchie, Hall, and Newton 1987). Drucker (1989) foresees an end to the long commutes from the suburbs to the city since jobs will move to people rather than the reverse.[7] Another scenario had headquarters shifting away from central locations (Solomon 1990). Others have forecast more home-based work, via "tele-working" or "tele-commuting" (Lozano 1989). However, many analysts have pointed out that just because it is possible to work at home or in some location distant from headquarters does not mean it is desirable (Forester 1989). Hall writes that "in an information society, the information you get in the corridor or the washroom or the cafeteria or the bar is still as useful as— often more useful than—the information that comes down the line and on the screen" (1989, p. 61). Also, much of the clerical work that is being performed at dispersed locations now may become unnecessary as new technologies, such as optical scanning, make data entry obsolete. Because cities have always been at key positions in information networks, their status and importance may be enhanced, according to some analysts (Goddard 1989).

Another technological change that will have a major impact on geography is the adoption of flexible manufacturing systems and other advanced automation technologies. As the cost of labor becomes less important as a factor of production, firms will no longer be compelled to site plants in areas of cheap labor. In other words, the standardized, mass-production phase of the classic product cycle could be eliminated. Where plants will locate and what factors will determine location remain to be seen.

Crisis in Regions/Crisis in Theory

Massey (1984, p. 3) has written: "Crises in theory are often a reflection of the real world in flux. In recent decades the spatial organization of industry, and the questions and problems it has raised have been trans-

formed, and the old theoretical structures have lacked the flexibility to respond."

The extraordinary global changes that have occurred in recent decades
have marginalized the older regional development theoretical frameworks.
The scope of geographic restructuring has been so great that it cannot be
explained by a single theory (Hepworth and Waterson 1988; Keeble
1976; Moriarty 1986; Stöhr 1986a). Thompson (1989, p. 136) writes
that the established frameworks "by stressing competition, crisis, and
rewards to innovation . . . tend to place high technology in a model market environment rather than in a real world home of historical legacies,
institutional constraints, and personal decisions." The more important
empirical studies of regional high-technology development have tended
either to ignore regional development theory or to give it merely lip service.[8] Neither have the established theoretical frameworks informed much
of high-technology public policy. Most governments that have attempted
to foster regional high-technology growth have used improvisational or
imitative policies. Higgins and Savoie (1988, p. 11) write that "by and
large, governments in Europe and North America have attempted to promote regional development by 'trying this and that.' Theoretical frameworks for defining measures have been singled out by governments but,
it appears, only for the benefit of annual reports or ministerial declara-
tions and speeches." Some of the particular difficulties with each of the
theoretical frameworks and their relevance to high-technology development are discussed below.

Neoclassical. Industrial location theory has largely fallen into disuse.
Many of its basic features—atomized decision makers, single-plant
firms—are increasingly out of place in today's business environment
(Scott 1988b). Its reliance on price competition as the critical issue in location decisions also appears no longer appropriate (Clark 1986).
Perhaps the most obvious weakness of neoclassical theory is the importance ascribed to traditional industrial location factors, such as transportation costs, access to markets, and access to raw materials. Labor is
viewed as homogeneous. To apply to newer industries, neoclassical theory must be recast. Locational attributes do matter to new industries,
whether they are services or high technology, but these factors are not the
same ones that apply to traditional manufacturing industries (Ady 1986).

Many studies have speculated on the nature of these factors.
Transportation costs are not critical for most high-technology or service
industries because of the high value per unit of their products (Kutay
1988a). However, because product cycles tend to be compressed in these
industries, products must be delivered to markets quickly. Thus, access

to an international airport is important. Access to raw materials and energy sources also is not a major factor because high-technology industries typically use little of either.[9]

Factors generally assumed to be important to newer industries are a skilled labor force, high-quality educational and research institutions, access to venture capital, physical and cultural amenities, and other "quality of life" attributes (Malecki 1986; Armington 1986; Office of Technology Assessment 1984). These factors cannot be incorporated easily into standard neoclassical models. They are often vaguely defined and impossible to operationalize, and their relative importance is difficult to assess. Scott and Storper (1987) conclude: "In practice these factors turn out to be little more than ad hoc lists hopefully masquerading as analysis."

Yet another difficulty with neoclassical theory is the set of assumptions that must be made in order to develop functional models. Many of the obvious oversimplifications are dealt with in the more complex formulations. However, the assumptions that economic actors are omniscient and that information is freely available are still present in many models. This is a serious problem for neoclassical theory as it relates to high-technology development (Nicol 1985). In high-technology industries, information is a factor of production that probably ranks higher than transportation costs, access to raw materials, and other factors important in neoclassical theory. Information is a scarce and costly resource for high-technology enterprises.

The most serious problem with neoclassical theory, however, is its failure to capture the dynamics of global change (Clark 1986; Massey 1984; Malecki and Varaiya 1986). Geographic restructuring is "a dynamic process set in a world of uncertainty and disequilibrium," notes Clark (1986, p. 416). These forces are at odds with the basic attributes of neoclassical models.

Political Economy. Political economy approaches to regional development emerged, in part, as a reaction to the rigidities of neoclassical frameworks. Political economy has been more effective at grasping the dynamics of regional restructuring and global economic and technological change. However, political economy approaches have not succeeded completely in explaining the complexities of contemporary regional development.

The weaknesses of product life-cycle theory, which has been the most influential of the political economy approaches, have become increasingly apparent in recent years. Birch's exhaustive empirical study of U.S. companies found the growth predictions of product-cycle theory unconfirmed, prompting him to suggest that we "need to discard anthropomorphic inclinations and obtain a more sophisticated model of the economy" (Birch 1987, p. 28). Product life-cycle theory fails to recognize the differences among firms and industries (Storper 1985; Scott and Storper 1987). Many high-technology industries differ in fundamental ways from older industries and do not follow the same developmental patterns. Product cycles are much more compressed in high-technology industries. Standardization stages, in particular, are extremely short. Therefore, it may not be profitable for firms to shift production to the periphery late in the product cycle. Also, many high-technology firms that should be reaching maturity and decline are exhibiting considerable capacity for innovation. The development of flexible manufacturing and other advanced automation technologies also is weakening the logic of the product cycle (Rees 1989). New process technologies can provide firms with the responsiveness needed to meet the demands of collapsing product cycles, while at the same time reducing the importance of labor costs. The Japanese already have found that modernizing mature manufacturing industries is an alternative to shifting production to cheap labor countries.

Neo-Marxist approaches have been the most concerned with global restructuring and the most willing to reconstruct theory to account for changed environments. The work of Scott and Storper on flexible accumulation has gone beyond the limits of product-cycle theory to explain how new technology and the forces of global capitalism are altering the rules of regional development (Scott and Storper 1987; Scott and Cooke 1988; Scott 1988c). This literature has made important contributions to an understanding of the role of the world economy on regional development. The most serious problem with neo-Marxist frameworks is their neglect of matters of innovation and entrepreneurship (Rees 1989; Hall et al. 1987). Their focus is too often on declining regions (Bluestone and Harrison 1982; Massey 1984). Neo-Marxist approaches are better at explaining why the location of industries shifts around the world than they are at explaining why and how indigenous growth occurs. This is an important point for a study of the technopolis.

The movement of industry around the globe is only part—and perhaps not the most important part—of the process of high-technology industrial development, or any industrial development, for that matter. High technology-based regional development has been an entrepreneurial phenomenon. Birch's study (1987) found that for different regions in the United States, the rate of business failures varied little. What determined regional growth and development was the rate of new business formation. The important question for regional development then becomes: What makes some regions hotbeds of entrepreneurship and others not?[10]

A final criticism of neo-Marxist approaches is that they are of little utility to policy makers. If industrial location is determined by the shifting of global economic forces, there is little that local officials can do about it. The standard Marxist and dependency prescriptions—delinkage from the world economy and socialist revolutions—become ever more unrealistic in industrialized countries. This criticism, of course, does not invalidate any of the research or conclusions of neo-Marxist research. However, it does suggest that the search for lessons about effective high-technology policies must go beyond this analysis.

A CONCEPTUAL MODEL OF THE TECHNOPOLIS

Although the theoretical approaches outlined above provide insights into regional development, none offers a complete explanation. Global restructuring has occurred with such swiftness that it has overtaken the analytical capacity of established theory. Neoclassical industrial location approaches may have explained fairly well the traditional manufacturing industries of early twentieth-century America, but they cannot interpret modern service economies. Product life-cycle theory may have explained the locational patterns of multinational manufacturing firms in the 1960s, but it cannot account for the behavior of many of today's high-technology firms that are adopting flexible automation technologies.

All of the standard theoretical frameworks, from neoclassical to neo-Marxist, assume that the industries in question are composed of manufacturing firms. The relevance of these approaches must be questioned in societies in which 70 percent of the gross national product and 70 percent of employment come from services. Further, services are becoming increasingly technologically sophisticated and constitute a larger proportion of what are considered high-technology industries (Quinn 1987).

There is also a bias in many of the established frameworks toward traditional manufacturing industry, coupled with a neglect of high-technology manufacturing. High-technology industries, which are fast becoming the critical industries in the world, behave differently from traditional manufacturing enterprises. They have different locational requirements, and they respond to different competitive dynamics in the world economy.

The absence of a unified, coherent theory of regional economic development reflects the disarray in the larger realm of economic theory. Drucker (1989) argues that the complexities of the world today have made construction of comprehensive theories impossible. "Such a synthesis may not be possible," he writes, "however badly it is needed—at least not in the form of a scientific theory. An equation with many partially dependent variables cannot be solved, as any mathematics beginner is taught" (p. 167). Economic research should focus on explaining discrete, short-term phenomena instead of trying to develop overarching theories, Drucker argues. This, after all, is the way the fields of modern engineering and modern medicine functioned for many years, he states. This point of view is particularly appropriate for the field of regional development, especially given the underdeveloped state of theory. Sweeping theoretical constructs crafted to be internally consistent are likely to founder on rapidly unfolding non-paradigmatic events (Clark 1987).

The remainder of this chapter constructs a framework for understanding one aspect of global regional restructuring: the development of the modern technopolis. Insights from a number of different theoretical perspectives are used. The intended result is a coherent yet flexible model that can explain why, how, and where technopolises develop and what role policy can play in the process.

The Nature of the Technopolis

As a first step, a clear definition of a technopolis needs to be established. The term and its synonyms—high-tech centers, high-tech corridors, and any number of variations of Silicon Valleys, Glens, Gulches, and so on—have been used in different ways by different authors. For the purposes of this discussion, a technopolis is defined as *a region that generates sustained and propulsive economic activity through the creation and commercialization of new knowledge.* This is a narrower definition than that used by many authors. As the term is applied here, a technopolis is not merely a concentration of high-technology firms or research and development organizations. At the center of the technopolis is the creative process of developing new technologies and translating them into commercial products or processes. This activity sets in motion a sustained spiral of economic growth through the creation of new enterprises, the expansion of old ones, and the attraction of others from outside the region.

This more focused definition tends to raise doubts about the conclusions of a number of researchers (Tatsuno 1986; Miller and Côté 1987; Markusen, Hall, and Glasmeier 1986) that high-technology centers are quite abundant and that many areas can become the "next Silicon Valley." Much of the regional development and high-technology literature in the United States uses federal standard industrial classification (SIC) codes to determine where there are concentrations of high-technology industry. Three problems emerge from this practice. First, SIC data have been notoriously out of date and are poorly maintained by the federal bureaucracy (Warsh 1990). Second, they do not distinguish between firms composed almost entirely of high-technology workers and those with a small high-technology work force (Malecki 1989). Finally and most importantly, this methodology fails to capture the central dynamic of the technopolis: the interaction of science and industry to produce new commercial products and processes.

The number of places that could be considered technopolises is fairly small, and they are widely scattered: Silicon Valley, Route 128, London's M-4 corridor, Orange County in California, and a number of sites in Europe, North America, and Asia. The most important characteristic of a technopolis is entrepreneurship (Birch 1987; Miller and Côté 1987). The technopolis spawns a large number of new businesses at a fast pace. Entrepreneurship gives the technopolis its dynamism and drives regional economic growth. Many of the new firms are spin-offs from existing enterprises. New firms replace older businesses that die or move. Although large firms are important to the technopolis, it is small firms that contribute most to the region's innovative capacity (Rothwell and Zegveld 1982). The effects of the technopolis's growth radiate outward to nearby economic space. Much of this growth is transmitted to neighboring geographic space, creating regional growth and development.

Another key feature of the technopolis is that its firms are part of the core industries of the national and international economies (Scott and Storper 1987). Most technopolises are based upon microelectronics, computers, and a handful of other similar or related industries. These industries determine the competitiveness of other industries. They are fast-growing, and they employ many people. Also, each technopolis tends to specialize in one or a handful of industries or technologies, for example, semiconductors and microcomputers in Silicon Valley, minicomputers in Route 128. Scott and Storper refer to these groupings of related industries as "ensembles." Another distinguishing characteristic of a technopolis is the presence of a large technical and scientific labor force. This agglomeration of specialized labor, which is drawn first by the job opportunities in the technopolis, reinforces the growth of the high-technology region.

Origins of the Technopolis: Global Change

As indicated earlier in this chapter, the technopolis emerged as part of the worldwide restructuring that began after World War II and intensified in the late 1960s and 1970s. Global restructuring produced uneven, polarized growth and sharp regional inequalities. The technopolis represents one extreme on the growth spectrum. The technopolis became the geographic center of the core, propulsive industries of the new era, replacing in the geographic hierarchy the old centers of the manufacturing belt.

More specifically, the technopolis arose because of the knowledge revolution, the dramatic new developments in information technology and related fields. With this technological revolution came a shift in the nature of economic development. The most important factor affecting the growth of firms and industries suddenly became knowledge. Raw materials, energy, transportation, and even markets assumed a lesser role. Thus technopolises emerged because they were uniquely capable of generating knowledge.

The knowledge revolution is not merely another chapter in the evolving saga of world capitalism; neither is it another Kondratieff wave that will crest and be replaced by another. It is a fundamental change in the technological basis of society. New information technologies and their interaction with other forces are reordering the economy, geography, and politics of societies all over the world. Advanced information technologies are ubiquitous, found in ever more products and processes. In the economic realm, their impact is being felt by high-technology, medium-technology, and low-technology industries. Traditional manufacturing is being transformed by computers, robotics, and information systems. Agriculture also is profoundly affected. According to one estimate, the information content of a slice of pizza exceeds the agricultural content (Wright 1990).

Because this technological revolution is still unfolding, it is impossible to fully grasp its consequences for regions. However, the central role of knowledge in this transformation produced the rapid ascent of the technopolis to the top of the global geographic hierarchy.

Knowledge Centers

The technopolis emerged because of the knowledge revolution; the characteristics of regions determined the location of technopolises. At the core of each technopolis is an institution that creates new knowledge. In most cases, this institution is a university or a university-affiliated research institute. In principle, the knowledge center could be an industrial research organization, but in practice, the conservatism of these organizations usually precludes them from pursuing the technical breakthroughs that come from the propulsive core of a technopolis. Personnel at industrial research organizations also tend to lack the entrepreneurial orientation found at many research universities or contract research institutes. There are important exceptions. Many researchers from Digital Equipment Corporation, Fairchild Semiconductors, and Shockley Laboratories developed ideas into products and spun off new companies. These older high-technology companies are properly considered secondary knowledge centers that developed their own propulsive qualities.

For a knowledge center to function as a growth center, it must do more than produce new scientific discoveries. It also must have an entrepreneurial orientation. Many fine research institutions are not surrounded by agglomerations of high-technology businesses. The only comprehensive survey of high-technology regions in the United States found no correlation between research spending and high technology location (Markusen, Hall, and Glasmeier 1986). In the successful technopolises, the knowledge centers have made the commercialization of laboratory research a central part of their mission. MIT and Stanford University had long-standing policies promoting the commercialization of research, while many other universities elsewhere discouraged it.

The university or knowledge center functioning as a growth pole is a relatively new phenomenon and perhaps the most distinctive feature of the technopolis. Before World War II, important new products and processes were developed by inventors working on their own or in small companies. The model of organized research that emerged during the war changed the nature of invention. From that point forward, team research, conducted, for the most part, in universities or university-affiliated institutes, became the dominant way new products came about.

The knowledge centers in the successful technopolises have a long history. They did not spring up haphazardly in random locations. Their growth can be traced to the actions of key individuals over the years, the most important being Leland Stanford and Frederick Terman at Stanford University, and William Barton Rogers and the university presidents who followed him at MIT. The development of these institutions, when traced to their origins, does seem to have a certain happenstance quality. One can speculate what might have happened if Rogers had not come to Massachusetts or if Terman had moved to Texas. The actions of individual men and women do make a difference in history, and the progress of regional economic development is no exception. However, the actions of individuals and the outcome of those actions are shaped by broader environmental forces. For important sociohistorical reasons, Terman did not settle in Texas, and if he had, his efforts to create a university science park there would surely have had different consequences.

Innovative Environments

An environment that supports innovation is the second necessary condition for the development of a technopolis. A knowledge center set in an environment that does not support innovation either will fail to generate growth or will produce growth elsewhere in space. Aydalot and Keeble (1988, p. 9) suggest

local environments play a major if not determinant role as incubators of innovative activity, as prisms through which stimuli to innovation must pass, as networks of interactions channelling and shaping the imprint of technological change in particular areas. The firm is not an isolated agent of innovation: it is one element within the local industrial milieu which supports it.

The following discussion of innovative environments borrows a framework used by Aydalot (1988). He identified three aspects of the environment: local relations, markets, and labor force. A fourth has been added here: the knowledge infrastructure. Strong interactions exist among these factors, and their relative importance cannot be precisely assessed. The goal of this section is to define the role each plays sufficiently to inform the subsequent discussion of public policy.

The Nature of Local Relations. A major difference between a technopolis and an older industrial complex is the new set of relationships among the principal actors. Distinctive relations form between large firms and subcontractors, manufacturers and service firms, government and academia, business and community groups, and so on. These relationships are intricate and interwoven. The result is an environment that is "information-rich."

High-technology entrepreneurship emerges more easily in this environment (Malecki 1989; Sweeney 1985, 1987). Would-be entrepreneurs employed at a firm or research institution can obtain information about opportunities for new products. They also have better access to venture or start-up capital, which, despite the emergence of an international market, remains a strongly locally based resource. As information about job opportunities and employees circulates, labor mobility increases. Information about successful entrepreneurs or role models encourages others to follow the same path.

Cooperation among elites is important to the development of this network of relationships (Miller and Côté 1987; Sirbu et al. 1976). A study of North Carolina communities found that entrepreneurship was more likely to flourish where community leaders and the business elite were oriented toward entrepreneurship (Schell 1983). Broader studies have attributed the economic renaissance in certain U.S. states to support from political and business leadership (Osborne 1988; Fosler 1988; Eisenger 1988).

Elite support for entrepreneurship can take many forms: public-private partnerships, sensitivity to regulatory concerns of small businesses, reduced taxes on business, and attention to infrastructure. Although insufficient empirical evidence exists to establish the importance of each of these environmental supports for entrepreneurship, the issue merits further attention because it is an area that is manipulable by public policy.

Markets. The presence of product markets has been an important contributor to the growth of technopolises. Many high-technology firms grew on Britain's M-4 corridor to serve the markets of the British government research establishments (Hall et al. 1987). The universities and research institutions of Paris provided a market for the cluster of high-technology instrument firms that spurred the growth of Scientific City (Scott 1988c). Boston's hospitals promoted the growth of the medical instruments industry in that city (Hekman 1980a). Even in a global economy, local markets are important for firms in almost any industry. Communication with customers is faster and clearer, and product development proceeds more effectively (Porter 1990).

Not all technopolises emerged because of the pull of markets. In the most important and best-known examples, no markets existed for the products that became the heart of the technopolis. There was no preexisting market for semiconductors for Silicon Valley's first entrepreneurs; neither was there a preexisting market for Route 128's first minicomputers. In these instances, supply created demand. As the technopolis took shape, downstream markets clustered around the new high-technology firms. Thus while markets contribute to the development of a technopolis, they are not a necessary precondition.[11] Markets ultimately are required to sustain the growth of a technopolis, and the stability of markets, whether military or civilian, can determine the prosperity of a high-technology region. The sharp fluctuations that have become characteristic of high-technology markets has produced dramatic swings in regional fortunes—fast-paced growth followed by sharp down-turns.

Labor Force. A broad range of research has found that the characteristics of the labor force are the critical environmental factors for the location of high-technology industry (Malecki 1987, 1989; Ettlie 1980; Scott and Storper 1987; Castells 1985a). Unlike traditional industries, high-technology firms do not depend heavily on factors such as raw materials, land, and proximity to markets. Most of the traditional factors of production can either be attracted to or are already abundant in many different locations (Dorfman 1982). Large amounts of initial capital usually are not required. The most important factor of production for high-technology business is knowledge, which is still embodied foremost in people (Ettlie 1980).

The labor force qualities that most support the development of a technopolis vary according to the technopolis's industry, its stage of development, and other factors. It is generally assumed that a high proportion of technical, scientific, and professional workers is most desirable (Rees and Stafford 1984; Malecki 1987; Flynn 1988; Botkin, Dimancescu, and Stata 1982; Bollinger, Hope, and Utterback 1983). Also, it seems to help if these workers are willing to accept lower than average pay (Thurow 1988). A vast literature has detailed the kind of labor force that tends to stifle innovation (Massey 1984; Bluestone and Harrison 1982; Checkland 1975; Castells 1985a). Technopolises are unlikely to arise in areas where the labor force is predominantly blue-collar, politicized, and unionized.

Beyond these generalizations, different technopolises have different personnel requirements. Some need, in addition to technical and professional workers, disciplined employees who will work for low pay at routine manufacturing positions.[12] A wide range of skills is needed to fill positions in service industries that support high-technology firms.

Labor force attributes are perhaps best captured by the concept of human capital (Schultz 1981; Thurow 1970; Harbison and Meyers 1964). The physical contribution of labor to most economic activity in advanced societies is minimal in relation to the contribution of brainpower. This is even more true in the technopolis. The rarest and most valuable form of human capital needed by the technopolis is scientific, professional, and technical workers.

A second step in analyzing innovative environments and the labor force is to identify the kind of environment that appeals to scientific and technical workers. There is little doubt that the main attraction is the technopolis itself, or the job opportunities and income growth possibilities that are found in the region (Scott 1988c; Scott and Storper 1987; Sirbu et al. 1976). A technopolis's growth thus can feed upon itself, which is an important agglomeration advantage.

Beyond this point, certain kinds of environments appear to attract and hold scientific and technical workers. Research is only beginning to sort out the more important factors. Scientific and technical workers tend to be more mobile than other workers (Gentile and Stave 1988; Ladinsky 1967), although the increase in dual-career families is restraining some of that mobility. One study has discovered clear "migration routes" for professional people in different parts of the United States (Shapero 1985). Some workers prefer to locate where they attended college or graduate school.[13] As mentioned above, the presence of a large agglomeration of firms—high technology and others—attracts scientific and technical labor because it increases the job prospects for workers and spouses.

Another recognized attraction for critical high-technology labor is quality of life. This concept is necessarily vaguely defined. As Scott and Storper (1987) point out, what is considered a good quality of life in one culture or period of time may be quite different from that in another. Much speculation and some empirical research have identified many of these factors. Among the most commonly cited are a pleasant climate, good schools, cultural and natural amenities, and low-density neighborhoods (Malecki 1989; Graves 1980; Porell 1982; Keeble and Wever 1986). Ranking these by order of importance is impossible given the incompleteness of empirical research and the amorphous nature of the variables. However, the available evidence, some of it anecdotal, indicates that a meaningful correlation exists between the presence of quality-of-life factors and large concentrations of scientific and technical workers.[14]

As Scott (1988a, 1988c) points out, the chain of causation does not begin with the tastes of technical and professional workers. In some instances, workers first are drawn to an area for employment opportunities, and then quality-of-life factors, such as cultural and commercial activities and improved schools, spring up around them. However, quality-of-life factors may prompt workers or students to stay in an area after they have been drawn to it initially. The absence of these factors in other areas can repel workers. Similarly, the presence of strongly negative quality-of-life factors, such as crime, pollution, and political corruption, can block high-technology development regardless of the number of positive influences (Kasarda 1988).

Quality-of-life factors cannot create a technopolis. However, as they interact with other influences in a developing technopolis, they often become an important part of an environment that supports innovation and high-technology entrepreneurship.

Knowledge Infrastructure. A common characteristic of the technopolis is a well-developed, highly regarded knowledge infrastructure (Goldstein and Luger 1990; Andersson 1985). For a number of reasons, innovation tends to occur where high-quality educational institutions, from day care to graduate schools, are present. The most important factor of production for high-technology industry is human capital, which is developed by the knowledge infrastructure.

First, quality primary and secondary schools, as well as preschools, are strong considerations for technical and professional workers in their residential location choices within and among regions. Second, schools are the key factor in the development of the human capital required by a region. Primary and secondary schools develop workers for first-tier jobs and also prepare students for higher education. Colleges and universities turn out workers for the higher-skill and managerial positions. Graduate and professional schools produce the human capital needed for the most specialized, knowledge-intensive positions. All elements of the knowledge infrastructure are instrumental in the development of entrepreneurs.

As discussed earlier, top research universities are the institutions that most often produce the new knowledge that is central to the growth of a technopolis. Universities also help develop the information networks that sustain the dynamism of the technopolis. Colleges and universities play an indirect role by attracting the services and amenities that make communities appealing to technical and professional workers, such as bookstores, restaurants, concerts, and theaters.

Agglomeration Economies. As discussed earlier, agglomeration economies arise after the entrepreneurial phenomenon has been set in motion. They appear to be particularly intense in the technopolis and help give the region its propulsive growth.

Agglomeration advantages in the technopolis arise in great measure from the large pool of technical and scientific labor. In this way, the technopolis resembles the industrial cities of the nineteenth and early twentieth centuries (Oakey 1984). Manufacturers of that era built plants in cities because that was where the workers were. In the technopolis, the labor pool is smaller and more specialized, but there are fewer competing places with corresponding labor profiles.

Agglomeration economies in the technopolis also are the result of the "vertical disintegration" of high-technology industries, identified by Scott (1988a, 1988c). For a variety of reasons, high-technology businesses tend to rely on external suppliers instead of resources within the firm. Niches for small and medium-size firms proliferate in this environment. Spin-off enterprises are encouraged. This is a powerful agglomeration advantage that was not present in the previous industrial era.

A final agglomeration advantage unique to the technopolis results from the short product-life cycles in high-technology industries (Oakey 1984). In traditional manufacturing industries, it is advantageous to relocate production to far-flung locations to reap labor-cost advantages. The compressed product cycles in high-technology industries mean that production often needs to be kept close to research and development. A related factor is the declining share of routine labor costs in high-technology products, which reduces the value of relocating jobs to low-wage places.

It is also important to note that agglomeration disadvantages may arise in the technopolis. These typically are overheated housing and labor markets, environmental degradation, and distressed infrastructure.

Services. The development of a technopolis is usually accompanied by the development of a strong services sector. The lines of causation are circular: The technopolis fosters services growth and services foster the growth of the technopolis (Sheets, Nord, and Phelps 1987; Kirn 1987; OhUllacháin 1989). The two are interdependent and, in some cases, indistinguishable (Daniels 1988; Brotchie, Hall, and Newton 1987). Many high-technology firms are service companies. Indeed, the distinction between manufacturing and services (a residual category at best) is breaking down in the new industrial era.[15] Information has become the principal commodity traded in almost all advanced industries, whether they are classified as services or manufacturing (Goddard 1989).

The technopolis should not be thought of as purely a high-technology manufacturing center (Graham and Ross 1989). In addition to the strong research and development component, a large and diverse agglomeration of service firms is an integral part of the technopolis.

The Technopolis in the 1990s: Competition and Cooperation

This model describes the manner in which the technopolis develops and identifies the critical elements in that process. However, it must be remembered that the model is set in a dynamic external environment. The great lesson of political economy research is that the real world is in constant change, which continually restructures the development process. Global shifts in technology, politics, economics, and society influence the manner in which the technopolis develops and the relative importance of each of the elements in that process.

At the start of the 1990s, the global business environment entered a period of significant change, which has had an important impact on the development of the technopolis. The accelerating trend toward globalization of markets joined with rapidly unfolding political and technological change to create an intensely competitive arena for firms, regions, and nations. An important reason for the early successes of the original high-technology firms of Silicon Valley and Route 128 was that they functioned in highly favorable competitive environments. These firms developed new products, which found vast, largely uncontested markets. This environment facilitated the rapid growth of the early high-technology firms and the first technopolises. The situation no longer exists. In high-technology business, as well as in many other businesses, a crowded field of industry giants, established mid-sized firms, and nimble start-ups is competing for shifting and fragmented markets. Competition now can come from anywhere: first- and second-tier NICs as well as the developed countries of Europe and North America. Japanese firms are a potent threat in almost all high-technology industries. With the globalization of competition, few companies are safe from foreign rivals in home markets.

Collapsing product cycles have further heightened competition. Manufactured goods that once had a life span of five or six years now must be redesigned every two or three. The situation exists in virtually all industries, but the challenge is greatest in high-technology fields, such as computers and semiconductors, where products can become obsolete in a matter of months. The principal consequence for firms is soaring costs for research and development. Indeed, these costs have become so steep that markets for many products must be global for firms to have any hope of recovering their investment.

Against this backdrop of profound economic change, the international business arena was jolted in the late 1980s by a series of momentous events: the stock market crash, the collapse of communism in Eastern Europe, pressures for democratization in NICs, and the end of the Cold War. While the long-term effects of these happenings will take time to sort out, the immediate effect was to inject more instability into an already shaky situation. Firms at the start of the 1900s thus faced not only heightened competition but also greater uncertainty.

The response of key players in the global economy has been to push aside many of the traditional boundaries that have existed in advanced capitalist countries between competition and cooperation. By forming strategic alliances with other firms and by developing more cooperative relationships with governments, firms have discovered that they can overcome some of the burdens of competing in this environment. Thus, a new and important determinant of competitive advantage for firms is the capacity to forge these collaborative relationships. For mature and emerging technopolises, this new environment poses both risk and opportunity.

Collaborative relationships among firms, commonly known as strategic alliances, take many forms (O'Brien and Tullis 1989; Gupta 1991). Firms have formed alliances for research, marketing, and manufacturing. Although strategic alliances exist in a wide range of industries, they are most prevalent in high technology, where product cycles are shortest and competition is the most intense. Perhaps the most important form of strategic alliance is joint, premarket research and development (R&D). The numbers of R&D consortia in the United States have grown consistently since 1984, when Congress legalized them by passing the National Cooperative Research Act. More than 137 now exist in the United States, and they are increasing at a rate of one or two per month (Evan and Olk 1990). Firms involved in different aspects of information technology—semiconductors, software, hardware, electronic equipment—have been active in forming R&D consortia to gain access to innovation in related fields and to reduce overall product development costs. Among the earliest and best-known R&D consortia are the Microelectronic and Computer Technology Corporation (MCC), a consortium of computer and electronics firms, which were influential in passage of the 1984 law, and the Semiconductor Manufacturing Technology Institute (Sematech), a consortium of U.S. semiconductor firms developing advanced production processes for memory chips. Although joint research and development is a relatively new phenomenon in the United States, both Europe and Japan have had R&D consortia for many years, and the success of the Japanese in electronics has been due in part to the pooling of talent and resources for research and development.[16]

Equity investments, typically by large firms in small or start-up companies, are another important form of strategic alliance. Large firms have found that by buying into small companies, they can gain access to innovation and entrepreneurship. The small firm benefits from the prestige and marketing power of the large firm and from the infusion of capital, which has been harder to obtain from traditional sources since the stock market crash of 1987 and the recession in the United States and other developed countries in the early 1990s. Some of the largest and most diversified companies in the world are seeking competitive advantage by buying into new small firms. Between 1988 and 1991, International Business Machines (IBM) accumulated more than $500 million in equity investments (Hooper 1991). Large firm investments in small firms have become characteristic of the biotechnology field (Sharp 1990). Research and development costs are huge in biotechnology, with long time periods required to get a product to market. Few small firms can compete in this environment without the financial backing of the large pharmaceutical companies. For the big firms, the biotechnology start-ups are important reservoirs of skills and ideas, as well as a bridge to the basic research being carried out in universities.

Government has adjusted its orientation toward interfirm collaboration. In many of the R&D consortia, government is a direct partner, providing both money and organization. In the United States, the long-standing distrust of business collaboration, which is embodied in nearly a century of anti-trust laws, has softened. The passage of the National Cooperative Research Act was a watershed in the U.S. government's orientation toward cooperative business relationships. The Reagan administration pushed the boundaries further, abandoning anti-trust actions begun by previous administrations against both IBM and the big cereal producers, approving a round of airline mergers, and allowing joint ventures by U.S. and Japanese car makers. During the 1980s, the Supreme Court also liberalized its position on a broad range of anti-trust issues, and related decisions flowed from the lower courts.

This changing external environment has not altered the fundamental process by which a technopolis develops. The role of knowledge and an institution capable of generating new knowledge remain central, and the presence of an environment that supports innovation is still essential. What the new environment does is heighten the importance of the web of local relationships. A technopolis is more likely to emerge and then thrive in a region characterized by dense, complex relations among firms and individuals. In this environment, capital will flow from large to small firms, which no longer have to rely on venture capitalists. Companies can develop buyer-supplier relationships not simply on the basis of price but also for long-term strategic advantage. The informal relationships characteristic of the early technopolises can become formalized.

Geographic proximity is not a prerequisite for the establishment of strategic alliances among firms. Collaborative relationships can be formed by firms in opposite corners of the world. However, strategic alliances, which require breaking down traditional boundaries between firms, are more likely to come together where firms are clustered in space. In these regions, complex social, professional, and commercial networks can develop, and these networks can facilitate the transfer of information necessary to build new interfirm relationships. Thus the established technopolises are in a position to exploit the new competitive environment.[17]

This does not mean that continued success is predetermined for established technopolises or their most prominent firms. Indeed, there is evidence that the problems of Silicon Valley's older semiconductor firms and Route 128's minicomputer companies were due, at least in part, to their failure to forge different kinds of relationships with other actors in the business arena (Saxenian 1990). The beneficiaries of the new environment more often are the smaller firms that are pursuing specialized markets and that gain competitive advantage by establishing subcontracting, supplier, or other relationships with firms in the region. These firms are exploiting the innovative milieu that led to the emergence of the technopolis in the first place. In this manner, the technopolis is sustained by re-creating the growth cycle that began the development of the region.

CONCLUSION

The review of regional development theory in the first section of this chapter concluded that none of the established theoretical frameworks captures the sweeping changes that have occurred in economic geography in the past forty years. Rather than try to use an existing theory to explain the development of the technopolis, this study has constructed a focused model that draws on a number of different theoretical perspectives to explain how the modern technopolis came about.

The technopolis emerged in the years after World War II because of global economic, social, and political change and the revolution in information technologies. The technopolis has been on the cutting edge of this phase of global, capitalist economic and regional restructuring. However, its meaning is more profound than this neo-Marxist construction implies. The technopolis represents a new process of economic development and provides the clearest indication yet that a new technological basis of society is evolving.

Technopolises developed in regions that were home to centers of critical research and development. These centers of global knowledge generated new products and processes used by industries throughout the world. Knowledge centers created propulsive growth because they were surrounded by innovative environments. These environments were rich in information critical to the development of high-technology enterprises. They provided access to product markets, some of which had explosive growth potential. These environments also had a large number of scientific, technical, and professional workers, as well as other favorable labor force characteristics. A final distinguishing feature of these innovative environments was the presence of a highly regarded knowledge infrastructure: primary and secondary schools, colleges and universities, and research institutions.

Propulsive growth is not guaranteed to any region where these conditions are assembled. Regional economies are set in a dynamic global environment. Many forces, both cyclical and structural, can undermine the growth of established or emerging technopolises. In the 1990s, because of an increasingly competitive external environment, the capacity to forge strategic alliances emerged as an important new determinant of competitive advantage for firms in the international business arena. Technopolises, which have dense networks of people and information, are well positioned to exploit this new external environment. Further important environmental changes will have major impacts on regions in the future. The rise and fall of industries will tend to create a boom-bust cycle in regions that are specialized in certain technologies. Nevertheless, regions that possess a knowledge center and an innovative environment will continue to have long-term advantages in the competition with other regions for the economic rewards of the technological revolution.

NOTES

1.   The industrial location work of another German economist, Wilhelm Launhardt, preceded that of Weber. However, Weber's book had a much greater impact because it was the first translated into English.

2.   The U.S. Department of Labor has predicted that service-producing industries will provide 79 percent of all non-farm employment by 2000 (Personick 1989). Thurow (1990) is a dissenting voice. He argues that service jobs in the United States have probably reached their peak as a percentage of total employment.

3.   Daniels, noting the impact of the October 1987 Wall Street crash, writes: "It follows that while researchers are still trying to get to grips with the spatial, economic and social impacts of the growth of services it may also be necessary to undertake some work on the actual and potential consequences of contraction" (1988, p. 435). Between 1987 and 1990, approximately 23,000 jobs were lost on Wall Street (Winkler and Power 1990).

4.   Geography is not a dependent variable, however (Castells 1985b, 1989). The interaction of geography with technological, economic, and social change produced the global restructuring outlined above.

5.   The expansion in rural areas was not universal. Falk and Lyson (1988) argue that much of the rural South was left out of the Sun Belt boom.

6.   There has been relatively little research into the geography of services. This is remarkable, given the attention that has been paid to the geography of manufacturing. A handful of studies has appeared in the past few years on the location of services in Britain (Howells and Green 1988; Begg and Cameron 1988), Europe (Howells 1988), and the United States (Kirn 1987).

7.   Robert Noyce, one of the inventors of the integrated circuit, presented this vision of the future most clearly when he told an interviewer:

If you look out the window at the freeway there, you might ask yourself, now what are most of those automobiles doing? They're *not* carrying goods; most of them are carrying information in the form of brains from one place to another. If you want to get a little speculative, you could ask yourself, what earthly reason is there for carrying those brains around and burning all that gasoline? I think it's because we don't yet trust the computer-telephone linkup; our electronic information technology is not perfect enough yet. There's just no need for all those cars.

There's no need for a high percentage of our working population to be *here* to work, because they're only handling information (Hanson 1982, p. 129).

8.   See for example, Keeble (1976), Smilor, Kozmetsky, and Gibson (1988a); Miller and Côté (1987); Dorfman (1982). These studies develop eclectic explanations of case studies of regional economic development. Hall et al. (1987) and Markusen, Hall, and Glasmeier (1986) formulate a synthesis of theoretical frameworks to explain high-technology development in Britain and the United States, respectively.

9.   Since World War II, proximity to raw materials and energy also has diminished in importance for traditional industries. The most striking example is Japan, which developed its steel and automobile industries without any indigenous iron ore or coking coal. Similarly, some of the world's most important ore producers, such as Mauritania and Liberia, have no significant heavy industries (Dicken 1986).

10.   It should be pointed out that the phenomena of entrepreneurship and innovation are not addressed well by any of the major theoretical frameworks. Clearly, the configuration of market forces posited by neoclassical approaches does not explain why and where innovation occurs; neither does placing these factors outside the model address the problem. As Galbraith once observed in an attack on neoclassical instruction: "Changing technology, it is conceded, alters progressively and radically what can be obtained from a given supply of factors. But there is no way by which this intelligence can be developed at length in a textbook. So economic instruction concedes the important, and then discusses the unimportant" (1966, p. 46 fn.).

11.   Similarly, the absence of markets can hinder the growth of a technopolis, as Saxenian (1988) demonstrates in the case of Cambridge, England.

12.   In a survey of seventy-two manufacturers, Kobu and Bryer (1989) found that the skills needed by high-technology manufacturers are not much different from those needed by traditional manufacturers: manual dexterity and the ability to follow directions. One manager of a high-technology manufacturing firm confided that employees were hired not on the basis of qualifications or performance in an interview but on whether they could fill out an application and make it to the interview on time.

13.   The attraction of the Boston area to MIT graduates has been recognized as an important factor in the region's high technology renaissance (Botkin, Dimancescu, and Stata 1984).

14.   Part of Silicon Valley lore is that the electronics industry developed there rather than in Phoenix or Dallas because semiconductor companies could not hope to attract top engineers to the hot climates of Texas and Arizona. See Lindgren (1969), cited in Sirbu et al. 1976. Cox (1985) argues that high-technology industry has never developed in Knoxville, Tennessee, which has both a major government research facility and a large university, because of the region's isolation and its marginal attraction as a place to live. In their survey of high-technology firms, Sirbu et al. note that respondents said they preferred Edinburgh to Glasgow because of the "ugliness" of Glasgow (p. 51).

15.   The classification of the industry system widely used today was devised by Colin Clark in his 1940 work, *The Conditions of Economic Progress*. He divided the economic universe into three sectors: primary (agriculture and fishing), secondary (mining and manufacturing), and tertiary (services). The tertiary sector was basically everything not included in the primary and secondary sectors: commerce, transport, communication, finance, government, and so on.

16. Japan's most successful joint research and development project probably was

the VLSI (Very Large Scale Integrated Circuit) Research Association, a consortium of NEC, Toshiba, Hitachi, Mitsubishi, and Fujitsu. The project catapulted the Japanese ahead of U.S. semiconductor firms.

17. For a dissenting view, see Florida and Kenney (1990a, b). They argue that "chronic entrepreneurism," cut-throat competition, and high labor turnover in places like Silicon Valley and Route 128 waste resources and undermine national competitiveness.

Chapter 4

Evaluating Technopolis Policies

This chapter returns to the technopolis policies described in Chapter 2. Using the theoretical framework devised in Chapter 3 and the available empirical evidence, the study now evaluates technopolis policies. A number of questions are addressed: Have these policies achieved the immediate goals of their initiators? Have they furthered broader regional development objectives? What does the technopolis model predict will be the outcomes of these policies?

Answering these questions requires breaking new ground. Despite the abundance of technopolis policies, evaluations of their effectiveness have been sparse. The OECD (1987) and the U.S. Congressional Office of Technology Assessment (1984) compiled descriptive surveys of technopolis strategies. However, little formal assessment from government or other official entities has been attempted, even though billions of dollars in public money have been spent on technopolis initiatives (Evans and Triplett 1989). In the scholarly literature and the popular media, only scattered reports evaluating technopolis policies have appeared, and most of these have focused on specific programs or case studies.[1]

Advocates of technopolis policies often respond to the issue of evaluation by asserting that it is too soon to assess these programs: Building a technopolis takes time—ten to twenty years at least—and premature judgments could doom programs that would have brought results further down the road. While the general point may be valid, it should be remembered that some technopolis policies have been around for the ten- to twenty-year spans deemed necessary for results to appear. Research

Triangle is nearly thirty years old; Tsukuba Science City is twenty-five; Cambridge Science Park, nineteen; Sophia-Antipolis, sixteen. The first capital assistance programs—the Massachusetts Technology Development Corporation and the Connecticut Product Development Corporation—are more than a decade old. It may be too early to make a definitive judgment on all technopolis policies, but preliminary evaluations are warranted in many cases.

Another problem with evaluating technopolis policies is ambiguity in their objectives. By what standards should their accomplishments be measured? The most commonly used criteria offered by proponents of technopolis policies are the number of companies created, the number of jobs created, and the amount of private money leveraged (Feller 1988). The problem with these yardsticks is that they provide no clues as to whether these jobs and investments would have occurred anyway. Rarely are they measured against the financial cost of the policies or what might have happened if the money had been spent for some other public or private purpose.

Stöhr (1986b) developed general criteria for evaluating technopolis policies. He concluded that technopolis policies should be judged on their ability to upgrade the technological level of a region, produce more and better jobs, enhance the international competitiveness of a region, improve environmental quality, foster equitable income distribution, and generate self-sustaining growth. While these criteria may capture the intended benefits of technopolis policies and are, for the most part, quantifiable, the problem again arises of linking policies with outcomes. For example, regional income levels may rise after construction of a science park, but proving a causal link will be impossible because of the presence of so many other variables.

Another difficulty with evaluating technopolis policies is that outcomes have different meanings for different interests. The competitiveness of firms is an important measure for private enterprises, but less so for universities and government. Universities are more interested in scientific preeminence than are government or private firms. Governments are more interested in job creation than are private firms.

This study approaches the task of evaluating technopolis policies from two directions. First, they will be evaluated in the context of the model developed in Chapter 3. Policies will be examined to determine if they are consistent with the process by which a technopolis develops. Are policies creating effective knowledge centers? Do they support innovative environments? Second, the available empirical evidence will be reviewed to determine if technopolis policies are meeting the stated objectives of their initiators. Are science parks creating new jobs? Are business incubators hatching important new businesses? Because the empirical evidence is sparse and sometimes impressionistic, the conclusions must be tentative. Nevertheless, this represents a step toward determining whether these policies are working.

POLICIES AND PERFORMANCE

University Investments

As technopolis policies, university investments are designed to create or support a regional growth center. In theory, if a university research program can be strengthened sufficiently, it can produce new knowledge, which, in turn, can generate propulsive growth.

The biggest pitfall in such an approach is that many university programs cannot be elevated to the level of a knowledge center quickly or cheaply. Most of the knowledge centers in the successful technopolises evolved over many years, with large infusions of public and private funds. A university program that is to function as the core of a technopolis must have some existing capacity to generate new knowledge.

Effective university investments must be substantial and they must be sustained over long periods. Probably the most successful case of university investments promoting the emergence of a technopolis occurred in Texas, where state government poured millions of dollars in windfall revenues from the oil boom into the state university system. The Austin/San Antonio corridor has become the ninth-largest high-technology cluster in the United States by one estimate (Miller and Côté 1987). The University of Texas has ties to more than half of the high-technology small and medium-sized firms in the corridor (Smilor, Kozmetsky, and Gibson 1988c; Smilor, Gibson, and Kozmetsky 1989). Nevertheless, the failure of state government to maintain its level of investments in the university may jeopardize the growth process (Smilor, Gibson, and Kozmetsky 1989).

University investments have failed as technopolis policies where university research programs lacked the potential to become a knowledge center. However, this does not mean that regions should not invest in university research or higher education. University investments are an effective way of developing human capital, which is critical to virtually all regional economic growth strategies. Upgrading university research capacity can also be a long-range approach to technology development. The impact of such investments may be felt many years hence in ways that were unforeseen, in much the same way that MIT founder William

Barton Rogers never could have imagined that actions he took in the mid-1800s would lead, after a long train of events, to the development of the Route 128 technopolis. For most contemporary regions, however, investments in university research are not going to produce immediate economic growth.

Science Parks

A science park can be designed either as a growth center for a technopolis or as a component of an innovative environment (Goldstein and Luger 1990). The success of a science park may hinge on which of these roles its developers choose for it.

Science parks are unlikely to function as an effective knowledge center for a technopolis. Most of the knowledge centers in the existing technopolises evolved over many decades and even centuries, during which time considerable investments of public and private funds were made. Although it is possible to compress these time frames, the development of a research facility, which can function at the frontiers of science and technology, cannot be accomplished as easily or as quickly as building a science park. Goldstein and Luger, who surveyed 116 research parks, found that parks in regions with a prior concentration of research and development activity were the only ones likely to be effective: "A science/research park by itself is unlikely to serve as a 'seedbed' for stimulating a concentration of R&D activity in a region. Such a park is not likely to remain viable through the incubation stage" (1989, p. 7).

If conceptualized as part of an innovative environment, a science park is a more realistic approach (Goldstein and Luger 1989). As a public-private partnership that links university research and commercial exploitation, a science park can facilitate the flow of people and ideas in the innovation process that is at the core of a technopolis. When it functions in this manner, the science park facilitates the growth initiated by the knowledge center. The knowledge center must precede the science park. In other words, Stanford Industrial Park could not have existed without Stanford University's Electrical Engineering Department.

In practice, science parks have been designed to perform both roles, and the available evidence indicates that most have not been too successful in either. The science park as knowledge center is best exemplified by North Carolina's Research Triangle Park. Although it is often mentioned in the same breath as Silicon Valley and Route 128, Research Triangle has failed to demonstrate any self-sustaining capacity or to provide any linkages to the economy of the surrounding area (Whittington 1985a;

Goldstein and Malizia 1985; Luger 1984). Miller and Côté (1987) write: "On all accounts, the Research Triangle Park is an artificial cluster. It does not have much internal dynamism and grows mostly by the addition of outside elements. The Park was started some thirty years ago, and even today, it remains a very expensive experiment" (p. 6). Although it is far more ambitious than a science park, Japan's Tsukuba Science City represents the same phenomenon: transplanted research and development facilities with no propulsive capacity. Tsukuba's high-technology development has shown little ability to generate new firms or to upgrade the technological level of local industries. Moreover, like Research Triangle it is set in an environment that is not conducive to innovation.[2] Too often, science parks are used to house multinational corporations' branch plants, which have no capacity to spin off new firms or create backward or forward linkages in the local economy. In these instances, science parks represent subsidies of the multinationals (McLoughlin 1984).

Although science parks can function as an integral part of an innovative environment, many of them do not. The reasons are not easy to identify and probably differ from one science park to another. Joseph (1989) found that despite the intentions of science park developers, little interaction took place between universities and tenants in three parks in Australia. Macdonald (1987a) observed little interaction between industry and universities in British science parks. He attributes this to poor design and conceptualization of science parks: "Technology parks are fascinating; they are high technology as seen by urban planners, developers and architects, who have transmogrified something strange into something they can handle" (1987b, p. 367).

Another problem that has beset science parks is that even when they attract firms, these tend to remain small and have little employment effects on the surrounding region. New Haven Science Park houses about 100 firms, but its impact on the surrounding inner-city neighborhood, where unemployment is high and skill levels are low, has been minimal (Gupta 1990; Grassmuck 1990). Schamp (1987) found that science parks did not produce many jobs and did nothing to reduce regional inequality in Germany. Saxenian (1988) concluded that small firms in Cambridge, England, and Cambridge Science Park have been unable to grow because neither the British government nor the country's aging industrial base provides a large enough market for the firms' products.

Science parks also have encountered more basic problems. Many have had trouble finding tenants, leaving buildings vacant or sites undeveloped (Grassmuck 1990; Blumenstyk 1990; Macdonald 1987a, 1987b; Minshall 1984). The University of Delaware and the state of Delaware spent more than a million and a half dollars developing a research park that has been vacant for eight years (Blumenstyk 1990). The city of Pullman, Washington, has spent more than half a million dollars publicizing a 147-acre research park built by the community and Washington State University in 1982. In 1990, the park had only one building (Blumenstyk 1990).

Other parks have been unable to turn a significant profit or have lost large amounts of money (Lowe 1985; Gupta 1990). This can threaten the viability of a park if one or more of its benefactors—most often local or regional governments—encounter rough financial times themselves and no longer want to continue subsidizing the operation.

Not all science parks have failed. Those set in innovative environments or linked to an existing knowledge center have done well. Sophia-Antipolis has flourished in large measure because of the attractiveness of its natural surroundings. Parks set in metropolitan areas that already have significant high-technology resources also have succeeded (Malecki and Nijkamp 1988).

Capital Assistance

In theory, capital assistance programs could be effective technopolis policies. As an element in the system of local relations, publicly sponsored capital assistance programs could link technical entrepreneurs with needed risk capital. In practice, however, these programs have not been significant factors in regional high-technology development. One obvious limitation is their magnitude. Most funds have stayed on a small scale and represent only a small fraction of the venture capital needs of an emerging technopolis.

They also function in ways that are fundamentally different from private venture capital (Oakey 1984). Unlike private venture capitalists, managers of private funds tend to be risk-averse. They usually expect full recovery of their investment, while private venture capitalists expect either to lose their investment or reap a huge profit (Malecki and Nijkamp 1988). Private venture capitalists also are able to provide firms with technical, management, and marketing advice throughout the start-up period. For public funds, this is not always the case. Miller and Côté (1987) also point out that the quality of managers of public funds is often considerably lower than that in the private funds simply because public funds cannot begin to match the salaries of private funds. Managers of public funds are usually paid slightly above the rate of upper-level government bureaucrats. Managers of private venture capital funds are among the highest-paid people in the society.

Empirical studies of the effectiveness of public capital assistance programs are virtually nonexistent. The only one reported in the recent literature is Fisher's analysis of the Connecticut Product Development Corporation (CPDC), a program founded in the mid-1970s (Fisher 1988). CPDC provides grants to firms to develop new products in return for royalties on the sale of the products. Fisher concluded that the fund has not generated enough revenue to pay for its operation and will likely continue to require a taxpayer subsidy. Of the fifty-eight products CPDC invested in during its first ten years of operation, only six had generated royalties that were close to or more than CPDC's original grant. None of the other fifty-two products had returned more than 40 percent of the grant amount. He concluded that the public benefits probably did not justify the long-term taxpayer subsidy.

Small-Business Incubators

Like capital assistance programs, small-business incubators could, in theory, be useful technopolis policies. They are designed as a means of creating and transmitting the information needed by entrepreneurs. They also are intended to lower the initial overhead costs for start-up firms by providing subsidized office or laboratory space and shared facilities.

However, practical problems, similar to those that have beset capital assistance funds, have plagued small-business incubators. Miller and Côté (1987) identify several common problems. First, managers of incubators tend to focus on office management problems rather than technical or business support. When that support is available, it is usually only right after the firm starts up. Second, incubators tend to attract "problem firms" that have little potential for growth. Finally, incubators lack the status that is part of commercial high-technology development.

An incubator is egalitarian: Long corridors with doors every thirty feet with third-rate signs on most of them, announcing little-two-bit operations. This is not a neighborhood for high-powered entrepreneurs. The real entrepreneur secretly dreams of having his corporate logo perched high "up there," showing the world with bravado how well he made it in the tough world of high technology. An incubator does not recognize this aspect of an entrepreneur's inner world. (Miller and Côté 1987, p. 125)

A recent survey by the accounting firm Coopers & Lybrand of incubator tenants found considerable dissatisfaction with the management of the facilities (Jefferson 1990). Nearly 40 percent of respondents stated that incubator managers should be better trained, devote more time to tenants, and provide better access to accountants, lawyers, and consultants. More than two-thirds said the facility did not play a major role in helping them gain financing.

Thus, small-business incubators have made little contribution to regional high-technology development. Firms that have emerged from incubators have tended to remain small. A study of fourteen incubators in the United States and Canada found that even after several years of operation, few firms either in incubators or incubator "graduates" created many jobs (Campbell 1989). The average number of jobs in incubator graduate companies was twenty. In recent years, incubators themselves have struggled, and a number of them in the United States have gone out of business (B. Brown 1989).

Infrastructure

Infrastructure development is important for a technopolis, whether it is the physical infrastructure or the telecommunications or information infrastructure. Transportation systems are important for the movement of both people and products. High-technology products tend to be small and lightweight; networks designed to transport large, heavy goods are not critical. However, because of compressed product cycles, high-technology products need to reach markets fast. This enhances the importance of international airports with good access roads and public transportation links.

Perhaps more important in the technopolis are systems designed to move people, who in a knowledge-based society continue to be the principal conduits of knowledge. Thus effective systems of roads, mass transit, airports, and, in some places, high-speed inter-city trains must be in place. Government involvement is essential if this infrastructure is to be built.

A large literature exists on the role of infrastructure generally in economic development.[3] The central point of this work is that the productivity of industry is determined by the sum of private and public investments. Stated another way, regional development results from the combination of private production factors and infrastructure. Munnell (1990) traces the decline in U.S. productivity growth to underinvestment in infrastructure.

The fact that we are shifting into a new technological era does not invalidate this point. However, as the technological transformation unfolds, the infrastructural needs of society change. Transportation networks must be capable of moving people from the knowledge center to peripheral areas and from new residential areas to the new locations of industry. With changes in economic geography likely to continue for some time, flexible transportation systems are advantageous. Many of the transportation networks in use today are fixed and oriented toward the old locations of people and industry.

Although infrastructure planning occurs routinely in most regions of the world, rarely is it viewed as a technopolis policy. Only in Japan has this happened. In most places, infrastructure development occurs to meet perceived existing or projected needs. This is a weakness in technopolis strategies. Attention to the infrastructure should be an integral part of the development of an environment that is conducive to innovation (Peterson 1987).

Similarly, technopolis policies generally have failed to address information infrastructure needs. In the United States, policies that affect telecommunications systems are developed by public utilities regulators and not regional planners or development specialists. The establishment of high-speed data transmission systems and supercomputer networks could play a major role in economic development in the future. Kasarda (1988) suggests that municipal governments purchase supercomputers and lease time on them to local businesses. He writes: "Wiring a city and linking local businesses to municipally owned supercomputer facilities will be as essential to urban economic prosperity in the computer age as were water, sewer, and power lines linking businesses to public works facilities in the industrial age" (p. 80).

Whether municipal governments should be running supercomputers for local businesses is questionable (especially given the problems many local governments have with less complex technologies like cleaning streets), but technopolis planners should be paying more attention to the information resources of regions.

Public-Private Partnerships

Knowledge-intensive technologies cannot be developed by market forces alone. Cooperative efforts are required involving government, business, labor, and universities. Public-private partnerships thus are an important technopolis strategy. They can shape long-range technology initiatives and increase the flow of information among concerned parties (Bassett 1990). When effective cooperative relationships have been forged, barriers to innovation can be identified and removed. Malecki (1989, p. 74) writes:

[G]overnment—more precisely, a few individuals in the public sector—can facilitate informal networks and contacts among government, business, and education in ways that can be especially productive. Such contacts can provide the initial sources of capital as well as the early purchase contracts so essential to the success of new firms. To foster such contacts itself can require a considerable effort, especially for government leaders, but the payoff to the local economy can be substantial in the long run.

A strategy that has been effective is the establishment of umbrella institutions to encompass interests that may have been antagonistic to each other in the past (Perrin 1988). This approach creates a new framework in which parties can relate to each other and was used effectively at Sophia-Antipolis.

Public-private partnerships must be seen as long-range technopolis policies that promote the evolution of new relationships important in an innovative environment. A question that merits further research is whether the direct approaches mentioned above (capital assistance programs, business incubators, science parks) may have important indirect effects because they foster cooperative relationships among parties that in the past have been adversaries. The Congressional Office of Technology Assessment suggested this in its 1984 report. Referring to technopolis policies, the study concluded: "Their principal achievement to date may be in terms of institutional rather than technical innovation—i.e., policy development, consensus building, and the encouragement of cooperative linkages among governments, universities and industry" (Office of Technology Assessment 1984, p. 11).

Quality of Life

Technopolis policies oriented toward improving or maintaining quality-of-life attributes of a region are important. Quality of life is critical to attracting and keeping the labor force needed by high-technology firms. Furthermore, many quality-of-life attributes, such as environmental protection and education policy, are matters that are largely outside the market and can be manipulated only through public policy. Like infrastructure policy, quality-of-life issues are rarely conceptualized as elements of technopolis strategies. Rather, they are dealt with in relation to other, broader societal goals. Regardless of how they are framed, policies that address quality-of-life matters are important to the development of the technopolis.

Technopolis policies or innovation policies in general cannot be developed separately from policies affecting housing, education, recreation, public health, and the environment. Many of the technopolis strategies mentioned above foundered because they defined the process of regional development too narrowly.

CONCLUSION

Technopolis policies have had mixed results during the past decade. The more direct approaches to high-technology regional development—science parks, small-business incubators, and capital assistance programs—have generally failed to achieve their objectives. Most of these policies misunderstood the process by which a technopolis develops. These initiatives often were created without appropriate linkages to a knowledge center, which is necessary for the emergence of a technopolis. They also tended to be set in environments that were not conducive to innovation. Further, they were supplied with resources insufficient for a major impact on regional economies.

These policies may be important as symbolism, however. To the extent that they are the product of new relationships among key individuals and institutions, they can further long-range technology-development objectives.

The more effective technopolis policies are those that deal with broader environmental goals. Policies directed at improving or maintaining a region's quality of life may be most significant. Attention to the physical and information infrastructures also is an important role for policy.

A final point is that the sheer number of technopolis policies that emerged in the 1980s has hampered their effectiveness. Most technopolis policies are generated by regional interests. This tends to produce anarchic competition among regions for high-technology resources. Presumably not all regions can be technopolises, given the finite markets for high-technology products. As technopolis policies proliferate, the more they are likely to fail, simply because they are competing for a scarce commodity.

Whittington (1985a) describes the U.S. states as being caught in a classic prisoner's dilemma: To have any hope of economic growth, they must attempt high-technology development. But the more they try, the more they will fail. This process may be at work with Japan's technopolis program as well. MITI had originally planned to have only a handful of technopolises but agreed to more than twenty under pressure from prefectural governments. In some respects, the Japanese technopolis program resembles the industrial development phenomenon known as "every region in Yugoslavia must have its own steel mill." The technopolises may find themselves competing with each other for what high-technology development is possible in the country (Glasmeier 1988).

The problem is exacerbated by the fact that in advanced countries, would-be technopolises also must compete with established high-technology centers that were unplanned. Small-business incubators in various parts of the United States have been frustrated by having their "graduates" leave and settle in Silicon Valley and Route 128 (Abetti, Le Maistre, and Wacholder 1988; B. Brown 1989). The Japanese technopolises must compete with Tokyo and Osaka, and Hsinchu must compete with Taipei for the skilled personnel critical to high-technology development.

NOTES

1. Thompson (1987) calls studies of state government high-technology initiatives in the United States "snapshots of experiments in process" (p. 419). He concludes: "In sum, most research on state HTD [high-technology development] efforts thus far has concentrated on individual programs, has been of a mere cataloguing nature, or contains analysis at the general qualitative level. A formal quantitative study of goal achievement and impacts is still lacking" (p. 421).

2. Onda (1988) writes, "Tsukuba Science City is presently considered an isolated island, remote from normal human society—a city of academics and education."

3. For literature reviews, see Kaplan (1990) and Rietveld (1989). Studies of the problems of U.S. infrastructure include Munnell (1990), Aschauer (1989), National Council on Public Works Improvement (1988), and Choate and Walter (1981).

Chapter 5

The Development of the Route 128 Technopolis

The emergence of the Route 128 technopolis was an important event in post-World War II regional development. Route 128 is one of the first and largest technopolises in the world. It was built on top of a decaying traditional manufacturing economy. The rise of this technopolis is also significant for the suddenness with which it occurred. In less than a decade, the region went from economic stagnation to industrial renaissance. The Massachusetts miracle, as this transition was labeled, was emulated all over the world.

In fact, the restructuring of the eastern Massachusetts economy was no miracle. It can be understood in terms of the framework set forth in Chapter 3 and the revolution in information technologies. In the years after World War II, the region was positioned to capitalize on opportunities created by the unfolding technological revolution. It was endowed with not one but two of the world's great knowledge centers: Massachusetts Institute of Technology and Harvard University. The area had an abundance of attributes that would nurture the innovation process. The existing industrial base also provided many of the factors of production—especially skilled labor—needed by the emerging high-technology industries.

The Route 128 experience is significant also because it illustrates the dramatic swings in regional economies that can accompany high-technology development. In 1975, the unemployment rate in Massachusetts approached 12 percent, nearly three points above the national average. Ten years later, the unemployment rate was 3.9 percent, the lowest of any state in the country. By 1988, the major civilian and defense markets for the state's high-technology industries had weakened, and by 1991, the state's unemployment rate was well above the national average.

The fact that Route 128 was an unplanned technopolis is well known and widely accepted. Even more than Silicon Valley, which was guided in its early years by Stanford Professor Frederick Terman, Route 128 seemed to develop spontaneously. Nevertheless, the Route 128 technopolis should not be seen as a triumph of unfettered, open markets. Policies of non-market actors—governments, universities, and private organizations—supported the emergence of the technopolis. Although the precise role of military spending is the subject of much debate, its considerable importance to the economic revival is not disputed. Once the technopolis clearly was emerging, state and local governments moved to sustain the process. Some of these policies succeeded, while others failed.

THE INDUSTRIAL HISTORY OF MASSACHUSETTS

Two aspects of Massachusetts' industrial past contributed to the rise of high-technology industry: the industrial revolution and the development of the pre-World War II science-based industries. Each helped set the stage for the emergence of the technopolis.

America's industrial revolution began in Massachusetts.[1] Although most early settlers in New England were farmers, agriculture steadily migrated from the region's rocky soil to the more fertile lands to the west. Left behind were skilled craftsmen who had made tools for agriculture, merchants who had grown rich on overseas trade, and poor farmers who were looking for a better way of life. This combination of human resources was precisely what was needed for the industrial revolution.

Because war and embargos had restricted investment opportunities for Boston's merchant capitalists, they decided to invest in what was then new technology. In 1811, Francis Cabot Lowell, a wealthy Boston merchant, visited textile factories in England, memorized the configuration of the power looms, and with some technical help, introduced the textile industry to the United States. In 1813, Lowell and his fellow investors developed the first fully integrated textile factory in America in Waltham, Massachusetts. Although Lowell died in 1817, his partners went on to develop on the Merrimack River what could be considered a nineteenth-century technopolis, the city of Lowell, Massachusetts. They built machines, factories, canals, and housing. They recruited struggling farmers, both men and women, who became the nucleus of a new industrial working class. The city of Lowell was America's first planned industrial community.

New England already had many skilled craftsmen who had made a variety of goods, including furniture, clothing, and tools for the preindustrial economy. In the eighteenth century, mechanics, millwrights, and dam builders had constructed saw mills and grist mills. These workers designed and built the factories of the industrial revolution, and they made possible the development of the machine tool industry.

Machine tools are critical in the transition from an agricultural to an industrial economy. All modern manufacturing industries depend on them. The military's demand for guns stimulated development of the machine tool industry in Massachusetts and also led to the establishment of a weapons industry in the region. Manufacturing industries that were established in New England during this period needed to be close to the makers of machine tools and thus tended to stay in the region instead of migrating in search of cheaper labor.

By 1860, the industrial boom in Massachusetts was at its peak. Boston's population had tripled in the preceding thirty years, and new cities had grown up around the mills. Textiles, shoes, machine tools, metalworking, and weapons were thriving new industries. After the Civil War, however, the industrial base began to erode. The development of interchangeable parts and the widespread use of steam power permitted textile production to move away from New England's machine tool industry and abundant water power. The most attractive location for manufacturers was the American South, where labor was considerably cheaper and more docile. Massachusetts' manufacturing industries faded steadily throughout the twentieth century. Although World War I and World War II provided temporary boosts, stimulating production of leather goods, clothing, machinery, and weapons, the downward trend persisted. The rise of the newly industrializing countries in the 1970s was the death knell for most of Massachusetts' struggling textile production. While all of the state suffered during this period, the mill towns were hardest hit (Mullin, Armstrong, and Kavanagh 1986). Heavily dependent on a small number of factories, these communities saw thousands of people put out of work with little alternative employment available.

Before the turn of the century, conditions were in place for the development of enterprises that were different in fundamental ways from the manufacturing firms of the industrial revolution. The new companies represented the high-technology industries of their day: electrical machinery, communications, and electronics. They were built on the region's manufacturing base and the expanding cluster of higher educational institutions. They were the first businesses to originate from scientific research conducted at universities.

The universities supplied the inventors and entrepreneurs who launched the firms. The existing industries provided both the financial and human capital the new firms needed. The machinists and engineers who had worked in manufacturing helped to develop the products of the new industries, and the fortunes made by manufacturers or merchants supplied the capital needed to start the new firms.

The invention of the telephone and the founding of Bell Telephone Company illustrate the influence of both the universities and the industrial base in the emergence of science-based industry in Massachusetts (Reich 1985; Bruce 1973; Coon 1939). Alexander Graham Bell was a professor at Boston University and his assistant, Thomas Watson, was a machinist when they produced the first telephone in 1876. Bell had gotten the idea for the device after viewing a "mechanical ear" at MIT.[2] John Murray Forbes, a Boston merchant, provided financial backing for research and development. After Bell obtained a patent for the invention, three men— Bell; his father-in-law, Gardiner C. Hubbard, who was a wealthy lawyer; and Thomas Sanders, a successful leather merchant—founded Boston Bell Telephone Company. Sanders and Hubbard put up the capital while Watson managed the research organization. The enterprise eventually would become the largest corporation in the world.

Another twentieth-century industrial giant with roots in Massachusetts is General Electric Company (Conot 1979; Hammond 1941; Passer 1972). Thomas Edison was a Boston free-lance inventor before he moved to the New York City area in the 1870s to found Edison Electric Company. Meanwhile, Thomson-Houston Company of Lynn, Massachusetts, was a thriving electrical machinery and lighting company. In 1892, Thomson-Houston, owned by a group of shoe and leather manufacturers, merged with Edison Electric to become General Electric. The company was based in Schenectady, New York, although the Lynn facility remained in operation as a branch plant.[3]

Another important science-based firm to emerge around this time was Raytheon Corporation, which developed a revolutionary new radio tube in the 1920s (Adams 1977; Scott 1974). Founded by MIT Professor Vannevar Bush and two other men, Raytheon would become a major defense contractor during and after World War II with its pioneering work in radar technology. Other major prewar firms include Polaroid Corporation, founded in 1937 by Harvard dropout Edwin Land (Olshaker 1978); General Radio Company, the first electronics manufacturer in the United States; and the scientific and engineering firm EG&G, founded by MIT Professor Harold E. Edgerton.

Although they were overshadowed by the traditional manufacturing concerns, science-based companies became major contributors of jobs and economic growth in Massachusetts in the first half of the twentieth century. In 1923, electrical machinery was the state's third largest employer (Ferguson and Ladd 1988). Many of these firms are still among the largest employers in the region.

Few clear linkages exist between these companies and the new high-technology firms, most of which trace their roots either to other post-World War II high-technology firms or to university research laboratories. The role played by the prewar science-based companies is indirect. First, they provided financial and technical support to the region's universities and research institutes, which enabled the institutions to upgrade their facilities. Second, they created a demand for engineers and science graduates, which the universities expanded to fill. Third, the companies attracted skilled labor to the area. Thus the prewar companies helped create a large pool of skilled labor and a strong knowledge infrastructure, both of which were necessary conditions for the development of the technopolis. A final point is that prewar science-based firms were among the first to locate on Route 128, providing anchors for industrial districts that would become the heart of the high-technology region.

THE EMERGENCE OF THE TECHNOPOLIS

Route 128 High-Technology Industry

The Route 128 technopolis arose with the emergence of new, knowledge-intensive industry in the region. The core industry of the technopolis was computers (Kuhn 1982; Dorfman 1982, 1983; Hekman 1980b). The leading companies were Digital Equipment Corporation, Wang Laboratories, Data General, and Prime Computer. Surrounding these key firms, all of which were founded after World War II, were many new, smaller, high-technology companies, which were involved in computers and related electronics fields. This new, entrepreneurial high-technology sector was the engine that drove the Massachusetts economy after the 1960s. Although the service sector also grew dramatically during this period, it was not a primary cause of regional economic growth. Its main function initially was to serve high-technology manufacturing (Norton 1987).

The history of Digital Equipment Corporation (DEC) is probably the most celebrated entrepreneurial success story of Route 128 (Rifkin and

Harrar 1988). It illustrates the roles played by technical entrepreneurs, venture capitalists, and MIT and its research laboratories in the development of Route 128. In 1957, Kenneth Olsen, a researcher at MIT's Lincoln Laboratories, persuaded General Georges Doriot, president of a Boston venture capital firm, to invest $70,000 in a plan to develop a small, interactive computer. The company grew slowly but steadily until 1965, when it introduced the PDP-8, a small computer that would revolutionize the industry. The size, price, and technical features of the PDP-8 made computing accessible to thousands of people in business and in scientific research. This was the birth of the minicomputer industry, and during the next two decades, DEC experienced spectacular growth. By 1988, DEC was an $11 billion company and the second biggest computer maker in the world.[4]

No less astonishing was the story of Wang Laboratories, founded by a former Harvard researcher with only $600 of his personal savings. An Wang's company pioneered the development of word processing systems, the first product to bring computers to office workers. The phenomenal success stories of An Wang and Kenneth Olsen inspired countless other Route 128 entrepreneurs.

The new high-technology firms of Route 128 soon spawned new generations of firms. In 1968, Edson de Castro, who had headed the PDP-8 project for DEC, left the company with two other young DEC engineers and founded Data General (Tarcy 1991; Kidder 1981). The company set up shop in a former beauty parlor in the mill town of Hudson, Massachusetts. Data General's first computer, the NOVA, was an inexpensive and powerful machine that launched the company into a decade of growth unsurpassed in the industry. By 1978, Data General was a Fortune 500 company and a challenger to DEC's supremacy in minicomputers.

In 1972, seven engineers left their jobs at the Boston computer operation of Honeywell to found Prime Computer. Prime built a new high-performance minicomputer aimed at specialized markets. The product made the company a leader in the industry.

Another Route 128 firm that surged into the minicomputer industry was Computervision (Weil 1982). The company was founded in 1969 to manufacture a computer sold as a component of a computer-aided design/computer aided manufacturing (CAD/CAM) system. A decade later, the firm had 3,600 employees and was a major player in the minicomputer industry and the market leader in CAD/CAM.

The attention garnered by these big, high-growth Route 128 companies obscured the presence of the hundreds of smaller high-technology firms that were central to the regional economic boom. Many of the small companies were suppliers or subcontractors to the big minicomputer firms, which represented a vast new market. Other small high-technology firms were in fields not tied to minicomputers. The 1970s saw a large growth in firms that made precision instruments: measuring and controlling devices, medical and scientific instruments, and optical instruments and lenses (Hekman 1980a; Dorfman 1982).

The economic growth that reshaped the Massachusetts economy in the 1970s was indigenous (Dorfman 1982, 1983). The companies that led the way were Massachusetts start-ups, founded by entrepreneurs who came out of local research institutions or firms. Little of the growth was due to the relocation of outside companies or the siting of branch plants.

Despite the diversity of the myriad firms that produced the economic revival, certain common traits can be identified. First, the companies clearly represented high technology, in all of the standard definitions of the term. They devoted significant portions of their resources to research, and a large percentage of their employees were scientists and technicians. The firms succeeded by developing new technologies. Second, the companies, for the most part, developed new products and not new processes (Dorfman 1982, 1983). They did not discover more effective ways of making existing products, as Francis Cabot Lowell and Henry Ford had done. They created new products for which there was no existing market. The products in effect created their markets, which were global in scope. This large, open territory, relatively free of competition, made possible the explosive growth that occurred. A third characteristic is that most of the products were sold to businesses (Dorfman 1983). Some also went to universities, research institutes, and government. Not many of the products developed by Route 128 companies in the boom years were targeted for mass markets. Many of the smaller firms found lucrative niche markets in the business arena.

Finally, the central role of minicomputers in the economic boom should be emphasized. The development of minicomputers, which occurred almost exclusively in Massachusetts, was a landmark event in the history of information technology. DEC, Wang, Data General, Prime, and other, smaller firms built products that made the power of computers accessible for the first time to millions of people in business. By creating and exploiting these new market opportunities, these firms became huge multinational corporations almost overnight. Scores of smaller firms sprang up to supply and service the minicomputer firms, which soon became spawning grounds for entrepreneurs.

Spatial Dimensions of the Technopolis

The development of high-technology industry in Massachusetts was not confined to a single definable region. The most concentrated and well-known agglomeration is along Route 128, a horseshoe-shaped highway that encircles Boston while passing through many suburban municipalities. Route 128 was built in several phases, the first of which was completed in 1951. Planned as a bypass to keep long-distance traffic off congested city streets, the road quickly attracted industrial development. The first firms to locate on the highway were older companies that had been straining in cramped, outdated facilities in the city. Cabot, Cabot, and Forbes, a Boston real estate firm, pioneered the development of campus-style industrial parks that attracted the new high-technology companies (Rand 1964; Adams 1977). Cabot, Cabot, and Forbes built adaptable, one-story buildings, attractively landscaped, with plenty of parking and easy highway access.

Between 1951 and 1957, the investment in new plants on Route 128 totaled $85 million, more than three-fourths of which came from companies relocating from Boston (Massachusetts Institute of Technology 1958). After moving to Route 128, companies increased their employment by an average of 25 percent. In the next decade, development on Route 128 accelerated. Older firms were joined by high-technology start-ups and service and distribution companies. In 1965, an estimated 600 companies were on the highway.

The high-technology boom was not confined to Route 128, however. Route 495, a circular highway west of Route 128, became home to many high-technology firms, including Data General. Some firms located in Boston and Cambridge to be near universities, hospitals, or urban amenities. In the 1970s, East Cambridge's Kendall Square, which is adjacent to MIT, drew some companies. Their numbers increased dramatically in the 1980s after major public and private redevelopment efforts. MIT researcher David Birch (1987) calculated that in the 1980s, more jobs were created in East Cambridge, a neighborhood of less than one square mile, than in thirteen states. In 1990, *Inc.* magazine labeled East Cambridge "the most entrepreneurial place on earth" (Gallese 1990). The area is the center of the region's software and biotechnology industries. Probably the best-known company in Kendall Square is Lotus Development Corporation, the business software pioneer. Founded in 1981 with three employees, Lotus was a $500 million company eight years later.

In general, however, the pattern of high-technology location has been one of migration from the city (Boston and Cambridge) to the suburbs. The progress of Wang Laboratories is illustrative. Founded in Boston in

1951, the company moved to Cambridge a few years later, then to several locations on Route 128, and finally to Lowell. Some high-technology industry also developed further afield. While research and development tended to remain within Greater Boston, production and warehousing facilities were built in southern New Hampshire and southern Maine. Some high-technology industry also developed in Rhode Island and the Worcester area.

The city of Boston has undergone transitions caused, in part, by the development of Route 128 and other high-technology areas outside the city. The exodus of businesses to suburban locations was followed by population migration. In the 1950s, Boston was a decaying city (Adams 1977). City government, controlled by Mayor James Michael Curley, was rife with corruption. In 1959, Moody's Investors Service rated Boston's bonds the worst in the country. With the city on the brink of bankruptcy, Boston's business and financial communities rallied, forming what was known as the "Vault." This closed group of the city's elite moved aggressively into politics and development. In 1959, John Collins, a business-oriented politician, won a surprise victory in the city's mayoral election. Under Collins' administration, an ambitious redevelopment program was begun, which continued under his successor, Kevin H. White.

In the 1970s, Boston's financial and business services industries grew dramatically (Ferguson and Ladd 1988). The development of new information technologies created global markets for these services. With its long history as a financial center, Boston was in a position to take advantage of these new opportunities. The region's high-technology industries also needed lawyers, accountants, and business analysts. Thus as manufacturing moved out of the city, the new service industries moved in, bringing with them new jobs. Throughout the 1960s, 1970s, and 1980s, Boston's revival continued, albeit with occasional setbacks—most notably the school busing crisis of 1974. Gentrification became a concern in once-decaying neighborhoods, as well-do-do professionals began to move to the city. High-rise office buildings, starting with the Prudential Tower in 1965, reshaped the city's skyline. Commercial development proceeded at a fast pace, spurred by the spectacular success of Quincy Market. Boston's revival made it, in the words of historian Russell Adams, "a fit companion of the dynamic age of new technology sprawling along Route 128" (Adams 1977, p. 309).

The economic renaissance did not reach all of Massachusetts. Some of the older mill cities, including Fall River, Lawrence, Brockton, and New Bedford, never fully recovered from the collapse of traditional manufacturing (Ferguson and Ladd 1988; Coakley 1991). The western part of the state received almost no high-technology industry or high-level producer services (Harrison and Kluver 1989). Some smaller cities, including Pittsfield and Lynn, were vulnerable to the actions of large, external firms that operated local branch manufacturing plants. Depressed minority areas of Boston and other smaller cities also were largely untouched by the economic boom around them.

CAUSES

Knowledge Centers

The Route 128 technopolis would not have emerged without the presence of a world-class knowledge center. MIT is the core knowledge institution of the technopolis, with Harvard playing a secondary role. These institutions created the knowledge that entrepreneurs adapted into new commercial products. This process of innovation established the technopolis.

MIT's role in the emergence of the technopolis was shaped by the institution's past.[5] Two characteristics have distinguished MIT throughout its history: its close relationship with industry and its ties to the military. MIT nurtured these relationships at first out of necessity. Because it did not have a large initial endowment, the institution had to seek support from outside sources in order to grow.

William Barton Rogers, a geologist from Virginia, founded MIT in 1865 with funding from the federal Morrill Act and a land grant from the Massachusetts legislature. His goal was to train engineers for the new manufacturing firms of the industrial revolution. Rogers and his successors at the helm of MIT rejected the notion of the university as a refuge from the world. MIT was an institute, not a university, and it always had a practical bent. As early as 1869, MIT students were working in machine shops at the U.S. Navy Yard in Charlestown. In the 1870s, students travelled to Colorado, Utah, and Wyoming to learn about mining and geology. Engineering students visited the steel, coal, and oil regions of Pennsylvania, while others observed the construction of bridges over the Ohio and Mississippi rivers.

MIT's relations with the military began after the Spanish-American War, when the institute contracted with the Navy to train top Naval Academy graduates in naval architecture. The first Reserve Officers Training Corps (ROTC) program in the United States was established at MIT in the early 1900s.

In the first half of the twentieth century, MIT's leaders transformed the institution from a training school for engineers to a center of scientific, industrial, and military research. The first research laboratories were established in 1903. In the 1930s, MIT President Karl Taylor Compton bolstered the faculty, added courses, and modernized laboratories. The timing of this effort could not have been more opportune. MIT found itself positioned to reap a large share of the military research money that the federal government would dispense during and after World War II.

A pivotal event in the history of MIT and postwar economic development in Massachusetts was the establishment by military contract of the Radiation Laboratory in 1940 (Killian 1985). The laboratory, the largest research organization in the world to that time, developed microwave radar, which was crucial to the war effort. MIT's success with the laboratory demonstrated "the creative power of large, integrated research programs conducted in the benign environment of an educational institution" (Killian 1985, p. xviii). The Radiation Laboratory opened the gates to a flood of military funding to MIT. The Instrumentation Laboratory developed computing gunsights to defend ships against Japanese kamikaze pilots. This facility later became Draper Laboratories, a major research organization and spawning ground for high-technology entrepreneurs. In all, MIT received approximately 400 military contracts for the war effort.

One of the key facilities to emerge around this time was Project Whirlwind, under Jay W. Forrester. Although it was started with a military contract to build flight simulation systems, Whirlwind's focus soon shifted to development of the digital computer. In the 1940s, MIT's computer research had become stalled. Vannevar Bush, who headed the research, had focused on analog technology, which failed to yield significant computing power. Meanwhile, important advances were being made in digital computers at other universities. The University of Pennsylvania's J. Presper Eckert and John W. Mauchly, widely regarded as the inventors of the digital computer, and John von Neumann of Princeton led their institutions ahead of MIT in computer development. Project Whirlwind catapulted MIT back into the forefront. MIT researchers developed their own digital computer, which had a sophisticated magnetic storage system that represented a major breakthrough. MIT obtained a patent for the magnetic storage system and used it to receive large royalties from IBM and other computer companies.

After World War II, military contracts kept flowing to MIT. Special laboratories and projects were set up away from campus to perform classified research. Lincoln Laboratories, where DEC's Kenneth Olsen would get his start, was established in 1951 to perform work on air defense; Mitre Corporation received extensive defense and NASA contracts.

Government funds made the research possible, but MIT policies transferred the fruits of this research to the region's industry. MIT's Division of Industrial Cooperation and Research, established after World War I, was one of the institution's first large-scale initiatives to transfer laboratory research to industry. The university's patent policy, adopted in 1932, allowed researchers and the institution to share the profits of inventions. By contrast, Eckert and Mauchly received no royalties from their invention of the digital computer because the University of Pennsylvania had no patent policy.

MIT also encouraged its students and staff to get involved with business. Faculty members may spend 20 percent of their time on outside activities (Simon 1985). Joint research projects have been established with industry and university researchers. MIT students and faculty, especially those at the government-sponsored research institutes, have moved easily from the university to business. MIT is the largest source of high-technology entrepreneurs in the Route 128/Greater Boston area. A survey in 1986 identified more than 400 MIT spin-off companies, representing sales of more than $29 billion and employment of 175,000 (Lampe 1988). Companies whose founders had MIT connections include Digital Equipment Corporation, EG&G Inc., Teradyne Inc., Analogic Corporation, SofTech Inc., Apollo Computer Inc., Software Art Inc., Lotus Development Corporation, Symbolics Inc., Biogen Inc., Analog Devices, and Bose Corporation.

Harvard University shares with MIT a history of scientific excellence. The Lawrence Scientific School, founded at Harvard in 1847, was one of the first university science departments in the United States. The prestigious Graduate School of Arts and Sciences opened in 1872. With research facilities that are among the best in the world, Harvard has produced many scientific breakthroughs and Nobel laureates.

Harvard did not generate entrepreneurs the way MIT did, mainly because the university discouraged commercialization of university research, while MIT promoted it (Dorfman 1982). The philosophy at Harvard was that research should extend the horizons of knowledge, not develop commercial products. Nevertheless, Harvard did generate propulsive growth for the regional economy, although unintentionally. A number of technical entrepreneurs emerged from Harvard, the most important being An Wang, who resigned as a research fellow when the university deemphasized computer research because computers were becoming commercially viable (Wang 1986).

As the technopolis matured in the 1970s and 1980s, it became less dependent on its original knowledge centers. Many entrepreneurs emerged from high-technology firms. The best-known example is Data General, founded by employees of DEC. The large firms that did function as incubators of new high-technology entrepreneurs can be looked on as secondary knowledge centers. Nevertheless, most of the important new firms seemed to have some connection to MIT. Adams wrote, "Like some biblical patriarch, MIT begat companies that begat companies in a chain reaction that seemed to have no ending" (1977, p. 284).

Innovative Environment

The environment in the Greater Boston area during the formative stage of the technopolis was highly conducive to entrepreneurship and innovation. These conditions nurtured the growth stimulated by the knowledge centers.

Local Relations. The web of local relations needed by high-technology industry was well developed in the Route 128 technopolis. During the formation of the technopolis, information flowed freely among firms, universities, and research institutes. Most of the relationships were informal. The intricate connections among MIT researchers and key personnel at DEC and other companies facilitated the high rate of innovation that characterized the emerging computer industry in Massachusetts (Rifkin and Harrar 1988; Kidder 1981).

The importance of local relations was nowhere more evident than in the region's venture capital industry. Because the development of new technology carries great risks, venture capital has been critical to the growth of a technopolis. Despite the emergence of national markets, most venture capital remains a strongly local phenomenon. Some regions have abundant venture capital; others have none at all. Venture capitalists like to be close to the companies in which they invest so they can monitor and advise firms. One study found that although Boston-based venture capitalists export considerable capital from the region, one-third of it remains in New England (Florida and Kenney 1988).

In 1946, Ralph Flanders, president of the Federal Reserve Bank of Boston, developed the concept of the modern venture capital firm to stimulate the regional economy (Bylinsky 1976; Liles 1977; Jacobs 1969). With a group of industrialists, financiers and officials from MIT, Flanders founded the American Research and Development Corporation (ARD). The firm raised $5 million by issuing common stock, which was purchased by financial institutions, individual investors, and universities. General Georges Doriot, a Harvard Business School professor, was named president of the company. Doriot, aided by advisers from the MIT faculty, worked closely with the young high-technology entrepreneurs who came forward in the 1950s. He gambled on inventors who had little or no business experience, guiding them through the difficult process of developing products and finding markets. The company's most famous and most profitable investment was a $70,000 stake, or 77 percent ownership, in Kenneth Olsen's Digital Equipment Corporation.

Like the firms it invested in, ARD spun off new enterprises as staff and others connected with the company left to start new venture capital firms. Boston Capital, Palmer, Greylock, Charles River Partnership, and Morgan-Holland all have ties to ARD. ARD's success also stimulated the creation of new, unrelated venture capital firms and convinced established financial institutions to free up risk capital. In the 1950s and 1960s, the Bank of Boston financed many high-technology start-ups and was one of the first banks to allow federal grants to be used as collateral (Ferguson and Ladd 1988).

Boston, along with San Francisco and New York City, has become a center of the U.S. venture capital industry. In the 1980s, branch offices of venture capital firms began to move to the area. In 1988, greater Boston had an estimated sixty firms, controlling approximately $2 billion in capital. This represented approximately 12 percent of the total venture capital assets in the country (Florida and Kenney 1988).

Labor Force. The technopolis was able to grow because it had a highly favorable mix of skills embodied in the regional labor force (Browne and Hekman 1981; Hoy 1988). The most important characteristic of the labor market was the presence of abundant scientific and technical personnel. Many of these workers were drawn to the area by the concentration of prewar science-based industries. By coincidence, a slump in some of these industries, particularly those in aerospace and defense, occurred as the high-technology firms entered their time of greatest demand for labor (Dorfman 1982; Lampe 1988). This made available considerable technical labor at relatively low costs (Dorfman 1982; Thurow 1988).

The major reason for the concentration of scientists and technicians in the Route 128 area, however, was the unique concentration of colleges and universities. The Boston area produces a disproportionate share of the nation's engineers and scientists (Hoy 1988; Dorfman 1982). New England produces almost twice as many doctorates in engineering and the physical sciences per capita as the national average. Engineers are educated not only at Harvard and MIT but at Northeastern University, the University of Lowell, Worcester Polytechnic Institute, and other institutions. Northeastern has one of the largest engineering training programs in the country.

Many of these workers decide to remain in the area after completing their education (Gentile and Stave 1988). No empirical studies have been conducted of why these workers have stayed, although anecdotal evidence abounds. In addition to the obvious pull of job opportunities, other factors cited in the literature include the region's distinctive package of services and amenities (bookstores, theaters, restaurants, and sports, arts and music attractions), easy access to other East Coast metropolitan centers, good primary and secondary schools, an attractive natural environment, and a long history as a world center of culture and ideas (Dorfman 1982; Browne and Hekman 1981; Dukakis and Kanter 1988; Kohut and DeStefano 1989). Also, until the early 1980s, affordable housing could be found in attractive suburbs with good municipal services.

High-technology industry in the Greater Boston area also needed skilled machinists and metal workers, especially in the early years of the technopolis. Massachusetts had an abundant supply of these skilled workers, who had been employed in the machine tool business and other older manufacturing industries that once dominated the region.

The final class of workers required by high-technology firms is routine production and assembly workers. Qualities sought by high-technology firms are discipline, an ability to follow directions, and a willingness to work for low pay in a non-union setting. The collapse of traditional manufacturing had depressed wages considerably in Massachusetts and New England as the technopolis emerged. Workers were willing to accept low-paying jobs. Hard times softened the militancy of the dwindling industrial working class of the region (Harrison 1984; Harrison and Kluver 1989). Joining the working force during this period were unorganized immigrants and women. Most of the Route 128 high-technology firms successfully resisted unionization efforts. Furthermore, these workers were literate, disciplined, and quite capable of handling routine tasks. As pay scales increased in the Route 128 region, some firms relocated production to lower-cost areas. Some routine production remained in New England, especially southern New Hampshire, while other operations were shifted elsewhere in the United States and overseas.

Markets. No established market existed for minicomputers, the core industry of the Route 128 technopolis. Supply preceded demand for minicomputers. Once the industry emerged, the principal customers, who were found all over the world, were businesses, research organizations, and governments. As the technopolis emerged, the growing cluster of high-technology businesses, especially the minicomputer companies, became an important market for new and established local firms. The web of supplier and service firms represented a dynamic, expanding market.

Although the military was not a major customer for minicomputer companies, defense spending was an important market for other high-technology businesses in the technopolis. Many small companies that made instruments, computer hardware, information systems, and software sold their products to the military. Raytheon, General Electric, and other older, advanced-technology firms also did considerable defense business.

Whether military expenditures played a major role in the economic revival of the region is the subject of much scholarly and political debate. During the 1988 presidential campaign, Democratic candidate Michael Dukakis claimed credit for the state's economic success, while critics countered that the military build-up of President Ronald Reagan really was responsible for the Massachusetts miracle. Scholarly evidence is mixed. Dorfman (1982) examined patterns of military prime contract awards and determined that "they did not contribute greatly to the high tech boom" (p. 101). Barff and Knight (1988) looked at similar data as well as employment patterns and concluded that while defense spending may not have caused the economic renaissance, it did determine its timing. Crump (1989) argues that military spending was the main factor in the turnaround. Dismissing the idea of a Massachusetts miracle, Crump writes, "It is no miracle when a state which receives a yearly average of $334 in MPCAs [military prime contract awards] per capita for twenty years (1965-1985) enjoys an economic boom in military-dependent, high-technology industries" (p. 60).

A more difficult and perhaps more important issue is the extent to which defense spending nurtured high-technology firms by serving as early markets for high-risk products. Many firms may have shifted into civilian markets after receiving an early and critical boost from military spending, a process that clearly was at work in the development of the semiconductor industry of Silicon Valley. Although the minicomputer firms of Massachusetts emerged without significant defense markets, other smaller, high-technology industries in the region may have received important boosts from defense spending. The question, however, cannot be answered by analyzing aggregate data; information specific to firms must be used.

Knowledge Infrastructure. The region's abundant and high-quality colleges, universities, and primary and secondary schools are an essential part of the environment that nurtured the Route 128 technopolis. The unique agglomeration of institutions of higher learning and research is especially noteworthy. Approximately sixty colleges and universities are located within Route 128. These institutions produce entrepreneurs, skilled workers, and new ideas. They are sources of information for key personnel in high-technology industries and provide technical and business assistance for high-technology firms. Collectively, the Boston area's higher education institutions produce a creative environment that is attractive to high-technology entrepreneurs and their employees.

Like the agglomeration of high-technology firms that developed after World War II, the cluster of educational institutions in Greater Boston was unplanned. In the nineteenth century, religious groups founded many of the schools, including Boston University, Tufts University, and Boston College. During the next century, these universities would become secular institutions. Northeastern University, which pioneered the practice of work-study education, began at the Boston YMCA. Worcester Polytechnic Institute was established by a tinware manufacturer.

Massachusetts' public primary and secondary schools are financed mainly by local property taxes. Thus the quality of public education varies widely among the state's 351 municipalities. The wealthier suburban communities, where most high-technology professionals reside, have highly regarded public school systems. Greater Boston also has a large number of private and parochial schools that provide excellent education, albeit at a high price.

The Industrial Base. The Boston area's pre-World War II industries, the science-based firms and traditional manufacturers, contributed to the development of the technopolis in a number of ways. Although few of the high-technology firms founded after World War II have lineages to prewar industries, indirect linkages have been important (Hekman and Strong 1981). First, MIT probably would not have existed without the support of both the region's mill-based industries and the prewar science-based firms. These enterprises made enormous financial contributions to MIT and also supplied faculty and provided jobs for students. MIT would not have been in a position to capitalize on the opportunities of the post-World War II knowledge revolution if it had not been shaped by the institutions of the industrial revolution.

A second contribution of the industrial base to the technopolis was the development of labor markets. A skilled, educated work force formed to work in traditional manufacturing industry, and a large pool of scientific and professional labor developed to serve the science-based firms. These labor force traits were desirable to the emerging high-technology industry. Third, the prewar machine shops and circuit board-makers produced components for computers. In the early stages of the computer industry, these firms were critical suppliers (Dorfman 1982).

Finally, the abandoned factories of the industrial revolution provided cheap buildings for the new high-technology firms. DEC was founded in a former mill, and many of the new firms in East Cambridge are housed in renovated factories.

Agglomeration Factors. As the forces described above came into play and the region grew, agglomeration advantages started to develop. It is a well-documented phenomenon that early in the product cycle, growth feeds on itself. In the Boston area, the concentration of high-technology firms attracted job-seekers and venture capital firms. Backward and forward linkages—suppliers and buyers—became more abundant. Successful entrepreneurs became role models for others. As the universities and research institutes received more government and private funds, their reputation for excellence grew, which attracted more funds. Fueling the process was the multiplication of spin-off companies and research organizations.

Agglomeration externalities can become negative, as happened in the Route 128 area in the 1980s. The concentration of economic activity drove up the price of housing and labor, strained the physical infrastructure, and damaged the natural environment. This trend tended to disperse growth away from the Route 128 center to areas that had been on the periphery of the region's high-technology development.

THE ROLE OF POLICY

Although no master plan guided the development of the Route 128 technopolis, many diverse policies by individuals and institutions had a hand in the process. Some policies succeeded, others failed, and some had unintended consequences.

Investments in the Knowledge Infrastructure

After World War II, Massachusetts state government created a large network of public higher education institutions. These colleges and universities, while not producing many entrepreneurs, have supplied a significant share of the middle-level and high-skilled employees needed by advanced-technology firms. Some research departments in state universities have achieved excellence in a number of scientific fields. State government also provided critical financial support to MIT when the institute was founded in the nineteenth century. Without the legislature's grant of land for MIT, William Barton Rogers' vision of a school for engineers in Boston might never have become a reality. Also in the nineteenth century, state government appropriated money on several occasions to sustain both MIT and Harvard through hard financial times.

Most of the public support for the science and engineering departments of universities has come from the federal government, and most of that from the military. Money spent by the Pentagon, the National Science Foundation, the National Institutes of Health, and other federal agencies at Boston-area research institutions was crucial to the emergence of the technopolis. The military-funded institutes at MIT produced the entrepreneurs and top technical talent that spearheaded high-technology regional development. Although the federal government's intent in sponsoring university-based research programs was not to promote regional development, this was the result.

Massachusetts state government also operates one of the most ambitious worker-training systems in the United States (Office of Economic Development 1987). Programs are aimed primarily at workers who have lost their jobs. The major programs are the Employment and Training (ET) Choices program, which assists welfare recipients; the Bay State Skills Corporation, which funds public-private training partnerships; and the Industrial Services Program, which trains and places workers who lost their jobs because of layoffs or plant closings.

The framework developed in previous chapters predicts that public policies representing investments in the regional knowledge infrastructure will promote the development of the technopolis. This, indeed, appears to be the case. Although they were made long ago, state government investments in Harvard and MIT helped create the technopolis's knowledge centers. The network of state colleges and universities has helped develop an attractive labor force for high-technology industry. State and local investments in primary and secondary education and worker training also have enhanced the quality of the work force and the quality of life in the region.

Technology Transfer

Scientific and technical excellence alone is insufficient to create regional economic development. Knowledge must be transferred to commercial products and processes. This can be accomplished only through deliberate policies. MIT is rare among U.S. universities in its longstanding commitment to technology transfer. Faculty and staff were encouraged to work with business and to start their own firms. Explicit policies were established regarding patents, outside consulting and sharing of research findings—all designed to foster commercial development of laboratory research. This institute-wide culture of closeness with business nurtured a generation of entrepreneurs following World War II.

In terms of the technopolis model, these policies were effective because they promoted the development of an information-rich environment. MIT policies fostered the flow of information among firms, researchers, investors, and civic and governmental leaders.

Physical Infrastructure

Government at all levels—state, regional, and national—helped build the physical infrastructure needed for the emerging technopolis. Analyses of the development of the Route 128 area often overlook the importance of the road itself. Route 128, which was built almost entirely with state money, became almost immediately a magnet for old and new firms. The road provided access to low-priced commercial and industrial land close to the city and attractive suburbs (Massachusetts Institute of Technology 1958). The road also expanded the regional labor market by making it practical for people to commute over long distances.

Other roads built or reconstructed in the postwar years contributed to the development of the technopolis. Route 9, Route 2 and the Massachusetts Turnpike were spokes, linking the Route 128 arc with the universities, financial institutions, and industries of Cambridge and Boston. Route 495, another circular highway west of Route 128, drew high-technology firms. Routes 3 and 24 opened up rural areas south of the city, expanding the metropolitan housing and labor markets. Logan International Airport and its access roads were major public investments critical to the growth of high-technology industry. These infrastructure projects were not deliberate technopolis policies but rather incremental responses to perceived needs over long periods. Infrastructure development was a reaction to growth rather than an effort to stimulate it.

The effectiveness of these infrastructure investments is consistent with the technopolis model. They helped create an environment that supports innovation by expanding labor and product markets and by facilitating smoother and faster movement of people, goods, and information.

Another area of infrastructure development important to the emergence of the technopolis was the revitalization of commercial districts in Boston and Cambridge. The redevelopment of Boston's Quincy Market, the Prudential Center, Downtown Crossing, and other sections attracted the financial and business services needed by the region's high-technology firms. Most of these projects were initiated by Boston Mayor Kevin H. White's Redevelopment Authority. White faced considerable public criticism for his focus on downtown development and neglect of urban neighborhoods, and he was replaced in 1983 by Raymond Flynn, a neighborhood-oriented politician. Whether White had indeed abandoned the neighborhoods, the impact of his downtown redevelopment policies on the economy of the city and the region deserves recognition. Without redevelopment, many of the high-level services probably would have followed high-technology industry and migrated to the suburbs.

The redevelopment of Kendall Square in Cambridge also stimulated the growth of the technopolis and shifted its focus from Route 128 toward the city. Before redevelopment efforts there began in the mid-1970s, Kendall Square was an old industrial area with shuttered factories surrounded by poorer neighborhoods. The banks of a canal that ran through the area were used for storage by a state highway agency. A combination of public and private interests accomplished the redevelopment: city and state government, the regional transportation agency, MIT, and private developers. Kendall Square now is home to offices, laboratories, trendy shops, and restaurants. Condominiums and offices line the canal. The attractions of the redeveloped Kendall Square to high-technology firms are many. Proximity to MIT is perhaps the most important factor. Improvements in the road and rapid transit networks also have enhanced the desirability of the area. Finally, Kendall Square offers in great abundance the upscale quality-of-life factors desired by successful professionals.

Land-Use Regulation

Local governments played an important part in directing growth within the Route 128 technopolis. This was accomplished mainly by zoning regulations. Eastern Massachusetts is a highly balkanized region with scores of local governments, each determining the location and density of development within its boundaries. Developers and high-technology firms seeking to build new facilities faced myriad governmental entities, each with unique requirements. Some municipalities were essentially wide open, permitting development with few restrictions. Others permitted development in clearly defined areas, while preserving the rest of the community as it had been. Still other towns tried to keep out growth altogether (Saxenian 1985b).

As Hall et al. (1987) observed in the Greater London area, perverse effects can result from these municipal growth policies. Communities that kept development out became even more attractive to developers precisely because they were not densely developed. These communities typically became embroiled in conflict, and many were forced to accept development. This outcome is consistent with the technopolis model because it underscores the importance of quality-of-life factors in the technopolis. Areas that maintained a good quality of life attracted development even when they did not want it.

State Industrial Policy

Starting in the mid-1970s, Massachusetts, like many other states, developed programs designed to foster high-technology-based economic development. Initiatives include nearly a dozen different capital assistance programs, training programs, export assistance, business incubators, public-private partnerships, and centers of excellence. Although these programs received considerable attention, particularly during Dukakis' bid for the presidency, no hard evidence exists to indicate they played a direct role in the economic turnaround, which was already well under way when these programs were devised (Ferguson and Ladd 1988; Dorfman 1982). Moreover, the scale of these programs has not been great enough to have a major impact on the regional economy. All of the capital assistance programs combined are not large enough to have any serious effect on the capital requirements of business in the state.[6]

A more important question, though, is whether these policies, taken as a whole, helped sustain the growth of the technopolis or furthered its long-range prospects. Lampe (1988, p. 16) argues that these programs represented most importantly an "attitudinal shift" for state government in its relationship with business. Prior to this time, government often was perceived as hostile or indifferent to business interests. It is indeed doubtful that the state's economic revival could have been sustained with the business climate that existed in the early 1970s. State industrial policies played a symbolic role by announcing government support for industrial innovation and by involving business leaders in economic development planning (Graham and Ross 1989). Business and labor were formally represented in many of these programs. State industrial policy opened new channels for political participation by business interests.

Thus as efforts to enhance local relations and improve the climate for innovation over the long term, state industrial policies, in the aggregate, have been well conceived. As one of the first states to develop such programs, Massachusetts developed a reputation as a center of policy innovation (Osborne 1988). This has probably boosted the state in national and international competition for attracting and keeping high-technology industry.

Some of the specific programs, however, have struggled because of fundamental design flaws. The Centers of Excellence Program, one of the best known of the Dukakis industrial policy initiatives, underestimated the difficulty of creating an effective knowledge center for an emerging technopolis. Established in 1985, the Centers of Excellence Program targets four regions outside of the Route 128 area for the development of high-technology industry or the promotion of innovation in older industries. Joint public-private funding is provided for research at state universities based in these regions. Other elements of the program are business incubators, export assistance, technical training, and academic-industrial liaison programs. The Centers of Excellence Program is the most explicit industrial policy of Massachusetts government in that it identifies specific industries for special state assistance. The program has been hampered because the research programs at most state universities are not sufficiently advanced to function as the knowledge center of a technopolis. With the exception of the University of Massachusetts-Amherst, these universities have not achieved a level of excellence comparable to the world's leading universities. Although some successful businesses capable of finding niche markets may be created, it is doubtful that any regional economies can be reshaped by the Centers of Excellence or similar programs.

A more realistic approach would have been to devise policies to capture for Massachusetts more of the economic development that radiated outward from the Route 128 core. Despite the Dukakis administration's much-heralded "geographic targeting" efforts (Ferguson and Ladd 1988; Osborne 1988; Dukakis and Kanter 1988), a large share of the propulsive growth from Route 128 wound up in New Hampshire and, to a lesser extent, Maine (Harrison and Kluver 1989). Geographic targeting focused on Massachusetts' older, distressed cities. The Dukakis administration used a range of tools, including infrastructure development, capital assistance, regulation, and siting of state facilities to promote development in these communities. While these tactics may have helped to revitalize some of these older cities, the policies failed to capitalize on the resources of the Route 128 technopolis.

New Hampshire captured this growth because of perceived tax advantages, good transportation links to Route 128 and Boston, and cheaper traditional factors of production. Most of this development was in the form of production and warehousing facilities. Research and development, of necessity, stayed close to the knowledge centers of metropolitan Boston. For Massachusetts to have attracted this growth to its older cities or other disadvantaged areas beyond the technopolis, more traditional economic development strategies, such as recruitment, tax incentives, and the development of transportation networks, would have had a better likelihood of success.

Public-Private Partnerships

Most of the public-private partnerships developed during the growth of the Route 128 technopolis, notably the Dukakis-era industrial policy initiatives, are best viewed as long-range strategies, the main consequence of which has been to improve the climate for innovation and entrepreneurship. One partnership, however, did have a direct and powerful impact on regional development: the American Research and Development (ARD) venture capital enterprise.

American Research and Development backed financially many of the key high-technology companies and triggered the establishment of other Boston-area risk capital firms. The establishment of ARD should be considered a technopolis policy because it was designed as an instrument to promote regional economic development based on advanced technology. ARD was not created by a group of financiers looking to get rich quick. The idea for the company came from Ralph Flanders, president of the Federal Reserve Bank of Boston and a future U.S. senator. MIT was heavily involved in the firm from the start. A number of the founders, advisers, and officers of ARD were from MIT. Other key people in ARD were wealthy businessmen.

In 1956, ARD President Georges Doriot wrote in a newspaper article:

The men who created American Research were all men of great achievement in their respective professions. They were not in need, and they had great reputations. The easiest thing for them to do was to enjoy what they already had. . . . By pioneering in the field of venture capital, they felt they could be helpful to others. They had much to lose and relatively little to gain. (Liles 1977)

In order to accept investments from certain institutions, ARD had to be set up as a profit-making organization. However, there is substantial evidence that profits were secondary. In its early brochures, the company cited its objectives as expanding production and employment and increasing the standard of living (Liles 1977, p. 32). In ARD's early years, it had to defend itself in the press against charges that it was a philanthropic organization. To be sure, the firm's investment in Digital Equipment Corporation and other successful companies brought its owners great wealth over time. But in its early years, ARD is most accurately viewed as an instrument, designed by a business-university partnership, to foster economic development through the commercialization of new technologies.

ROUTE 128 IN THE 1990s: EVOLUTION
OF A MATURE TECHNOPOLIS

While other regions throughout the world were trying to replicate the success of the Route 128 technopolis, the economy of Massachusetts and most of New England experienced a steep and sudden downturn, raising questions about the meaning of the region's prior prosperity and the prospects for the future. Answers were hard to find. Route 128 is one of the few mature technopolises in the world and the first to experience such a sharp reversal in its fortunes. Although the changes in the region were not as profound as the shift that had occurred twenty years earlier from a traditional manufacturing to a knowledge-based economy, the Route 128 technopolis at the start of the 1990s was in the midst of a significant transition.

Miracle or Mirage?

Evidence that all was not well with the Massachusetts economy surfaced in the summer of 1988, when Governor Dukakis prepared to go to the Democratic Convention in Atlanta to accept his party's presidential nomination. As the governor and legislature tried to close the books on the fiscal year, officials revealed that the state budget was more than $400 million in the red. To avoid painful choices and to protect Dukakis' bid for the presidency, the Democratic-controlled legislature and the governor downplayed the significance of the shortfall and borrowed money to cover the gap. However, the budget deficit, which was triggered by slow growth in state revenue, was a warning that the miracle economy of the 1980s was in trouble.

Even before the 1988 state budget gap, signs of more difficult times ahead were present, although they were widely ignored amid the euphoria of the boom and the excitement of Dukakis' presidential bid. Beginning in 1984, overall job growth in Massachusetts slowed considerably, falling below the national average, while high-technology employment stalled completely (Harrison and Kluver 1989). Later analyses revealed that much of the 1980s employment boom was not the result of high-technology renaissance but of expansion in construction and real estate (Moscovitch 1990). The spectacular growth of the financial services industry, which had become an important component of the regional economy, skidded to a halt after the October 1987 Wall Street crash. In the mid- and late 1980s, the regional economy also displayed classic signs of overheating: inflated real estate prices, environmental degradation, transportation gridlocks, and chronic labor shortages. In June 1988, Frank Morris, president of the Federal Reserve Bank of Boston, told a group of bankers that the commercial real estate boom was likely to collapse and that the Massachusetts economy would underperform the nation's for the next decade. "Most booms do end in busts," he warned. "Developers will continue to build as long as bankers will lend them the money. Some banks are going to lose money when developers go bankrupt. I hope that none of them are yours" (Warsh 1988).

The cracks in the state economy were revealed most clearly in state government's protracted fiscal crises. State budgets in the United States are highly sensitive to economic slowdowns. First, their principal revenue sources—sales and income taxes—are affected immediately. Second, demands on government increase, with higher expenditures required for unemployment compensation, welfare, health care, and social services. The media tend to focus on state government, and in Massachusetts that scrutiny was especially intense because of Dukakis' stature as a former presidential nominee and his campaign claims regarding the state's economy. In early 1989, Dukakis announced he would not seek reelection as governor, and he set about the task of resolving the state's deepening fiscal crisis. Several traumatic and politically divisive rounds of budget cuts and tax increases failed to keep pace with plunging state revenues. In 1989 and 1990, the state ended its fiscal years in the red, covering the shortfalls with costly borrowing. The state's credit rating fell to just above junk bond status, the lowest of any state in the nation.

In 1989, the state fiscal crisis shared center stage with the woes of Massachusetts' minicomputer companies. Firms that had driven the region's high-technology revival began to struggle. Announcements from the big minicomputer makers of massive losses and layoffs became commonplace. Digital Equipment Corporation tried a voluntary severance program to trim its work force but eventually turned to layoffs, ending a thirty-three-year no-layoff tradition. Wang Laboratories and Data General slashed more than a third of their employees in the late 1980s. Some of the smaller firms, weakened by losses and desperate for cash, were taken over by out-of-state conglomerates. Prime Computer swallowed up Computervision Corporation, and then was itself acquired by a New York investment firm.

Other high-technology firms struggled as well. Apollo Computer Inc., a pioneer in the development of work stations, was overwhelmed by Silicon Valley's Sun Microsystems. While Sun took off in the late 1980s, Apollo recorded big losses. Cullinet Software Inc., for more than a decade one of the fastest-growing companies in Massachusetts, went into a sharp decline in 1986 and had to lay off hundreds of workers. Lotus Development Corporation, perhaps the region's brightest new star in the 1980s, stumbled when it failed to deliver its update to its popular 1-2-3 spreadsheet software on time.

The swift end to the Cold War jolted the big military contractors, which slashed thousands of jobs at facilities throughout the region. Although many regions in the United States have been hurt by defense cuts, New England's plight was especially acute because of its greater reliance on defense spending.[7] Lack of contracts forced slowdowns and layoffs at several Raytheon and General Electric weapons plants in Massachusetts, as well as at the General Dynamics Electric Boat Co. division in Groton, Connecticut, and the Bath Iron Works in Maine. Smaller defense subcontractors and suppliers suffered as well.

Simultaneously, the state's high-level business and financial services industry began to struggle. In 1988, Fidelity Investments, Boston's high-flying mutual fund company, laid off 800 employees; the New England insurance firm halted its health insurance business and transferred 500 employees; and Bain & Co., an important consulting firm, cut its work force by 10 percent.

The next to suffer were developers, builders, and virtually any business with ties to the real estate industry. New office towers in the overbuilt center city and the suburbs remained vacant for months, and half-finished shells of high-rise offices and condominiums dotted the landscape. Boston's biggest landlord, Harold Brown, filed for bankruptcy. Throughout the region, sales of homes and property values fell. In 1990, the median cost of a Boston area house dropped approximately 10 percent. Banks that had loaned to developers paid a heavy price when the loans went sour. In 1990, sixteen New England banks fell, including eleven in Massachusetts. The first five months of 1991 saw the collapse of thirty-six New England banks, most of them small institutions. The biggest banking casualty was Bank of New England, one of the region's largest banks. In 1991, the Federal Deposit Insurance Corporation declared the institution insolvent and sold its assets to Rhode Island-based Fleet/Norstar Financial Group.

Between November 1989 and November 1990, 125,000 jobs, approximately 4 percent of total employment, were lost in Massachusetts. Unlike the state's deep recession of the early 1970s, the victims of which were mainly traditional manufacturing firms and their workers, the economic decline of the late 1980s and early 1990s cut across industries and job categories. Joining blue-collar workers in unemployment lines this time were engineers, managers, stockbrokers, construction workers, secretaries, and government bureaucrats. The *Boston Globe* labeled the recession "an equal opportunity un-employer" (Loth 1991). By early 1991, the unemployment rate was nearly 10 percent, still two points below the rate at the depths of the recession of the early 1970s but a dramatic shift from the near full employment conditions of five years earlier and nearly three points above the national average.

In the summer of 1991, the relentless flow of bad news on the state's economy abated briefly. For the first time in four years, state government, led by a new Republican governor, former federal prosecutor William Weld, finished the fiscal year in the black. Tax revenues exceeded expectations for several months. Home sales picked up, although the construction industry remained at a virtual standstill. Some high-technology firms were growing, having found new or niche markets in a broad array of fields. Even the battered minicomputer industry had some success stories. A restructured, redirected Data General Corporation recorded two straight profitable quarters and celebrated by throwing a mammoth pizza party for the 2,500 employees at its headquarters in Westborough. Nevertheless, the economy appeared not to have hit bottom. A procession of business leaders and economists told a legislative committee in May that the skid would likely continue in 1992, and the following month, the state's two biggest employers, Raytheon and Digital Equipment Corporation, announced within days of each other that they would lay off hundreds of employees. Wang Laboratories also revealed plans to dismiss up to 4,000 workers, half of them in Massachusetts.

Causes of the Decline

The precipitous fall in the region's fortunes has been attributed to many different factors: military spending cuts, which began in the Reagan administration and accelerated under President Bush; state government's chronic fiscal problems; deterioration of government services, particularly education; the high cost of living and doing business in the region; and the onset of the national recession. Each of these influences no doubt played a role. However, to understand the dynamics of the regional economy, the performance of the core or driving industries and their part in the onset of the recession must be isolated and assessed first.

Moscovitch (1990) found that the base industries of the New England economy—those industries that export goods or services out of the region—stopped growing in 1984 and also lost market share to firms in other parts of the United States. This study, based on a shift share analysis, does not break down the base industries beyond broad categories: insurance, education, machinery, instruments, electric and electronic equipment, and others. Porter (1991) disaggregated the industrial base further, assessing the performance and prospects of four core "clusters" of linked industries that drive the regional economy. Porter's clusters—health care, information technology, financial services, and knowledge creation services—represent 35 percent of Massachusetts' total employment. The problems of the minicomputer companies stand out. Loss of market share to work stations and microcomputers in the second half of the 1980s forced the state's minicomputer firms to cut costs and employment dramatically. Digital Equipment Corporation, Wang Laboratories, Data General, and Prime all recorded large losses and laid off employees. Minicomputers led the region to the heights of the miracle, then took it back down.

Two broad trends that swept the global computer industry in the latter part of the 1980s triggered the sharp decline of the minicomputer firms. Smaller, less expensive desktop computers—work stations and microcomputers—had become increasingly powerful and could be linked in sprawling networks. The move to distributed processing undercut the market for minicomputers from below, while IBM and other mainframe computer-makers kept constant pressure from above. The second industry-wide trend was the shift away from proprietary computer hardware and software designs to so-called "open systems," running Unix, software programs that can operate most makes and sizes of computers. The Route 128 minicomputer firms were heavily invested in proprietary systems.

The problems of financial and business services also contributed greatly to the regional downturn. The industry was an important driver of the economy in the 1980s, with its payroll doubling during the course of the decade. The stock market crash and the ensuing tightening of credit jolted most segments of the industry to a halt. The troubles of the minicomputer firms and other high-technology businesses based in the region spelled further problems for regional financial and business services, which have important links to these firms. Asset management companies, which had been one of the biggest growth sectors of the financial services industry in Massachusetts, saw employment decline by 2.7 percent between 1988 and 1990. The insurance industry was a mixed picture, with some firms remaining profitable while others, in particular those that expanded into real estate, suffered big losses. Travelers Corporation of Hartford lost $499 million in the third quarter of 1990 alone, and Monarch Capital Corporation was forced into bankruptcy proceedings. Meanwhile, John Hancock Mutual Life Insurance Company had record gains of $196.6 million in 1989 and $214 million in 1990. However, profitability did not necessarily translate into jobs. In 1991, Hancock laid off 400 employees in Boston as part of a restructuring.

The declines in the financial and business services and minicomputer industries eliminated many of the best-paying jobs in the region and triggered serious problems in supplier and service industries. The rippling effect through the economy was swift and profound. Because many jobs in these industries are high-paying, the earlier expansion of these industries had a strong multiplier effect on the regional economy. However, when those industries contracted, the impact on the economy was equally strong in reverse.

Although the underlying reason for the decline in the regional economy was the problems of the core industries, the suddenness and severity of the fall was due, in large measure, to overexpansion of the real estate industry. In the 1980s, the industry had experienced rapid and unsustainable growth, far outpacing the growth of the core industries of the region. Real estate, although it is influenced by external capital markets, still is dependent on local economic conditions, in particular the strength of the core industries. While the core industries were growing slowly or retrenching in the 1980s, real estate took off, with employment expanding more than 8 percent a year until 1988. When the problems in the core could no longer be avoided, the real estate industry went into a sharp downturn. Vacancy rates in downtown office buildings more than tripled in a span of three years. New office towers and luxury condominiums sat empty, while developers, contractors, and landlords went bankrupt. The real estate slump affected a wide range of large and small businesses, from architectural firms to office furniture dealers to newspapers that sell real estate advertising.

The plight of the region's banks was directly related to the real estate industry's troubles. Massachusetts banks were heavily invested in construction and commercial real estate, and when those industries started to slide, they took many banks with them. Statistics compiled by Porter (1991) reveal that 61.6 percent of non-performing loans of Massachusetts banks in 1990 were in real estate, approximately twice the percentage of California banks. For Bank of New England, the biggest banking casualty of the regional slump, more than 80 percent of its problem loans were in real estate. Few banks in the region escaped trouble in the late 1980s and early 1990s. A *Boston Globe* survey identified only four large banks in Massachusetts that did not lose money in 1990, and two of them barely broke even (Rosenberg 1991).

The problems of banks and savings and loans had direct and indirect impacts on the regional economy. Many struggling or failed smaller banks were acquired by larger banks, and restructuring and layoffs became commonplace in both large and small financial institutions. The acquisition of Bank of New England by Fleet/Norstar alone resulted in a thousand layoffs when operations of the two institutions were merged. The banking industry's troubles also triggered a credit squeeze, which constrained expansion and start-up possibilities for businesses throughout the region. After years of expansion, credit availability declined in 1990, and Massachusetts ranked last among the fifty states in domestic deposit growth (Porter 1991).

The onset of a national recession compounded these problems. Beginning in early 1989, the U.S. economy entered a period of sluggish growth, which worsened for the next two years. At a time when Massachusetts firms desperately needed new external markets, the national economy offered few opportunities.

The Future of the Technopolis

Although the economic difficulties of Massachusetts were severe in the late 1980s and early 1990s, they have not meant the demise of the Route 128 technopolis. In analyzing Massachusetts' plight and its lessons for other regions, the problems caused by cyclical or aberrant forces must be separated from those that are the result of some inherent weakness in the technopolis itself. The failures of a particular firm or even an entire industry should not be interpreted as the failure of a region.

The technopolis remains viable. The core knowledge institutions, Harvard and MIT, are still preeminent in scientific and technical fields. Despite challenges from newly upgraded universities and research institutes elsewhere, Harvard and MIT have remained leaders in a broad array of disciplines. They are still producing knowledge that is being translated into new or improved products and processes. New businesses founded by technical entrepreneurs continue to emerge from the universities.[8]

The environment is still innovative, despite the adversity brought on by the recession. The labor force remains highly skilled, characterized by the presence of a large number of scientists and engineers. The downturn in the economy and the Route 128 layoffs have prompted some fears that skilled labor will migrate from the region for better jobs elsewhere. Although this is a danger, migration sufficient to alter the region's labor profile clearly has not happened yet and is unlikely to occur unless job opportunities remain poor for a protracted period. Many workers are tied to the area by investments in homes, careers of spouses, and commitments to their children's school systems. Some scientists and engineers are able to find jobs within the region in related fields, while others strike off on their own and start new businesses. Indeed, the labor surplus helped many new and small companies by allowing them to hire highly skilled workers they could not have afforded if the general economic conditions had been more favorable.

The long-term prospects for markets for Route 128 firms remain favorable. The diversified cluster of high-technology firms represents a strong local market for many firms, especially the new and smaller companies. Other high-technology markets are global in scope and are the same ones for which firms all over the world are competing. More immediate problems regarding markets for Route 128 are the national recession and the decline in defense spending. When the national economy recovers, opportunities will improve for the region's high-technology firms. The military cuts, however, are not cyclical and are likely to continue at least into the mid-1990s (Henderson 1990). Defense contractors in Massachusetts, as well as in other parts of the United States, will have to develop new civilian or government markets to remain profitable.

The web of local relations and flow of ideas that characterized the technopolis during its earlier development remains strong. The agglomeration of firms, the formal and informal ties among high-technology businesses and research institutions, and the complex networks of people are among the region's greatest assets. The regional venture capital industry, although weakened by industry-wide trends, is one of the largest in the United States and has strong links to high-technology industry. Both large and small firms are establishing strategic alliances to exploit opportunities in niches of high-technology fields.

The knowledge infrastructure also is intact despite turmoil in a number of areas of education. The state budget crisis resulted in reduced funding and program cuts in public higher education; however, reorganization and consolidation triggered by the budget problems may ultimately strengthen the system. In any case, the agglomeration of public and private higher education institutions remains one of the largest and most important in the world. State budget cuts also have hurt public elementary and secondary education, and great disparities persist among local school systems, each of which has its own administration and resource base. However,

Massachusetts public education in general still compares favorably with public school systems across the United States, and excellent private schools exist for those who can afford them.

New England also has a diversified economic base, which includes not only information technology firms, but also health care, education, and high-level business and financial services (Rosengren 1990; Simons 1990; Porter 1991). Although these industries have links to the high-technology sector, they are not dependent on it. Diversification cushioned the blow from the collapse of the minicomputer industry and is likely to hasten the region's recovery.

Route 128 also is spawning a new generation of high-technology firms (Brandel 1991; Edelman 1991b; Stein 1991). These companies tend to be small, focused enterprises that are carving out profitable niches in the high-technology marketplace. Like their predecessors in the technopolis, they were established by technical entrepreneurs who came from either the universities or established high-technology firms. Because of the more competitive external environment and their pursuit of narrower market strategies, these businesses are unlikely to achieve the spectacular growth of the region's first high-technology firms. However, taken together they represent a significant source of growth for the region.

Although they still employ only a small number of people, biotechnology firms have been one of the fastest-growing segments of the regional economy and have even greater growth potential. Massachusetts has become a center for biotechnology applications because of the region's agglomeration of hospitals and medical research institutions. Massachusetts has 137 biotechnology companies, 13 percent of the firms nationwide (Porter 1991). Many of these companies could see rapid growth in profitability and employment as they bring to market products that have been undergoing long periods of research and development.

The software industry grew steadily and rapidly throughout the 1980s, and most firms are expecting growth to continue. In early 1991, the Massachusetts Software Council reported its members anticipated sales gains of 15 to 20 percent for the year despite the recession (Edelman 1991a). Demand for software worldwide has been strong because of the proliferation of computers in a wide range of fields and the need for software packages to operate and coordinate complex hardware. Massachusetts, which has more than 800 software companies, is one of the centers of the world software industry and is well positioned to capitalize on global developments in software.

Other firms have carved out successful niches in diverse areas of information technology. A brief description of some of the leading growth companies of Route 128 illustrates the kind of businesses that are succeeding in Massachusetts in the early 1990s. Cambex Corporation, which the *Boston Globe* labeled the most profitable Massachusetts firm in 1990, manufactures memory boards that are compatible with IBM mainframes. Stratus Computer, which enjoyed strong growth throughout the 1980s and in 1991 had 1,400 Massachusetts employees, makes fault-tolerant computer systems for on-line transaction processing. Cognex Corporation is a world leader in artificial intelligence for manufacturing systems. Thinking Machines Corporation is the second largest manufacturer of supercomputers in the United States. IPL Systems Inc., one of the fastest-growing and most profitable firms on Route 128, makes IBM peripherals.

The future of the mature minicomputer companies is uncertain. Their broad strategy has been first to restructure their work forces and cut costs dramatically, resulting in large numbers of layoffs. Second, the minicomputer makers, like the newer and smaller companies of Route 128, have tried to find profitable niches in some area of information technology. Recognizing the imperative of developing open systems, they have begun making new open systems hardware while opening existing proprietary software. For most of the minicomputer firms, strategic alliances with smaller firms and industry leaders have been an important part of their strategies. Digital Equipment Corporation has broadened its product line dramatically to include software, mainframes, personal computers, and network systems. The company also reported plans to enter the field of massively parallel processing. Digital has used strategic marketing and manufacturing alliances with other information-technology firms as its principal vehicles for entering these new markets. Prime Computer has shifted its focus from minicomputers to the CAD/CAM systems and software. Data General developed the Aviion work station, a product that enjoyed early success and lifted the firm back to profitability. Wang Laboratories in 1991 signed a far-reaching agreement to market computers made by IBM, which made a $100 million investment in the struggling company. Wang was prepared to all but abandon the hardware manufacturing side of its business and focus on the development of software.

The economic policies announced by Governor Weld, who assumed office in January 1991, were aimed at improving the environment for business through resolution of the state fiscal crisis, limited taxation, streamlined regulation, physical infrastructure development, and stimulation of the economy through large, federally supported construction projects, reminiscent of the federal Works Projects Administration of the

1930s. The two biggest projects, both of which were initiated during the Dukakis administration, were the construction of a massive sewage treatment plant for Boston Harbor and a new highway and tunnel through downtown Boston. Weld appeared less inclined to promote the more interventionist industrial policies developed by Dukakis, although he did not move to dismantle the institutions established by the former governor.

NOTES

1. Sources for the history of the industrial revolution in Massachusetts are Hekman and Strong (1981), Ferguson and Ladd (1988), Warsh (1989), and Botkin, Dimancescu, and Stata (1984).

2. Hall and Preston (1988) write that this event was "an early example of the serendipitous effect of urban agglomeration in innovation."

3. An interesting sidelight to the General Electric and Bell Telephone stories is that both Alexander Graham Bell and Thomas Edison began their careers as inventors in Boston but moved to New York City to set up their businesses. Hall and Preston (1988) maintain that this pattern reflected Boston's position as the center of science and invention and New York's as a center of commercial innovation. After World War II, when the link between science to industrial development became stronger, Boston would overtake New York as a center of high technology.

4. DEC slipped to number three in 1990, when it was surpassed by Fujitsu.

5. Sources for the history of MIT are Wildes and Lindgren (1985), Prescott (1954), and Wylie (1975).

6. Graham and Ross (1989) point out that the capital assistance programs were conceived when the state was thought to have a "capital gap" that was hurting business. By the time the programs were functioning in the early 1980s, there was an abundance of capital available from private sources. However, problems in the banking industry in the late 1980s and early 1990s renewed fears that a capital shortage had developed.

7. For the nation as a whole, defense spending represents 6 percent of the gross national product, while it is 8 percent of New England's (Henderson 1990).

8. Fulman (1990) reports that the slowdown in the economy may actually be stimulating the formation of new businesses by MIT alumni. With a shortage of job opportunities at established firms, many MIT graduates may see entrepreneurship as their best alternative. According to Fulman, a Bank of Boston study found that MIT alumni started more companies in the depths of the 1982 recession than after the economy had picked up and that the flow of businesses from MIT remained steady during the latest slowdown.

Chapter 6

The Development of the Silicon Valley Technopolis

Silicon Valley is the preeminent high-technology region in the world. Its record of growth and development is unmatched in the post-World War II era. In little more than two decades, the region was transformed from a largely rural, agricultural area to the center of global electronics. Silicon Valley has become a model and a symbol of regional high-technology development.

This chapter examines the evolution of Silicon Valley, from its beginnings as a home to pre-World War II science-based industry to its emergence as the focus of the semiconductor, microcomputer, and other high-technology industries. The reasons the region developed as it did are suggested, and in this context, the role of policy is assessed. The chapter concludes with a comparative analysis of the Silicon Valley and Route 128 complexes.

THE EMERGENCE OF SILICON VALLEY

Science-Based Industry

Silicon Valley is an approximately thirty-by-ten-mile strip of land extending from the southern tip of San Francisco Bay south to San Jose. Before the region received its high-technology moniker, it was known simply as Santa Clara County. In the late nineteenth and early twentieth centuries, the valley was a major farming region, producing cherries, plums, pears, and apricots. In 1940, it was ranked among the fifteen most productive agricultural counties in the United States (Saxenian 1985a). The cities and towns in the area were oriented toward agriculture, with San Jose, which was the only large city, functioning as the regional service and distribution center.

In the midst of this farmland was Stanford University, in Palo Alto at the northern end of the valley. Founded in 1885 by railroad magnate and U.S. Senator Leland Stanford, the university started out with a substantial $20 million endowment. The university also was rich in land: Leland Stanford donated his 8,800-acre stock farm in Palo Alto for the school's campus.

At first, Stanford gained a reputation as a "country club" school, where children of the landed aristocracy studied instead of journeying back East for their education. In the early 1900s, however, an electrical engineering program was established, and the school began to generate its first science-based industry. Poulsen Wireless Telephone and Telegraph was founded in 1909 by Cy Elwell, a Stanford graduate who invented a small, wireless radio. Elwell convinced university President David Starr Jordan to invest $500 in the start-up company. Stanford faculty became advisers to the firm. Within two years, the company, which changed its name to Federal Telegraph Company, was one of the largest electrical firms in the country.

Federal Telegraph, which later became part of ITT, is best known as an incubator for inventors and entrepreneurs. In 1912, Lee DeForest, while working for Federal Telegraph, invented the vacuum tube, which made possible radio, television, and countless other electronic devices. The first commercial radio station in the United States, San Jose's FN (now KCBS), was founded in 1909 by Dr. Charles Herrold, who worked with DeForest. Magnavox Company was founded by two former Federal Telegraph employees in 1913. Charles Litton established Litton Engineering Laboratories, a maker of precision glass vacuum tubes, when Federal Telegraph shifted its operations to the East Coast in 1932. Litton Industries later became a manufacturer of military electronics systems and a billion-dollar corporation.

In the 1920s, Stanford dramatically upgraded its research program (Rogers and Larsen 1984). In 1924, Dr. Harris Ryan, one of the best and most prominent teachers at Stanford, established a radio communications laboratory in the attic of the university's Electrical Engineering Building. He asked Frederick Terman, now commonly referred to as the "godfather of Silicon Valley," to run it.[1] Terman, the son of a Stanford professor, had graduated from Stanford and then gone to MIT for his doctorate. At

MIT he studied under Vannevar Bush, who encouraged him to think of the university as a source of commercial innovation and not as an ivory tower. After receiving his degree, Terman accepted a position at MIT, but before starting the job he returned to Palo Alto for a visit. While there, he was stricken with tuberculosis and spent a year recuperating. Believing that the California climate would be better for his health, he accepted Ryan's job offer.

Terman was a brilliant teacher and administrator, and throughout the 1920s and 1930s his lab drew the best students. Although not a great researcher or inventor, he was effective in helping students develop ideas and translate them into commercial products. He found jobs for his students and helped them start businesses in the community.

Terman, who would eventually become dean, provost, and vice president of Stanford, also was committed to improving the quality of the electrical engineering program and the research capabilities of the university more generally. He skillfully and aggressively raised millions of dollars for the university from government and industry sources. Using contacts made while heading a major World War II research project at Harvard, he won big defense contracts for Stanford. The emerging electronics industry in the region also became a major source of funding for the electrical engineering program, which in turn became an important supplier of key personnel. In the 1960s, Stanford's electrical engineering program became known as one of the best in the country.

By the early 1940s a significant number of small, innovative firms had clustered around Stanford in Palo Alto and nearby communities. These firms would play an important part in the development of the regional economy during and after World War II. The most important prewar firm was Hewlett-Packard. Until Steve Jobs and Steve Wozniak arrived on the scene in the late 1970s, the saga of David Packard and William Hewlett was probably the most renowned success story of Silicon Valley.

The two men, who were students of Terman, became friends while undergraduates at Stanford in the 1930s. After graduation, Packard went to work for General Electric in Schenectady, New York, while Hewlett enrolled in a master's program at MIT. Terman eventually lured both back to Palo Alto. He obtained a job for Hewlett building an electroencephalograph for a doctor, and he offered a fellowship at Stanford to Packard. Reunited in Palo Alto, Hewlett and Packard set up a business in a one-car garage at Packard's house. They first built an array of electrical products, from signaling for a bowling alley to an automatic harmonica tuner to a motor drive for a telescope. In 1939, they invented the audio oscillator, a device that generates electrical signals of varying and controllable frequencies. That year, ITT bought the foreign patent rights to the product and assisted the two men in getting a U.S. patent. Sales of the audio oscillator grew rapidly, and in 1940 Hewlett-Packard (the firm was incorporated in early 1939) moved out of the garage to a small building a few blocks away. During the next two decades Hewlett-Packard would become one of the largest electronics firms in the world, and the two founders would become millionaires many times over.

Another important early Silicon Valley company was Varian Associates, which was established by two brothers who grew up in Palo Alto and studied with Stanford Physics Professor William Hansen (Malone 1985; Bylinsky 1976). Sigurd and Russell Varian invented the klystron tube, a critical device in radar systems. At an early stage in the invention process, the university gave the brothers $100 for supplies in return for a share of any future profits. Varian Associates grew and prospered and is now a world leader in radar, microwave devices, and semiconductor manufacturing equipment. Stanford's $100 investment returned millions (Bylinsky 1976).

World War II provided an enormous boost to the emerging regional industrial economy. The military became a major market for Hewlett-Packard's electronic instruments and equipment, and by the end of the war, the firm was a $2 million company with 200 employees. Stanford's laboratories were a magnet for wartime research funds on electronic components and equipment. The war even transformed elements of the agricultural economy. San Jose's Food Machinery and Chemical Corporation shifted from tractor assembly to tank production (Saxenian 1985a). The war also brought thousands of servicemen through the San Francisco area on their way to the Pacific theatre. Many of these men returned to the area to live after the war ended.

An aerospace industry also emerged in the area around the end of World War II. In 1940, the National Advisory Committee for Aeronautics, the forerunner of the National Aeronautics and Space Administration, established the Ames Research Center in the Santa Clara County community of Mountain View. In 1956, Lockheed Aircraft Corporation, a Southern California-based firm, moved one of its subsidiaries to Sunnyvale, near the Ames Research Center. For many years, Lockheed was the largest employer in Silicon Valley (Malone 1985).

Several large, prewar electrical and electronics-related firms, including General Electric, Sylvania, Philco-Ford, Westinghouse, and Admiral, opened divisions in the area. IBM established a major research center in San Jose. The magnetic data-storage disk was invented at IBM's San Jose facility.

Stanford was not the only university or research institution in the area. The University of California at Berkeley became a major source of engineers for firms in the region. Later, the university's research laboratories would develop close ties with Silicon Valley industry. San Jose State and Santa Clara College developed instruction in electronics fields. In addition, Stanford in 1946 created Stanford Research Institute (later renamed SRI International), which became a large and influential think tank.

Another ingredient in the mix that helped to create the Silicon Valley technopolis was Frederick Terman's brainchild, Stanford Industrial Park. In 1951, Terman, working with university President Wallace Sterling, developed a plan for what would be the first science park in the world. Stanford Industrial Park was a product of the university's need to dispose of excess land (which could not be sold under the terms of the Stanford family gift) and Terman's twin goals of raising money for the university and promoting local entrepreneurship. The university developed the site, which was adjacent to the campus, and granted leases to high-technology enterprises. Firms were lured by the promise of close ties with the university's faculty and access to research facilities. Revenue from the park was funneled back to the university to recruit faculty or to improve facilities. The first tenant was Varian Associates. In 1954, Hewlett-Packard moved in. As the park grew, it became an important vehicle for transfering technology from the university's research laboratories to the marketplace. Stanford Industrial Park, since renamed Stanford Research Park, now has nearly 100 tenants and has become the model for science parks all over the world.

Thus by the mid-1950s, conditions were in place for the development of new high-technology industry in Santa Clara County. At the core of the regional high-technology economy was Stanford, a world-class research institution and an incubator of new firms. An emerging cluster of advanced technology firms was starting to create agglomeration advantages. An entrepreneurial tradition had been established, and a physical infrastructure and a large pool of technical talent were in place. The region also offered an ideal climate, undeveloped land, and a large number of non-unionized, migrant workers. Santa Clara County was well positioned to capitalize on perhaps the most far-reaching invention of the twentieth century: the silicon chip.

The Semiconductor Industry

The important inventions in microelectronics—the transistor, the integrated circuit, the microprocessor—were not the work of single individuals, although they are often attributed to one or two men. These, like most modern inventions, came about as a result of many years of accumulated scientific wisdom and painstaking research conducted by teams of researchers (Saxenian 1985b). In microelectronics, many of the big discoveries happened at about the same time in different parts of the United States. However, because of the resources of the region and the behavior of its firms, Silicon Valley was the place that semiconductor technology was commercialized most successfully, and it was Silicon Valley that became the center of this important new global industry.[2]

A pivotal event in the history of the semiconductor industry in Silicon Valley was the return of William Shockley. Shockley, who grew up in Palo Alto, was a member of the research team at Bell Laboratories that invented the transistor. He left that organization to start his own company to pursue his ideas about the development of the transistor. With a group of scientists handpicked from all over the country, he established Shockley Laboratories in Palo Alto in 1954.[3]

Shockley Laboratories, which had close ties to Stanford, struggled after it was established. Although he was a brilliant scientist, Shockley was considered a poor manager, and dissatisfaction among employees was high. The semiconductor production process used by the laboratory was ineffective, and competition from Dallas-based Texas Instruments was heightening.

In 1957, seven key employees from Shockley Laboratories decided to defect and develop their own production process. With East Coast financing, they connected with Connecticut-based Fairchild Camera and Instrument Company and formed a semiconductor branch of the firm in Mountain View. Shortly thereafter, Robert Noyce, Shockley's most brilliant scientist, also defected to Fairchild, and the new enterprise was off and running.[4]

Fairchild Semiconductor became caught up in a race with Texas Instruments and Motorola in semiconductor product and process technologies. The integrated circuit was invented at Texas Instruments, but Fairchild was close behind and was the first to develop the new planar assembly-line manufacturing process. As research and development began to yield viable products in the early 1960s, Fairchild and Texas Instruments began looking for customers. Televisions were still made with vacuum tubes. Computer makers bought some integrated circuits, but that market was not large enough to sustain the emerging industry. The government, which had funded little of Fairchild's research and development effort, was the customer that gave Fairchild and the semiconductor industry in general the boost they needed. The space program and the high-technology military build-up purchased large amounts of integrated circuits at a critical period in the industry's development.

Fairchild proposed building the guidance system for the Minuteman Intercontinental Ballistic Missile with planar transistors and integrated circuits instead of transistors. The military accepted the plan, and Fairchild's fortunes soared (Hanson 1982).

The most important part Fairchild played in the emergence of the technopolis was its role as an incubator of new companies, or "Fairchildren," as they came to be known. "Throughout the sixties, bright young engineers spun out of Fairchild Semiconductor like so many enterprising Minervas from the head of Zeus," wrote Hanson (1982, p. 110). Venture capital was pouring into the valley, and enterprising engineers and executives had little trouble setting up new businesses. Among the firms that came out of Fairchild were Rheem Semiconductor, Signetics, Teledyne, and General Microelectronics. In 1967, Charles Sporck, Fairchild's manufacturing specialist, left to become head of the revitalized National Semiconductor. Jerry Sanders, Fairchild's marketing director, quit and later founded Advanced Micro Devices. Almost all of the Silicon Valley semiconductor firms present in the 1970s could trace their roots to Fairchild.

The most important Fairchild spin-off was Intel, founded by Noyce, Gordon Moore, and Andrew Grove. The goal of Intel was to design an integrated circuit with advanced memories that could replace earlier chips. An Intel design team, headed by Ted Hoff, in 1971 produced the microprocessor or "computer on a chip," a powerful device that would revolutionize information technology (Braun and Macdonald 1982). At first, Intel did not know what to do with the microprocessor, which it had developed while trying to solve a problem for a Japanese calculator company. The military was not an immediate buyer. But customers soon came from everywhere. The first microprocessors were used in music, agriculture, slot machines, and manufacturing (Hanson 1982). Soon a parade of companies began making microprocessors: Advanced Micro Devices, Fairchild, and Signetics in Silicon Valley, and elsewhere in the United States, RCA, Rockwell, Motorola, Texas Instruments, and Mostek. Five Japanese firms also entered the market, as did Siemens and Phillips of Europe. However, in the 1970s, the Silicon Valley firms, which had a commanding lead, dominated.

The blossoming of the semiconductor industry transformed Santa Clara County into Silicon Valley. Farm land was bought up by developers for housing tracts and commercial and industrial projects. Municipalities built industrial parks. New services for businesses and individuals sprouted and flourished. The valley produced thousands of jobs for lawyers, accountants, public relations specialists, journalists, and consultants. Malone writes: "For every way there was of making a fortune from the flow of electrons in Silicon Valley, there were probably ten equally effective ways that required absolutely no knowledge of electromagnetic theory at all" (1985, p. 333).

In the late 1970s, Silicon Valley's grip on the semiconductor industry loosened as firms from elsewhere captured the first big consumer markets for microprocessors: calculators and digital watches. Silicon Valley companies, which had sold primarily to the military and to businesses, were ill-prepared to compete in consumer markets.

The most serious competition to Silicon Valley industry came from Japan (Hart 1989). Between 1976 and 1979, the Japanese government and five private firms—Hitachi, Fujitsu, Mitsubishi, Nippon, and Toshiba—launched a major VLSI (Very Large-Scale Integration) research program in semiconductor memories. Japanese firms also were large, vertically integrated concerns with consumer electronics operations. Unlike the merchant firms of Silicon Valley, Japanese chip producers had their own internal markets and, because they were diversified, could ride out industry slumps. Preferential purchasing by the Japanese Ministry of Posts and Telecommunications further boosted the position of the Japanese firms.

The maturation of the industry and foreign competition changed the geography of semiconductor production in line with the product-cycle hypothesis. Silicon Valley ran out of room in the late 1970s, and labor costs also began to soar relative to producers in other areas. Firms shifted their manufacturing operations to other parts of the United States, mainly to the West or South, in order to remain competitive (Saxenian 1984; Scott and Angel 1987; Scott 1988a, 1988c). The movement offshore began in 1963, when Fairchild built an assembly plant in Hong Kong. Assembly operations increasingly were shifted to low-wage countries in Asia.

In the mid-1970s, governments all over the world began to see semiconductors as a vital national industry. By 1976, every major industrial nation had established a semiconductor industry (Warshofsky 1989). One way to acquire a semiconductor industry was to buy one, and Silicon Valley firms became the targets of buyouts from foreign and domestic firms. Siemens of West Germany bought Litronix and 20 percent of Advanced Micro Devices. NEC of Japan bought Electronic Arrays; Honeywell bought Synertek; Northern Telecom bought 24 percent of Intersil. In 1979, Schlumberger Ltd. of France purchased Fairchild for $350 million in cash.

Another reason for the wave of acquisitions was the changing capital needs of the industry. It had become increasingly expensive to set up production operations, and smaller firms needed a cash-rich partner. The trend continued in the 1980s. In 1982, IBM bought 12 percent of Intel and later expanded its ownership to 30 percent.

Thus for a range of reasons—most often the need for capital or cash for one party and technology for the other—Silicon Valley firms were acquired by outsiders. A study of 250 firms established in Silicon Valley in the 1960s found that 32.4 percent had been acquired by 1980 (Bruno and Cooper 1982).

The 1980s saw another shift in the industry with the development of the new gate-array production process, which allowed manufacturers to produce customized chips without large initial capital costs. This brought another round of small companies and start-ups to Silicon Valley. Leading this "second wave" of Silicon Valley chip firms was LSI Logic, founded in 1980 by Wilfred J. Corrigan, a former Fairchild executive (Bylinsky 1985; Wilson 1985). In its first four years, LSI Logic grew faster than had Intel and Advanced Micro Devices at a similar stage of development. Other important custom chip start-ups include Integrated Device Technology, founded by three Hewlett-Packard engineers, and Cypress Semiconductor, started by an executive at Advanced Micro Devices. Larger semiconductor firms in Silicon Valley and elsewhere also entered the custom chip market.

The growth of the custom chip industry in Silicon Valley occurred as the larger mass-production chip firms of the region and the United States were losing their competitiveness. Throughout the 1980s, U.S. semiconductor firms lost market share to the big Japanese companies, and by 1990, the Japanese controlled more than 40 percent of the world chip market and 70 percent of the basic dynamic random-access memory (DRAM) chip market (Warshofsky 1989; Wrubel 1990). The Semiconductor Industry Association was formed in response to these pressures. The association, in cooperation with the Defense Department, the National Science Foundation, and the Commerce Department, created the Semiconductor Manufacturing Technology Institute (Sematech), a consortium trying to develop new manufacturing technologies to head off Japanese domination of the industry. Robert Noyce was named head of Sematech, and he waged a vigorous fight for political support for the organization and its goals. However, lukewarm backing for the effort from the Bush administration and the death of Noyce in 1990 left doubts about the future of Sematech.

The semiconductor industry stimulated the development of Silicon Valley and gave the technopolis its name. The industry has undergone remarkable competitive shifts and spatial transformation. These changes, despite the dislocations they may have caused, have not undermined the status of the technopolis. First, Silicon Valley has remained a center of corporate control and research and development for the semiconductor industry. Second, and perhaps most important, the technopolis has spawned new industries that have reduced the region's dependence on semiconductors.

The New Industries of Silicon Valley

Although the inventors of the microprocessor knew they had created an extraordinary product, they did not really know what to do with it at first: "The old marketing wisdom of pinpointing a need and then building a product to fill it was giving way to a new approach—building a product so universal in application as to fulfill a rainbow of needs, many of them unforeseen by its designers" (Hanson 1982, p. 109). Eventually, almost every manufactured product, from watches to microwave ovens to automobiles, would have a microprocessor embedded in it somewhere.

The manifold uses of semiconductors shaped the development of Silicon Valley. The principal consequence was that the semiconductor industry drew into its orbit a number of industries that relied on semiconductors as a critical component. As these industries grew, they became less dependent on the initial cluster of semiconductor firms.

The instruments industry, which preceded the semiconductor industry in the region, was probably the first to grow rapidly as a result of the development of semiconductor technology. The microprocessor made possible "smart" instruments for testing, measurement and diagnosis in medicine and industry. Among the instrument firms that arose or experienced rapid growth in the 1970s as a result of the microelectronics revolution were Hewlett-Packard, Diasonics, Xonics, Acurex, and Measurex (Malone 1985).

The video game industry was another early consequence of the development of the microprocessor. The game "Pong" was invented in 1972 by Nolan Bushnell, a former University of Utah student who came up with the idea while working in an amusement park. He developed the concept while working for Ampex in Silicon Valley. Finally, he set out on his own, founding Atari, a phenomenally successful company that for a time defined high-technology industry.[5] Atari brought computers into the home and launched the video game industry, which propelled the regional economy forward.

The microprocessor also made possible dramatic improvements in computers. In the 1960s and early 1970s, IBM dominated the computer market in the United States with its powerful mainframes. However, with the development of the minicomputer, the computer industry extended to Boston, Minneapolis, and a few other locations. Some of the Silicon Valley semiconductor firms made early forays into computer-making. One of the first computer success stories of the valley is that of Gene Amdahl, a former IBM engineer who started his own company to compete head-to-head with the computer giant. Amdahl developed a "plug-compatible" computer that could be used with an IBM system but was more technically sophisticated than anything IBM offered. Other companies also began developing plug compatibles. Amdahl Corporation had enormous success until IBM developed a new series of computers that made the generation of plug compatibles obsolete.

The next step in the evolution of the computer, the personal or home computer, was unforeseen by either the video game makers or the semiconductor firms, which were the logical companies to develop them. IBM and the minicomputer companies of Route 128 also overlooked the opportunity. The development of the personal computer fell to a pair of college dropouts, Steve Wozniak and Steve Jobs, who belonged to a "hackers" computer club in Palo Alto.

The personal computer actually had its origins in the 1950s, when engineers working for companies or research laboratories would take home equipment and patch together their own machines (Malone 1985). The first commercial personal computer was offered by Altair, a New Mexico firm, in 1975. In 1977, several other companies offered personal computers: Commodore International, Radio Shack, and Heath Company, maker of do-it-yourself electronic "Heath Kits."

Jobs, who worked for Atari, and Wozniak, who worked for Hewlett-Packard, came to know each other at the Home Brew Computer Club, which held monthly meetings on the Stanford campus. Wozniak designed and built their first small computer in Jobs' garage in Los Altos. The prototype cost $1,300 and was financed with the sale of Jobs' Volkswagen microbus and Wozniak's Hewlett-Packard programmable calculator (Malone 1985). They took their plans for the first Apple computer to their respective employers, but both Atari and Hewlett-Packard rejected the proposal (Rogers and Larsen 1984).

Jobs, who was then 21, and Wozniak, 25, founded Apple Computer in 1977. Jobs was the entrepreneurial wizard, while Wozniak provided the technical expertise. They hired the top public relations expert in the valley, Regis McKenna, who helped them obtain seed money. Eventually, start-up funds were obtained from venture capitalist Arthur Rock, Venrock Associates, and the Bank of America. Mike Markkula, former marketing director at Intel, was hired and became a key official in the company.[6] He also put up $250,000 of his own money in exchange for a one-third ownership of the company. The Apple II was a huge success. When the company went public in 1980, Jobs' shares were worth $165 million and Wozniak's were worth $88 million.

Competition in the personal computer business heated up in the 1980s. Atari and Texas Instruments were among the first to enter the market. Soon IBM, Digital Equipment Corporation, AT&T, and Hewlett-Packard offered personal computers. Meanwhile, Apple stumbled after the phenomenal success of the Apple II. The Apple III was a year later and widely unpopular. IBM's PC, introduced in 1981, made major inroads into Apple's territory. In the early 1980s both IBM and Apple introduced unsuccessful products: IBM's PCjr and Apple's Lisa. Finally, Apple broke open the market in 1984 with the Macintosh, introduced with its striking "1984" television advertisements in the Superbowl. Within hours after it hit the market, the user-friendly, graphically oriented Macintosh had produced $7.5 million in sales. Fifty thousand machines were sold in seventy-four days. It had taken two and one-half years to sell that many Apple II's (Sculley 1987).

The emergence of the small computer industry set off a new round of growth in Silicon Valley just as the older semiconductor firms were starting to falter. Silicon Valley firms also began to succeed at work stations, powerful, mid-sized desktop computers. The most successful work station company was Sun Microsystems, founded in 1982 in Mountain View, and now the industry leader. Computers also created demand for software, which represented another new growth industry for the technopolis.

Other high-technology industries have emerged in Silicon Valley. The region is a center of laser technology (Bylinsky 1985). Varian Associates spawned laser companies in much the same way that Fairchild produced chip firms. Spectra-Physics, the first and largest laser firm, is a Varian spin-off. The second biggest laser company is Coherent Inc., a spin-off of Spectra-Physics. The Silicon Valley laser cluster also includes Liconix, General Photonix, XMR, Cooper LaserSonics, Quantel, Uniphase, Cyonics, and Continental. One of the two American co-inventors of the laser, Arthur Schawlow, teaches at Stanford, while the other,

Charles Townes, is at Berkeley. Graduates of both universities have contributed greatly to the growth of the industry.

The greater San Francisco area, including Silicon Valley, is a center of biotechnology and pharmaceutical industries (Bylinsky 1985). The biotechnology industry traces its roots to the entrepreneurial efforts of Dr. Alejandro Zaffaroni, a researcher for Syntex, a drug company that moved to Palo Alto in 1961. Zaffaroni created several new firms, including Syva, Zoecon, and Alza. Genentech, the pioneer biotechnology firm, was founded in South San Francisco by Robert A. Swanson, a San Francisco venture capitalist, and Herbert Boyer, a biochemistry professor at the University of California Medical School in San Francisco.

The Dynamic Technopolis

Silicon Valley shifted from a resource-based economy to a knowledge-based economy in less than three decades. This transition occurred without an intervening stage of traditional manufacturing (Henton and Waldhorn 1988). Thus Silicon Valley, as well as other high-technology regions in California, are examples of technological leapfrogging.

The synergistic growth of Stanford University and local science-based industry in the first half of the twentieth century created agglomeration advantages that facilitated the emergence of the semiconductor industry in Silicon Valley. The semiconductor industry stimulated the growth of a broad range of high-technology industries, including video games, personal computers, instruments, custom chips, and software. Surrounding these core industries were important networks of supplier and service firms.

The region has become a remarkable incubator of new companies and new industries. As older firms decline, new firms grow. As the industries that fueled the growth of the technopolis mature, new industries are being born. The next section explores why Silicon Valley became such a dynamic industrial region.

CAUSES

The emergence of Silicon Valley can be understood in terms of the model presented in Chapter 3. The technopolis arose because of the existence of a world-class knowledge center and an environment that was highly conducive to innovation.

Knowledge Centers

The initial knowledge center of Silicon Valley was Stanford University. This institution set the region apart from other predominantly agricultural areas in the 1940s. Because of the presence of Stanford, electrical and electronics-related industry clustered in the Palo Alto area. The electrical engineering and physics laboratories at Stanford produced many of the key early inventions of the electrical revolution. Stanford graduates were the technical entrepreneurs who founded the early firms of the technopolis. Stanford faculty provided advice on technical and business matters to their students who were starting new firms. By the early 1950s, Stanford Industrial Park was a magnet for new technology-based companies. Few high-technology firms that emerged in the critical World War II and postwar years did not have some important link to Stanford.

As the technopolis grew, Stanford's role changed. The key inventions came not from university laboratories but from the high-technology firms. The firms also became the incubating environments for entrepreneurs. Stanford graduates continued to start new firms and make technological breakthroughs, but they usually did so after serving an apprenticeship at an existing Silicon Valley company (Malecki 1986). Thus secondary knowledge centers developed, the most important early ones being Shockley Laboratories, Fairchild Semiconductor, and Intel. In the 1970s, virtually every semiconductor firm in the valley traced its roots to Fairchild.

As the technopolis matured further, the importance of a central knowledge center diminished. The agglomeration advantages that had developed were so strong that the technopolis no longer depended on Stanford or a handful of companies. The vast network of diverse high-technology firms, as well as a rich milieu of supplier and service companies, ensured a steady stream of technological innovation and new company formation. Thus in the case of Silicon Valley, a knowledge center and several secondary knowledge centers were critical to the emergence of the technopolis, but after the technopolis matured, no single institution served as a growth pole. The internal dynamism of the technopolis came from its large cluster of firms and research organizations. Although the initial growth pole, Stanford, remained vital to the technopolis, its role had become less central.

Innovative Environment

The environment in Silicon Valley during the formative stage of the technopolis was highly conducive to entrepreneurship and innovation. These conditions nurtured the growth initiated by the knowledge centers. The different aspects of the environment identified in Chapter 3 are discussed separately below.

Local Relations. Local relationships evolved in Silicon Valley in a way that supports a high level of innovation. The clustering of spin-off firms in the area has contributed to the development of a rich and continuous flow of information and ideas. Patterns of interaction among high-technology executives and personnel also have built up this aspect of an innovative environment. Rogers and Larsen state: "One ought to think of Silicon Valley not as just a geographical place, nor simply as the main center of the microelectronics industry, nor even as several thousand high-tech firms, but as a *network*" (1984, pp. 79-80).

An important way that information is exchanged in Silicon Valley is by the movement of personnel from firm to firm. With a few exceptions the bonds between employers and employees are weak, and personnel jump easily to new firms. Turnover among executives and engineers was estimated to be as high as 30 percent a year in the early 1980s (Rogers and Larsen 1984). Housing costs are so high that most people who do not already own homes in the valley cannot afford to buy in; personnel movement thus tends to occur among people who already have jobs in the region (Grove 1987). Since the most important technological and business information in Silicon Valley is carried by people, this rapid movement of people from organization to organization creates a rich environment of information exchange.

The spatial proximity of firms in Silicon Valley also facilitates the diffusion of information. Executives and personnel are more likely to have contact with each other in formal and informal settings in such a dense concentration of firms. Stanford also represents a neutral arena in which individuals from different firms meet and develop relationships.

A number of organizations have served as formal settings in which information has been exchanged and important relationships forged. The Home Brew Computer Club, founded in 1975, served as a critical meeting place for the computer enthusiasts who launched the personal computer industry (Rogers and Larsen 1984). Club members started twenty-two microcomputer companies, including Apple, Cromemco, and North Star. Many software pioneers also came from the club. Similarly, Fairchild served as the information hub for semiconductor technology, as did Atari for video games.

Another crucial element in the Silicon Valley milieu is the large venture capital industry. After Fairchild succeeded, money poured into the region for entrepreneurs with plans for new products. In some cases, the credentials of the founders were all that were needed to obtain financing. Noyce once said that he and his partners never had a formal business plan when they received financing to start Intel. Proximity to San Francisco, which was already a major financial center, facilitated the growth of venture capital. Venture capitalists became the gatekeepers of Silicon Valley, deciding which enterprises would have a chance. Venture capitalists provide not only money but also technical and managerial assistance. The large concentration of venture capital and the network by which it is allocated have maintained the vitality of the region. Venture capital is probably the most important element in what Rogers and Larsen (1984) call the "Silicon Valley maternity ward"—the sophisticated system of supports for new and growing companies.

Labor Force. As the technopolis was taking shape, Silicon Valley possessed an almost ideal mix of skilled and unskilled labor needed by high-technology industry. A unique and critical feature of the region's labor characteristics was the concentration of scientific and technical personnel. Probably no other place in the world had such a large assembly of engineers, scientists, and technical labor. These specialized workers had been drawn to the region by the early science-based companies, university research organizations, and military establishments.

The large firms that established branches in the region, including Lockheed, IBM, ITT, Sylvania, and General Electric, recruited engineers from a national market. This vast technical labor pool was invaluable to the emerging semiconductor industry. The new high-technology firms often simply stole employees from the big firms (Saxenian 1985a).

Stanford has been a major factor in the development of the labor force. The university is one of the largest producers of advanced engineering degrees in the country. The University of California at Berkeley also became a large source of engineering graduates for Silicon Valley industry.

Engineers and scientists drawn to the area for education or an initial job had strong incentives to stay. The growing industrial milieu provided extraordinary job opportunities for high-technology workers and their spouses. Further, the region offers an attractive suburban lifestyle with good schools and housing. San Francisco is a short drive away with its extraordinary cultural offerings. The valley also is blessed with an almost perfect climate and attractive natural surroundings.

A plentiful supply of cheap, non-unionized labor also was available for the routine assembly and manufacturing positions required by high-technology industry. Large numbers of immigrants from Latin America and Asia settled in the area. The mechanization of agriculture also brought surplus labor to the region from other parts of California.

The absence of a trade union tradition and a male blue-collar class increased the attractiveness of the region for new industry. Unionization efforts in Silicon Valley were weak and ineffective. Even at Atari, where 1,700 workers were laid off in 1983 when manufacturing was shifted offshore, a union election failed that same year.

Markets. Proximity to markets was vital to the growth of high-technology firms in Silicon Valley. The important early markets for semiconductor firms were military contractors and subcontractors. Northern California was home to several large military and aerospace establishments and their dependent aircraft and aerospace contractors. The complexity and innovative nature of semiconductor technology required frequent interaction among chip makers and customers. The spatial proximity of semiconductor firms in Silicon Valley to their military customers was an important competitive advantage over firms located elsewhere (Saxenian 1985a).

Eventually, civilian markets for semiconductors emerged, especially after the development of the microprocessor. Many of these markets were found in Silicon Valley initially, although they soon became global in scope. Makers of instruments, video games, computers, and electronic equipment set up operations in Silicon Valley to be close to semiconductor firms. The result was an increasing concentration of industry in the region.

Knowledge Infrastructure. At the center of the knowledge infrastructure is Stanford, which functions as a developer of entrepreneurs and high-technology personnel, as well as a source of technological breakthroughs and a focus of community life. The University of California at Berkeley is an important supplier of talent to the high-technology region. The university also boasts some of the world's leading research laboratories. Stanford and Berkeley both have large engineering education programs, and the San Francisco area is the largest producer of engineering doctorates in the United States (Malecki 1986). California's large public higher education system also has helped to supply human capital to high-technology firms in the technopolis.

Public and private schools in Silicon Valley provide good quality education at the primary and secondary level. These schools are an important attraction for key personnel at high-technology firms.

The Industrial Base. Although Silicon Valley is often said to have emerged in a virgin industrial area, the region's existing industry did contribute to the growth of the technopolis. The most important contribution, cited above, was the concentration of scientific and technical personnel that developed in the region to serve the early science-based industry.

Another factor was the presence of specialized suppliers and services needed by the semiconductor industry. The prior concentration of industry had brought firms that made the chemicals, testing equipment, silicon, and special production equipment needed in semiconductor manufacturing (Saxenian 1985a). The new firms probably would not have been able to provide these supplies and services in house.

The Role of Policy

The Silicon Valley technopolis was an entrepreneurial phenomenon, driven by the activities of profit-seeking individuals and institutions. However, deliberate policies by universities, governments, and other actors outside the market also played important roles in the development of the technopolis.

University Policy. The policies of Stanford University in supporting innovation and entrepreneurship were critical to the growth of the technopolis. Faculty and students were encouraged to commercialize their research. Stanford's policies of vigorously seeking government and industry support for its research programs also helped to transform the university into a world-class knowledge center, which was critical to the early growth of the technopolis.

The activities of Frederick Terman, recounted earlier in this chapter, were vital to the emergence of the technopolis. His support for William Hewlett and David Packard was by itself an enormous contribution. But Terman also inspired and assisted many other student entrepreneurs. He raised millions of dollars to upgrade the university's faculty and research facilities, and he created Stanford Industrial Park, an important piece of the physical and institutional infrastructure of the technopolis.

Federal Government. Federal policies played a critical but indirect role in the development of the technopolis. The presence of Ames Research Center and Moffett Field Naval Air Station, both in Mountain View, were important to the early development of a defense and aerospace industry in the region. Federal support for education and research was essential to the development of Stanford and other higher education institutions in the region. Nearly all scientists with doctorates received some form of federal support for their research.

The most important role of the federal government, and perhaps the most important factor in the emergence of the technopolis, was procurement (Saxenian 1985a, 1985b; Markusen, Hall, and Glasmeier 1986). The government market for Silicon Valley's electronics firms grew dramatically after World War II. Semiconductors became an important component of missile and defensive systems. In the early 1960s, the government purchased nearly all of the semiconductors made in the United States. This support permitted the industry to develop until civilian markets emerged.

A final federal policy that helped create the technopolis was the relatively low tax rate for capital gains in the 1950s and 1960s. This ensured a plentiful supply of venture capital to fuel the growth of new firms during the time that the technopolis was taking shape.

State Government. California state government policies have been widely viewed as playing a minor and indirect role in the development of the Silicon Valley technopolis (Henton and Waldhorn 1988; Osborne 1988). The major accounts of the evolution of Silicon Valley barely mention state government at all (Hanson 1982; Rogers and Larsen 1984; Malone 1985; Saxenian 1985a; Bylinsky 1976). Nevertheless, four general activities of state government that may have had some bearing on the direction of the technopolis have been identified in the literature: infrastructure development, support for education, support for entrepreneurship, and state industrial policy.

After World War II, California embarked on an extraordinary infrastructure construction program (Henton and Waldhorn 1988; Kotkin and Grabowicz 1982; Osborne 1988). The state's coffers overflowed during the war because of taxes reaped from the expansion of the defense industry. Governor Earl Warren hoarded this money and used it to finance the construction of roads, bridges, schools, hospitals, prisons, and water projects. The next big surge in infrastructure development occurred during the administration of Governor Pat Brown, from 1958 to 1966. Brown oversaw the construction of California's massive freeway system, three new universities, and a major water project.

These infrastructure investments were critical for economic development throughout California, including Silicon Valley. They made possible the population growth that accompanied the development of high-technology industry. The road networks facilitated the movement of people and goods and helped to develop labor markets and product markets for the technopolis.

Since the late 1960s, infrastructure investments have not kept pace with development, and Silicon Valley and much of California have suffered from the familiar deglomeration factors of mature technopolises: clogged road networks, environmental degradation, and an inadequate housing supply (Henton and Waldhorn 1988; Saxenian 1984; Malone 1989).

From the 1940s through the 1960s, California made massive investments in its system of higher education (Henton and Waldhorn 1988; Osborne 1988). A consolidated system of nine universities, nineteen colleges and 106 community colleges was established. California has the largest higher education system of any state, and it draws students from all over the country.

A new higher-education master plan adopted by the legislature in 1960 led to the construction of three new universities, including the University of California at Irvine in Orange County and the University of California at San Diego. These two schools became top research institutions that have stimulated regional high-technology development: biotechnology around UC-San Diego, and aerospace and electronics in Orange County. The University of California at Berkeley, one of the older universities in the state system, has established some of the world's top scientific laboratories.

California's higher education system contributed to the development of human capital for high-technology industry. The system also produced some Silicon Valley entrepreneurs, although not nearly as many as Stanford.[7] The government's commitment to education also enhanced the attractiveness of California for business.

In the post-World War II years, California was highly supportive of entrepreneurship. This has been attributed to a number of factors, including the frontier/gold rush tradition, a heritage of rugged individualism, the free-wheeling California lifestyle, and the emergence of impressive role models, such as William Hewlett and David Packard (Kotkin and Grabowicz 1982; Rogers and Larsen 1984; Malone 1985). The role of state government in creating this environment is difficult to discern, although it is reasonable to expect that it played some part.

Henton and Waldhorn (1988) credit state government with fostering entrepreneurship through investments in education, transportation, communication, and other infrastructure. The efforts of the state's governors to create a "good business climate" also have contributed to the entrepreneurial environment, according to Henton and Waldhorn. The policies of California governors since World War II have varied widely. Governor Ronald Reagan's approach to economic development was to limit government's role, particularly in areas of taxation and regulation. Governor Jerry Brown, after shedding his initial anti-growth posture, adopted an activist approach characterized by research and development investments, education and job training programs, and public-private partnerships. Governor George Deukmajian's strategy returned to the Reagan approach of limiting government involvement in the economy. He also developed a comprehensive marketing program to sell California as a location for new business.

During much of the evolution of the Silicon Valley technopolis, state industrial policy did not exist. Reagan and Deukmajian rejected the concept, and Pat Brown did not have any explicit economic development strategy until the end of his administration. Jerry Brown, however, did develop a comprehensive and innovative approach to industrial development. Many of the features of Brown's strategy were copied by other states, and some of the policies and programs still have an impact in California.

Brown was a member of what David Osborne (1988) calls the "class of '74" elected officials, which included Michael Dukakis, Paul Tsongas, Gary Hart, Christopher Dodd, Richard Lamm, and Bruce Babbitt, all elected that year. Of all of these leaders, Brown was probably the most innovative—and unpredictable. He began his governorship espousing the limits of growth and was initially hostile to business interests. However, in his third year in office, he underwent a transformation. He became increasingly concerned about economic development and developed a series of initiatives to promote industry.[8] In the late 1970s, Brown became the first politician of national stature to advocate an explicit industrial policy (Osborne 1988).

Brown instructed his planning office to streamline the permit process for industrial sites. Calling for greater cooperation among business, government, and labor, he created a job-training program for firms that were expanding or opening new plants. He also set up a retraining program for workers who were losing their jobs because of economic or technological change. This program was funded with unemployment taxes and represented the first time unemployment taxes had been used for anything other than support checks for workers (Osborne 1988). Brown also set up a $25 million network of centers to train teachers in the use of computers. Other Brown initiatives were capital assistance programs for new businesses, reduced capital gains taxes, and diversification of public pension-fund investments.

In 1981, Brown appointed the California Commission on Industrial Innovation, which was comprised of business and labor leaders, including Steve Jobs and David Packard. The commission contributed to the establishment of the university-industry research program, Microelectronics Innovation and Computer Research Operation (MICRO), at the University of California at Berkeley (Osborne 1988; Henton and Waldhorn 1988; Office of Technology Assessment 1984).

As in the case of Route 128, state industrial policies had little, if any, impact on the emergence of the Silicon Valley technopolis, which had already taken shape before the policies were designed or implemented. State industrial policies may have improved the climate for innovation and entrepreneurship, and thus helped to sustain the technopolis once it was under way. Brown's policies also may have fostered more cooperative relations between business and government. The dramatically different orientations of the state's governors in the post-World War II years and the seemingly marginal impact of these shifts on high-technology industry in the state would tend to cast doubt on the significance of state industrial policy on the development of Silicon Valley.

Local Government. Much of the physical infrastructure for the technopolis was built by local government. After Stanford Industrial Park began to attract industry to Palo Alto, several nearby communities—Mountain View, Cupertino, and Santa Clara—built industrial parks (Saxenian 1984). These developments, along with road, sewer, water, and other infrastructure improvements, provided sites for high-technology firms. Local governments also built much of the infrastructure necessary to accommodate population growth.

City government in San Jose encouraged the transformation of the city into a regional center for the emerging high-technology industry. Saxenian (1984) reports that city leaders were committed to turning San Jose into the "Los Angeles of the North." Through infrastructure development, zoning, and annexation, city government made possible rapid residential and commercial development. San Jose's population jumped from 95,000 in 1950 to 683,000 in 1984. It is now more populous than Pittsburgh, Cleveland, or St. Louis and nearly as large as San Francisco.

SILICON VALLEY IN THE 1990s

As the 1990s began, Silicon Valley faced considerable adversity: the national recession, cuts in military spending, and relentless technological change affecting its core industries. The real estate market slumped, and unemployment inched upward. Many Silicon Valley companies, in particular the older semiconductor and computer firms, were in turmoil, facing internal restructuring and repositioning in the high-technology marketplace. However, despite the problems of particular firms, the region as a whole remained vital. Entrepreneurship continued to spring from Silicon Valley, producing jobs and wealth. In the 1980s, employment increased by 35 percent, and the informal boundaries of the technopolis expanded to San Mateo to the north, Fremont to the east, and Santa Cruz to the south (Saxenian 1990). According to one estimate, from 1986 to 1990, the market value of firms in northern California increased by $24 billion, more than double the wealth creation of any other region.[9] By renewing itself through innovation and small-firm creation, Silicon Valley remained the preeminent high-technology region in the world.

The region's resilience was due in part to its strong foundations: the presence of Stanford, the existing concentration of diverse high-technology firms, and the highly innovative environment. The region's dense networks of people and information may have been the main factor in Silicon Valley's success in the 1990s. Would-be entrepreneurs find themselves in an environment populated by consultants, venture capitalists, trade associations, established firms looking for strategic alliances, and highly skilled workers eager to jump to a new firm. Under these conditions, entrepreneurship flourishes. Saxenian (1990, p. 95) attributes Silicon Valley's performance to "a regional environment that is not only rich in skill and know-how, but one which fosters new firm formation and collective learning."

The new firms that have driven the renewal of Silicon Valley are different from the previous generation of high-technology firms that were long the core of the regional economy. The older firms are centralized enterprises that developed and manufactured products that found vast new markets. The new firms of Silicon Valley are smaller, focused organizations that are finding profitable niches in some specialized segment of their business. They often form strategic alliances with new or established firms for marketing, production, or research and development.

In a detailed study of the new semiconductor firms of Silicon Valley, Saxenian (1990) describes the revitalization of the region. In the 1980s, more than 85 new chip makers emerged, most of them founded by entrepreneurs who had come from the large, first-generation semiconductor firms and who were dissatisfied with the bureaucratic rigidities of those organizations. The new firms produced custom, high-performance chips, largely for niche markets. Their flexible design and manufacturing technologies enabled them to respond quickly to changing market conditions, and their relations with other firms in Silicon Valley gave them a strong competitive edge. Drawing on the rich network of people and institutions in Silicon Valley, the new semiconductor firms unbundled their operations, subcontracting out the different phases of their businesses. This has allowed firms to stay focused on their central missions. Saxenian writes: "Each firm remains at the leading edge of its particular expertise—be it chip design, fabrication processes, engineering and design services, or fast turnaround manufacturing—and has access to the products and services of equally sophisticated and specialized suppliers" (1990, p. 94).

The dense networks of local relationships have been valuable in supplying the capital needs of Silicon Valley start-ups. For a number of reasons, including tighter capital markets and divergent interests of financiers and high-technology entrepreneurs, the importance of venture capital in financing high-technology enterprises diminished in the late 1980s. Venture capitalists have become less patient with the long research and development phases in many high-technology fields, which delay the introduction of new products and push back public offerings on new firms. Entrepreneurs increasingly are turning for initial financing to established firms, which want a stake in new technologies they are unable to generate internally. Silicon Valley's complex web of existing firms and entrepreneurs and the free flow of market information in the region has greatly facilitated this process (*Economist* 1991). Many large firms, such as Hewlett-Packard, as well as some medium-sized firms are spinning off new companies by bankrolling employees who want to leave and start their own businesses. Because of the support systems in Silicon Valley, most of these firms stay in the region.

A final point in understanding Silicon Valley's success in the 1990s is that the broad changes that have occurred in high-technology fields in the past half-dozen years have favored the region. Silicon Valley was not heavily invested in declining industries, such as minicomputers. Although one big industry of Silicon Valley has struggled—commodity chips—its decline was neatly paralleled by the rise of custom chip producers. Other important industries concentrated in Silicon Valley, microcomputers, work stations, and pharmaceuticals, have been on the upswing. The region also is well positioned to compete in emerging technologies, such as palm-top computers, software, and biotechnology (Markoff 1991).

COMPARATIVE ANALYSIS OF SILICON VALLEY AND ROUTE 128

Common Themes

The Route 128 and Silicon Valley technopolises emerged at about the same time—the immediate post-World War II years, when the revolution in knowledge-intensive technologies began to change the nature of regional economic development. Both areas were well positioned to take advantage of this shift. At the core of each technopolis was a primary knowledge center (Stanford and MIT), as well as an institution that played a secondary role in generating regional growth (University of California at Berkeley and Harvard). Both regions had the important ingredients of highly innovative environments: a skilled technical labor force, a well-developed web of local relations, access to markets, and a high-quality knowledge infrastructure. Prewar science-based industry was present in both technopolises and provided a solid foundation on which to build new high-technology industry. World War II, the Korean War, and the Cold War defense and aerospace build-ups stimulated the development of both technopolises.

In both, the policies of the principal universities played a central role in the emergence of the technopolis. Unlike most other top universities in the United States at that time, Stanford and MIT strongly encouraged students and faculty to commercialize their research. Both universities nurtured relations with industry and the military. Stanford and MIT also were responsible for major policy innovations. The world's first science park was established at Stanford. The first venture capital firm was organized by MIT officials and several other individuals.

During the formative years of the Silicon Valley and Route 128 technopolises, state government was largely unaware of the emergence of regional high-technology development and took no deliberate actions to encourage or sustain it. After the transition was well under way, innovative governors—Jerry Brown in California and Michael Dukakis in Massachusetts—developed industrial policies aimed at encouraging high-technology development.

The Role of Military Spending

Military spending played important though somewhat different roles in the development of Route 128 and Silicon Valley. For Route 128, defense spending created the big laboratories and research projects of MIT. These laboratories produced the entrepreneurs and inventions that created the new industries of the technopolis. However, the military did not provide critical early markets for the post-World War II high-technology firms of Route 128. Minicomputers, which were the mainstay product of the technopolis, were sold mostly to businesses and scientists.

In Silicon Valley, the military did not fund much of the early basic research that produced semiconductors. That work was conducted within private firms: Shockley Laboratories, Fairchild Semiconductor, and others. However, after the integrated circuit was developed, the military became a critical market for semiconductors. By purchasing nearly all of the semiconductors U.S. firms produced until the early 1960s, the military sustained the industry during the time that civilian markets were forming. The invention of the microprocessor, which found vast civilian markets, freed the industry from its reliance on military purchasing.

Both Silicon Valley and Route 128 did receive significant prime contract awards from the military throughout the development of the two technopolises (Markusen, Hall, and Glasmeier 1986; Markusen 1988; Saxenian 1985a, 1985b). These money infusions clearly helped to sustain the technopolises. During the formative years, however, it was military-funded research that provided the boost for Route 128 and military purchasing that carried Silicon Valley.

The Semiconductor Industry

A second significant difference between Silicon Valley and Route 128 is the nature of their core industries. The semiconductor industry had more propulsive capabilities than minicomputers, although both stimulated the development of a large web of backward and forward linkages. Semiconductors became a fundamental building block of virtually all subsequent electronic products. The presence of the semiconductor industry in Silicon Valley promoted the growth of new industries in the region. The microprocessor launched the video game and personal computer industries. Personal computers stimulated the growth of the software industry in Silicon Valley.

As a consequence, Silicon Valley developed a more diversified industrial base than did Route 128 and thus has been better able to withstand downturns in the fortunes of particular firms or industries. Route 128, however, became dependent on minicomputers, and when that industry slumped in the late 1980s, the regional economy experienced a sharp decline.

NOTES

1. Terman's contribution to the development of Silicon Valley was vital. Hall and Markusen write that "to an extraordinary degree, Silicon Valley resulted from the drive and imagination of one man: Frederick Terman" (1985, p. viii). Rogers and Larsen state that "without Fred Terman, Silicon Valley might never have happened" (1984, p. 31).

2. Scott (1988c) argues that the post-World War II resources of Silicon Valley—a major research university, an existing electronics industry, and military/aerospace installations—were not unique. He contends that several other areas, including Phoenix and Dallas, had similar resources. Why the semiconductor industry arose in Silicon Valley is unclear, he states: "It may be that the particular corporate structures of Motorola in Phoenix and Texas Instruments in Dallas discouraged horizontal and/or vertical disintegration (spin-off) and encouraged the internalization of new product and process innovations, whereas Shockley Laboratories and later Fairchild Semiconductors in Silicon Valley, were unable at the outset to achieve the same level of organizational control" (p. 91). See also Scott and Angel (1987).

3. The following year, Shockley received the Nobel Prize for his work on the transistor.

4. Although Shockley had created the conditions for the birthplace of the semiconductor industry in Silicon Valley, the company he founded never had a major impact. Shockley Laboratories was sold to Clevite Laboratories in 1960 and then to ITT in 1965. Shockley himself went on to gain notoriety for his unorthodox views on race and intelligence.

5. Liberals in Congress who supported industrial policy to promote high technology became known as the "Atari Democrats."

6. In addition to his formal role in marketing, Markkula played an important part in developing the company's financing. In later years, he was a stabilizing force. Markkula was known as the "fifth Beatle," who never obtained the fame of Wozniak or Jobs. John Sculley wrote: "The world never figured out how two young college dropouts could put together, nurture, and run a large company. In fact, they didn't. Mike Markkula did" (1987, p. 268).

7. Steve Wozniak was a Berkeley dropout when he and Jobs started Apple. After he became a millionaire many times over, he went back and finished his degree. A Route 128 parallel is Edwin Land, founder of Polaroid and Harvard's most famous dropout.

8. Osborne (1988) attributes Brown's conversion to Dow Chemical's decision in 1977 to scrap its plans to build a petrochemical refinery north of San Francisco because of the long and costly state-permit process. Osborne also notes that Brown also was influenced by a trip he took to Japan shortly thereafter.

9. This figure was reported by the *Economist* (1991), which attributed it to the California computer magazine *Upside*.

Chapter 7

Conclusion

The challenges of regional development planning may never have been greater than in the 1990s.Competition is intensifying among regions not only for high-technology resources but also for more traditional kinds of economic development. Cyclical changes and sudden shifts in global markets are jolting regional economies. Despite nearly half a century of regional development efforts in the United States, regional inequality has increased.[1] Old development strategies have been discredited, and doubts are surfacing about the newer ones. Policy makers are searching for answers.

A technopolis strategy can be an effective approach for some regions. It promises rapid growth and new prosperity, but it also carries great risks. The technopolis is not immune to the cycles that affect other regions. Indeed, the consequences can be even more severe, as the vaunted multiplier effect of high technology becomes a "reverse-multiplier," sending the regional economy into a tailspin. However, a technopolis can overcome these problems eventually. Hard times, in fact, can spur innovation, as entrepreneurs leave struggling companies to start new firms. If a region has an effective knowledge center and an innovative environment, it can produce another generation of technologies that will spark a new round of growth.

Another drawback to technopolis strategies is that success creates its own problems. Environmental degradation, overheated housing markets, and strained infrastructure often undermine the quality of life in a technopolis and threaten its future prosperity. Another consequence may be heightened inequality, with society split between a technical-professional elite and an underemployed lower class.[2]

The most important technopolises to emerge in the post-World War II era were Silicon Valley and Route 128. Silicon Valley arose in a predominantly agricultural area; Route 128 developed in a traditional manufacturing region. Each had at its core a world-class university and a significant cluster of prewar science-based firms. The rapid growth of Silicon Valley and Route 128 occurred because specialized technologies emerged in these regions and found applications all over the world. Semiconductors were the initial core industry of Silicon Valley, while minicomputers were at the heart of Route 128. Powerful agglomeration advantages arose in both technopolises, as an intricate web of suppliers, customers, and services emerged. A large pool of technical, scientific, and professional labor also formed.

As the Route 128 and Silicon Valley technopolises grew, they became more diversified. New industries, in both manufacturing and services, arose with either backward or forward linkages to the core industries. In Silicon Valley, development of the microprocessor made possible video games and microcomputers, which became important new regional industries in their own right. Firms that used computer chips in their products benefited from proximity to semiconductor firms because of the importance of face-to-face contacts during the research and design stages. In similar fashion, Route 128's minicomputer industry spawned software, high-level business services, network systems, and other electronics industries.

The universities of the two technopolises also expanded their areas of excellence. Engineering and physics programs at Stanford and MIT had propelled the early growth of high-technology industry in the two regions. As the universities became known as world-class institutions in these fields, they also built up programs in other scientific areas. This further diversified the regional economies, as new commercial fields, biotechnology in particular, emerged from scientific research.

Perhaps the most important factor promoting diversification of Silicon Valley and Route 128 was the large agglomeration of scientific and technical labor drawn to the core industries of the technopolises. These labor concentrations attracted a broad range of high-technology industries. Many different kinds of electronics firms could draw from the labor pools that formed around the semiconductor and minicomputer industries.

During the 1980s, both the semiconductor companies of Silicon Valley and the minicomputer firms of Route 128 suffered under severe competitive pressures. However, the diversification that had already occurred in the two technopolises enabled the regions to survive the downturns in their core industries. Silicon Valley has been in a stronger position because the products of its firms serve both consumer and producer markets, while Route 128 firms sell mainly to other producers.

Although both technopolises were unplanned, policies in each helped support and sustain the growth of high-technology industry. University administrations at MIT and Stanford set out to achieve scientific excellence and then transfer knowledge developed in laboratories to the commercial arena. Federal, state, and local governments built the physical and knowledge infrastructures needed by emerging high-technology industry in both regions. The federal government's procurement and research and development policies were critical to the emergence of industry in both regions. State industrial policy in California and Massachusetts helped create a climate of support for innovation and entrepreneurship.

For regions that hope to replicate the success of Silicon Valley and Route 128, the first step is to assess their resources (Nason, Dholakia, and McLeavey 1987). Perhaps the biggest mistake regional planners have made in the past decade has been trying to grow technopolises where they could never survive. There are two minimum requirements for the development of a technopolis. The first is a knowledge center that has the potential to make discoveries and advances at the frontiers of science and technology. The second is an environment that can, with some realistic interventions, support innovation. This means having in place a pool of skilled labor, a developed knowledge infrastructure, and significant information resources embodied in people and institutions.

For regions that have these assets, the first task is to develop an effective knowledge center. This is accomplished mainly by investing in research institutes or research departments of major universities. These investments must be of sufficient magnitude and must be sustained long enough to enable the knowledge center to achieve scientific preeminence. From a hypothetical standpoint, recruitment of government or industry research facilities is another way to develop a knowledge center. Many regions have taken this approach because of the enormous resources and long time horizons required to develop an indigenous knowledge center. In practice, however, this strategy rarely succeeds. Research and development centers that relocate to new regions usually are divisions of multinational firms or large government bureaucracies. These facilities rarely are effective incubators of the entrepreneurs who are vital to the emergence of a technopolis (Miller and Côté 1987). Personnel tend to have a managerial rather than an entrepreneurial orientation. They are unlikely to leave their organizations and create innovative firms. Also, industrial research laboratories are more likely to pursue conservative lines of research rather than the path-breaking endeavors of university-based research (Hall et al. 1987). Thus while recruited research and development facilities provide employment, they rarely have the propulsive capacity that stimulates regional development. In the worst case, transplanted research and development centers become enclaves that have no impact on traditional regional economies other than to drive up the costs of housing and services.

A knowledge center of a technopolis does not have to be a university or university-based research institute. Private firms also can perform the role. Fairchild Semiconductor and Shockley Laboratories served as knowledge centers in Silicon Valley, as did Digital Equipment Corporation in Route 128. These innovative private organizations produced technical entrepreneurs who developed new products or processes and then founded spin-off companies. Private research and development also have been at the center of Southern California's Orange County high-technology complex. Although the University of California at Irvine is now the research core of Orange County, high-technology industry in the region preceded the founding of the university (Scott 1988a). In most cases, however, private firms that function as regional knowledge centers were themselves the product of a university-based center. Without MIT, Digital Equipment Corporation would not exist; without Stanford, there would be no Hewlett-Packard. Particularly in the early stages of a technopolis's development, university-based research is vital.[3] Investment in indigenous university-based research is still the most realistic and effective means of developing the knowledge center of a technopolis.

The next step in fashioning a technopolis strategy is to devise policies that will support an innovative environment. Regional technology development policies must be broadly defined to include a range of activities that affect business conditions and not just "pure" technopolis policies, such as science parks and business incubators (Zegveld 1988; Nijkamp and Stöhr 1988). Probably the most effective strategy is to strengthen the regional knowledge infrastructure. Because it plays such an important role in the development of human capital and the quality of life, and because it is accepted as a legitimate role for public policy, the knowledge infrastructure should be the focus of technopolis strategies aimed at enhancing the environment for innovation.

One of the most important tasks in this regard is the development of skills in the labor force appropriate to new technologies (Rosenfeld 1987). Flynn (1988), in her study of the changes in the work force in Lowell, Massachusetts, concluded that product life cycles have parallel "skill training life cycles." In other words, as technological change occurs in an industry, the work force must acquire new skills. The capacity of local and regional education systems to develop these skills is critical to the success of industries and regions undergoing technological change. According to Flynn, education systems must monitor changing skill needs and then devise programs to reshape the work force. In the case of the technopolis, the most needed skills are in specialized scientific and technical fields. Programs to nurture these skills in the work force are critical to the development of a technopolis.

It is not enough to construct regional policies that will develop human capital. Skilled labor also must have compelling reasons to stay in a region. Although mobility of workers and families has decreased in the United States since the 1960s, due in part to the difficulty of uprooting two-career households, technical and scientific workers are among the most mobile of all workers (Malecki 1989; Gentile and Stave 1988; Ladinsky 1967). They are not bound to the region in which they were educated.

Investments in quality-of-life attractions are thus important technopolis policies, although they may be recognized by some other name, such as environmental policy, housing policy, education policy, or infrastructure policy. For example, if a major attraction of a high-technology region for key personnel is beaches and waterfront, policies to control water pollution are important not only for the environment but also for high-technology development. Similar arguments can be made for matters ranging from affordable housing to quality of schools to crime.

Quality of life is not a constant through space and time. What was considered a good quality of life in 1920 is obviously quite different from what is considered a good quality of life today (Scott and Storper 1987). Even within national boundaries, regional preferences vary widely. The quality-of-life attractions of suburban New York City are quite different from those of Huntsville, Alabama, although both areas have attracted high-technology industry. Thus it is important for planners to understand and capitalize on the quality-of-life strengths of their region. In some places it may be affordable, high-quality housing. In others, it may be cultural and recreational attractions, such as the performing arts, museums, major sports teams, restaurants, and shops. Natural surroundings may be the major draw in other regions. In general, it is some unique combination or "bundle" of amenities that gives an emerging technopolis its appeal (Malecki 1989). Attempting to re-create the amenities of Silicon Valley or Route 128 is not an appropriate strategy for most regions.

A quality of life that once attracted personnel to a region can deteriorate and, in the process, subtract an important regional comparative advantage. Indeed, the cycle of development tends to promote this process. An attractive natural environment can encourage growth, which in turn erodes the natural environment with overcrowding and pollution. Affordable, high-quality housing can attract growth, which drives up the cost of housing. Thus in established or growing technopolises, a major challenge for policy makers is to develop strategies to maintain regional quality-of-life advantages.

The approaches to developing a technopolis suggested above—support for research institutions, investments in the knowledge infrastructure, maintenance of quality-of-life attributes—must have long time horizons. They require patience as well as commitment. Because of the volatility of the external environment, there is no guarantee that they will bring the sought-after prosperity. However, if implemented effectively, they can guarantee that a region will be competitive in its pursuit of high-technology development.

Quick-fix technopolis approaches are unlikely to succeed. In this category are included most science parks, incubators, and capital assistance programs. These policies have created some successful businesses, but for a number of reasons these firms usually have not had a major impact on regional economies. Often, the programs are of too small a scale in relation to the whole of the regional economy to have any great effects. Sometimes, policy makers lack a long-term commitment to the policies. In many cases, the programs are set in environments inappropriate for high technology. Finally, inasmuch as they represent direct interventions in the internal workings of firms, they conflict with the political culture of most capitalist societies. Their greatest contribution may be that they improve the climate for innovation by bridging some of the gaps that separate the parties with a stake in high-technology development.

In addition to the specific steps outlined above, two broad approaches are required for the development of successful technopolis policies. First, relationships among business, government, universities, and labor must be reshaped. Barriers to cooperation need to be pushed aside further. This process too will take time as new coalitions emerge to replace those of the previous industrial order (Bassett 1990; Botkin, Dimancescu, and Stata 1984). However, the complexity and costs of developing knowledge-intensive technologies are so great that high-technology regional development will not occur if the rigid adversarial relationships that exist in many capitalist societies persist.

Second, policy makers must be aware of shifts in world markets and global technology (Harding 1989). Monitoring of the external environment is an important task for business, government, and universities. The most effective policies are those that are oriented toward change. Policies must be flexible enough to adapt to outside forces and to locate points of leverage in the environment.

Although building and maintaining a technopolis is a policy objective appropriate for a small number of regions, other paths to regional development exist. Older industries, whether they are traditional manufacturing, crafts, or agriculture, can be modernized through innovation. Although the regional development literature is filled with accounts of traditional economic regions overrun by technological change, history also records some successful adaptations, such as the Jura region of Switzerland, which made the shift from mechanical to electronic watchmaking, and the midwestern U.S. city of Milwaukee, which in the 1980s modernized its aging heavy industries (Bailey 1990).

The attraction of branch plants or relocated facilities of established firms is another option open to regions. By developing infrastructure and physical and institutional links to existing centers of industry, peripheral areas can capture some of the growth generated by core regions. Although this strategy will not re-create the dynamism of a technopolis, it can provide jobs. If sufficient environmental supports are developed, branch plants also can foster the growth of services and supplier firms.

Not every region can be a technopolis, but the experience of the technopolis does hold lessons for regions that seek to rebuild declining industries, attract outside firms, or foster indigenous growth that may not be of the high-technology variety. The technopolis succeeds by supplying conditions that support innovation, which is critical to any economic development strategy today. Policy cannot create entrepreneurs or compel an existing business to expand, but it can nurture an environment in which the central processes of development are most likely to occur.

NOTES

1. The U.S. Commerce Department found that regional differences in per capita personal income as a percentage of the national average widened in the 1980s. For the previous five decades, the differences had been narrowing (Garnick 1990).

2. Although the phenomenon is referred to often in the literature, the extent to which society has become split between rich and poor in the technopolis has not been measured. One U.S. study did not find strong evidence that polarization had occurred as a result of high-technology development (Klak 1989).

3. In general, a two-stage process occurs in the development of entrepreneurship in the technopolis. Universities train skilled researchers, who then go to work for a local firm. The firm is the incubating environment from which the entrepreneur then moves to establish his own firm (Malecki and Nijkamp 1988; Miller and Côté 1987; Cooper 1986).

Appendix

Tatsuno (1986) identifies the following regions as U.S. technopolises:

1. Portland (Silicon Forest)
2. Seattle
3. Sacramento/Roseville (Silicon Foothills)
4. Santa Barbara (Silicon Beach)
5. San Fernando Valley (Peripheral Valley)
6. Culver City, California (Byte Hill)
7. Orange County (Irvine Ranch)
8. San Diego (Golden Triangle)
9. Phoenix/Tempe (Silicon Desert)
10. Tucson
11. Salt Lake City (Bionic Valley)
12. Reno/Sparks
13. Boulder-Denver-Colorado Springs (Silicon Mountain)
14. Rio Grande Corridor
15. Fort Worth-Dallas-Austin (Silicon Plain)
16. San Antonio (Silicon Ranch)
17. Lafayette, La. (Silicon Bayou)
18. Little Rock (Technology Corridor)
19. Huntsville (Cummings Technical Park)
20. Knoxville/Oak Ridge
21. Indianapolis
22. Chicago (I-90/Route 41)
23. Minneapolis/St. Paul (I-494)
24. Detroit/Ann Arbor/Lansing
25. Cleveland (I-480)
26. Philadelphia (Route 202)

27. Gaithersburg, Md. (Satellite Alley)
28. New Hampshire Golden Triangle
29. Hudson Valley
30. Syracuse (Silicon Valley East)
31. Long Island (Tech Island)
32. Princeton (Telecom Belt)
33. Bethesda, Md. (Bio Corridor)
34. Northern Virginia (I-495)
35. Research Triangle, North Carolina
36. Atlanta (Silicon Pines)
37. Jacksonville/Daytona (Silicon Coast)
38. Gainesville (Robot Alley)
39. Orlando (Golden Girdle)
40. Dade/Broward/Palm Beach (Silicon Beach)

The twelve "Silicon Valleys" identified by Rogers and Larson (1984) are:

1. Silicon Valley
2. Route 128
3. Research Triangle, North Carolina
4. Salt Lake City
5. RPI/SUNY/Albany
6. Dallas/Austin
7. Colorado Springs
8. Portland
9. Phoenix
10. Minneapolis/St. Paul
11. Seattle
12. Orange County

Bibliography

Abetti, Pier A., Christopher W. Le Maistre, and Michael H. Wacholder. 1988. The role of Rensselaer Polytechnic Institute: Technopolis development in a mature industrial area. In *Creating the technopolis: Linking technology commercialization and economic development*, ed. Raymond W. Smilor, George Kozmetsky, and David V. Gibson, 125-44. Cambridge, Mass: Ballinger Publishing Co.

Adams, Russell B., Jr. 1977. *The Boston money tree*. New York: Crowell.

Ady, Robert M. 1986. Criteria used for facility location selection. In *Financing economic development in the 1980s: Issues and trends*, ed. Norman Walzer and David L. Chicoine, 72-84. New York: Praeger.

Aglietta, Michel. 1976. *A theory of capitalist regulation*. London: New Left Books.

Allen, David N., and Victor Levine. 1986. *Nurturing advanced technology enterprises: Emerging issues in state and local economic development policy*. New York: Praeger.

Alonso, William. 1988. Population and regional development. In *Regional economic development: Essays in honour of François Perroux*, ed. Benjamin Higgins and Donald J. Savoie, 131-41. Boston: Unwin Hyman.

Andersson, Ake. 1985. Creativity and regional development. *Papers of the Regional Science Association* 56: 5-20.

Armington, Catherine. 1986. The changing geography of high-technology businesses. In *Technology, regions and policy*, ed. John Rees, 75-93. Totowa, N.J.: Rowman and Littlefield.

Arnold, Erik, and Ken Guy. 1986. *Parallel convergence: National strategies in information technology*. Westport, Conn.: Quorum Books.

Aschauer, David A. 1989. Is public expenditure productive? *Journal of Monetary Economics* 23: 177-200.

Asian Finance. 1988. Singapore finds an answer to Silicon Valley. 14 (April 15): 78-79.

Atkinson, Robert. 1988. State technology development programs. *Economic Development Review* 6:29-32.

Aydalot, Philippe. 1988. Technological trajectories and regional innovation in Europe. In *High technology industry and innovative environments: The European experience,* ed. Philippe Aydalot and David Keeble, 22-47. London: Routledge.

Aydalot, Philippe, and David Keeble. 1988. High technology industry and innovative environments in Europe: An overview. In *High technology industry and innovative environments: The European experience,* ed. Philippe Aydalot and David Keeble, 1-21. London: Routledge.

Bailey, Jeff. 1990. As economy falters, old industrial city of Milwaukee shines. *Wall Street Journal* (November 29): A1, A6.

Bar-El, Raphael, and Daniel Felsenstein. 1989. Technological profile and industrial structure: Implications for the development of sophisticated industry in peripheral areas. *Regional Studies* 23: 253-66.

Barff, Richard A., and Prentice L. Knight III. 1988. The role of federal military spending in the timing of the New England employment turnaround. *Papers of the Regional Science Association* 65: 151-66.

Barkley, David L. 1988. The decentralization of high-technology manufacturing to non-metropolitan areas. *Growth and Change* 19: 13-30.

Bartik, Timothy J. 1989. Product development corporations and state economic development: The importance of R&D spillovers. *Economic Development Quarterly* 3: 327-28.

Bassett, Keith. 1990. Labour in the sunbelt: The politics of local economic development strategy in an 'M4-corridor' town. *Political Geography Quarterly* 9: 67-83.

Begg, Iain, and Gordon Cameron. 1988. High technology location and the urban areas of Great Britain. *Urban Studies* 25:361-379.

Bell, Daniel. 1973. *The coming of post-industrial society.* New York: Basic Books.

Berger, Suzanne, Michael Dertouzos, Richard K. Lester, Robert M. Solow and Lester Thurow. 1989. Toward a new industrial America. *Scientific American* (June): 241-56.

Birch, David. 1987. *Job creation in America: How our smallest companies put the most people to work.* New York: The Free Press.

Bluestone, Barry, and Bennett Harrison. 1982. *The deindustrialization of America.* New York: Basic Books.

Blumenstyk, Goldie. 1990. Pitfalls of research parks lead universities and states to reassess their expectations. *Chronicle of Higher Education* (July 5): A19, A24.

Bollinger, Lynn, Katherine Hope, and James M. Utterback. 1983. A review of literature and hypotheses on high technology firms. *Research Policy* 12: 1-14.

Bolton, Roger E. 1980. Impacts of defense spending on urban areas. In *The urban impacts of federal policies,* ed. Norman J. Glickman, 151-74. Baltimore: Johns Hopkins University Press.

Booth, Douglas E. 1987. *Regional long waves, uneven growth, and the cooperative alternative.* New York: Praeger.

Borrus, Michael, and John Zysman. 1986. Japan. In *National policies for developing high technology industries,* ed. Francis W. Rushing and Carole Ganz Brown, 111-42. Boulder, Colo.: Westview Press.

Botkin, James W. 1988. Route 128: Its history and destiny. In *Creating the technopolis: Linking technology commercialization and economic development,* ed. Raymond W. Smilor, George Kozmetsky, and David V. Gibson, 117-24. Cambridge, Mass.: Ballinger Publishing Co.

Botkin, James, Dan Dimancescu, and Ray Stata. 1982. *Global stakes*. New York: Penguin Books.

_____. 1984. *The innovators*. New York: Harper and Row.

Boudeville, Jacques. 1976. *French regional polarization and planning*. Paris: Pion.

Bradshaw, Ted K., and Edward J. Blakely. 1982. The changing nature of rural America. In *Rural policy problems: Changing dimensions*, ed. William P. Browne and Don F. Hadwiger, 3-18. Lexington, Mass.: Lexington Books.

Brandel, William. 1991. High tech's next wave. *New England Business* (April): 16-20.

Braun, Ernest, and Stuart Macdonald. 1982. *Revolution in miniature: The history and impact of semiconductor electronics*. New York: Cambridge University Press.

Breheny, Michael. 1988. Contracts and contacts: Defence procurement and local economic development in Britain. In *Defence expenditure and regional development*, ed. Michael J. Breheny, 188-211. London: Mansell Publishing.

Breheny, Michael J., and Ronald W. McQuaid. 1987. H.T.U.K.: The development of the United Kingdom's major centre of high technology industry. In *The development of high technology industries: An international survey*, ed. Michael J. Breheny and Ronald W. McQuaid, 297-354. London: Croom Helm.

Britton, John N. H. 1987. High technology industry in Canada: Locational and policy issues of the technology gap. In *The development of high technology industries: An international survey*, ed. Michael J. Breheny and Ronald W. McQuaid, 143-91. London: Croom Helm.

Brooks, John. 1973. *The go-go years*. New York: Weybright and Talley.

Brotchie, John F., Peter Hall, and Peter W. Newton. 1987. The transition to an information society. In *The spatial impact of technological change*, ed. John F. Brotchie, Peter Hall, and Peter W. Newton, 435-51, New York: Croom Helm.

Brown, Buck. 1989. Business incubators suffer growing pains. *Wall Street Journal* (June 16): B1.

Brown, Duncan. 1989. States, technology and jobs. *Technology Review* 92 (May/June): 16-17.

Browne, Lynn E. 1984. The New England economy and the development of high technology industries. *New England Economic Indicators*. August: A3-A6.

_____. 1988. The defense buildup and state economic performance in the 1980s. *New England Economic Indicators*. First Quarter: iv-x.

Browne, Lynn E., and S. Gavian. 1981. The importance of defense to New England. *New England Economic Indicators* (August): A3-A6.

Browne, Lynn E., and John S. Hekman. 1981. New England's economy in the 1980s. *New England Economic Review* (January/February). Federal Reserve Bank of Boston. Reprinted in *The Massachusetts miracle: High technology and economic revitalization*, ed. David Lampe, 169-87. Cambridge, Mass.: MIT Press.

Bruce, Robert V. 1973. *Bell: Alexander Graham Bell and the conquest of solitude*. London: Victor Gollancz.

Bruno, Albert V., and Arnold C. Cooper. 1982. Patterns of development and acquisitions for Silicon Valley startups. *Technovation* 1: 275-90.

Burns, Arthur F. 1934. *Production trends in the United States*. New York: National Bureau of Economic Research.

Burton, Daniel F., Jr. 1989. Economic realities and strategic choices. In *Vision for the 1990s: U.S. strategy and the global economy*, ed. Daniel F. Burton Jr., Victor Gotbaum, and Felix G. Rohatyn, 3-25. Cambridge, Mass.: Ballinger Publishing Co.

Bush, Vannevar. 1970. *Pieces of the action*. New York: Morrow.

Bylinsky, Gene. 1976. *The innovation millionaires: How they succeed*. New York: Charles Scribner's Sons.

_____. 1985. *Silicon Valley: High tech window to the future.* Hong Kong: Intercontinental Publishing Corp.

Camagni, Roberto. 1988. Functional integration and locational shifts in new technology industry. In *High technology industry and innovative environ-ments: The European experience,* ed. Philippe Aydalot and David Keeble, 48-64. London: Routledge.

Campbell, Candace. 1989. Change agents in the new economy: Business incubators and economic development. *Economic Development Review* 7:56-59.

Carroll, Richard R. 1986. The small business incubator as a regional economic development tool: Concept and practice. *Northeast Journal of Business and Economics* 12: 24-43.

Case, John. 1990. The most entrepreneurial cities in America. *Inc.* 12 (March): 41-48.

Castells, Manuel. 1985a. High technology, economic restructuring and the urban regional process in the United States. In *High technology, space, and society,* ed. Manuel Castells, 11-40. Beverly Hills: Sage Publications.

_____. 1985b. Preface. In *High technology, space, and society,* ed. Manuel Castells, 7-8. Beverly Hills: Sage Publications.

_____. 1988. High technology and urban dynamics in the United States. In *The metropolis era:* Vol. 1. *A world of giant cities.* ed. Mattei Dogan and John D. Kasarda, 85-110. Newbury Park, Calif.: Sage Publications.

_____. 1989. *The informational city: Information technology, economic restructur-ing, and the urban-regional process.* Cambridge, Mass.:Basil Blackwell.

Checkland, Sydney G. 1975. *The upas tree.* Glasgow: University of Glasgow Press.

Choate, Pat, and Susan Walter. 1981. *America in Ruins: Beyond the public works pork barrel.* Washington, D.C.: Council of State Planning Agencies.

Christaller, Walter. 1966 (1933). *Central places in southern Germany.* Translated by C. W. Baskin. Englewood Cliffs, N.J.: Prentice-Hall.

Clairmonte, Frederick F., and John H. Cavanagh. 1986. TNCs and services: The final frontier. *Raw Materials Report* 4:4-13.

Clark, Colin. 1940. *The conditions of economic progress.* London: Macmillan.

Clark, David. 1985. *Post-industrial America: A geographical perspective.* New York: Methuen.

Clark, Gordon L. 1986. Regional development and policy: The geography of employment. *Progress in Human Geography* 10: 416-26.

_____. 1987. Regional development and policy: Perspectives on foreign competition and the United States economy. *Progress in Human Geography* 11: 549-57.

_____. 1988. Regional development and policy: Emerging themes of research on labour, the firm and location. *Progress in Human Geography* 12: 549-59.

Coakley, Tom. 1991. The roots of a recession: State's manufacturing past helps create jobless present in New Bedford, Fall River. *Boston Globe* (April 21): 29.

Coates, Vary T. 1988. Office automation technology and home-based work. In *The era of home-based work: Directions and policies,* ed. Kathleen Christensen, 114-25, Boulder, Colo.: Westview Press.

Cobb, James C.. 1982. *The selling of the South: The Southern crusade for industrial development, 1936-1980.* Baton Rouge: Louisiana State University Press.

Conot, Robert. 1979. *A streak of luck.* New York: Seaview Books.

Conway, McKinley. 1989. Sites for science enter new era of global competition for high-tech locations. *Site Selection* (June): 652-54.

Cooke, Philip. 1988. Flexible integration, scope economies and strategic mediations: Social and spatial mediation. *Environment and Planning D: Society and Space* 6: 281-300.

Coon, Horace. 1939. *American Telephone and Telegraph: The story of a great monopoly.* New York: Longmans, Green and Co.

Cooper, Arnold C. 1985. The role of incubator organizations in the founding of growth-oriented firms. *Journal of Business Venturing* 1: 75-86.

_____. 1986. Entrepreneurship and high technology. In *The art and science of entrepreneurship*, ed. Donald L. Sexton and Raymond W. Smilor, 153-68. Cambridge, Mass.: Ballinger Publishing Co.

Coopers & Lybrand. 1987. *State policy and the telecommunications economy in New York*. New York State Office of Economic Development.

Courchene, Thomas J., and James R. Melvin. 1988. A neoclassical approach to regional economics. In *Regional economic development: Essays in honour of François Perroux*, ed. Benjamin Higgins and Donald J. Savoie, 169-89. Boston: Unwin Hyman.

Cox, R. N. 1985. Lessons from thirty years of science parks in the U.S.A. In *Science parks and innovation centres: Their economic and social impact*, ed. John Michel Gibb, 17-24. Amsterdam: Elsevier Science Publishers.

Crump, Jeffrey R. 1989. The spatial distribution of military spending in the United States 1941-1985. *Growth and Change* 20: 50-62.

Daniels, P. W. 1988. Some perspectives on the geography of services. *Progress in Human Geography* 12: 431-40.

Darlin, Damon. 1990. Taiwan, long noted for cheap imitations, becomes an innovator. *Wall Street Journal* Eastern edition (June 1): A1, A12.

Darwent, D. F. 1969. Growth poles and growth centres in regional planning—A review. *Environment and Planning* 1: 5-31.

Davelaar, Evert Jan, and Peter Nijkamp. 1989. The role of the metropolitan milieu as an incubation centre for technological innovations: A Dutch case study. *Urban Studies* 26: 517-25.

Davis, Neil W. 1984. MITI's technopolis project. *Japan Marketing/Advertising* 2: 40-41.

DePass, Rudolph E., and Howard L. Friedenberg. 1990 Regional perspectives. *Survey of Current Business*. U.S. Department of Commerce 70, no. 1 (January): 25-26.

Dicken, Peter. 1986. *Global shift: Industrial change in a turbulent world*. New York: Harper and Row.

Dorfman, Nancy S. 1982. *Massachusetts' high technology boom in perspective: An investigation of its dimensions, causes and of the role of new firms*. Cambridge: Center for Policy Alternatives, MIT.

_____. 1983. Route 128: The development of a regional high technology economy. *Research Policy* 12: 310-33.

Drucker, Peter F. 1985. *Innovation and entrepreneurship: Practice and principles*. New York: Harper & Row.

_____. 1989. *The new realities*. New York: Harper & Row.

Dukakis, Michael S., and Rosabeth Moss Kanter. 1988. *Creating the future: The Massachusetts comeback and its promise for America*. New York: Summit Books.

Dyckman, J. W., and Eric A. Swyngedouw. 1988. Public and private technological innovation strategies in a spatial context: The case of France. *Environment and Planning C: Government and Policy* 6: 401-13.

Economist. 1991. How grey is my valley? (March 23): 71-72.

Edelman, Lawrence. 1990. Wang posts $496.7m loss in quarter; layoffs planned. *Boston Globe* (July 31): 49-50.

_____. 1991a. Computers still need lots of software. *Boston Globe* (January 20): A4.

_____. 1991b. Route 128 awakening to a brave 'new tech' world. *Boston Globe* (June 30): 1, 8.

Edgington, David W. 1989. New strategies for technology development in Japanese cities and regions. *Town Planning Review* 60: 1-27.

Eisinger, Peter K. 1988. *The rise of the entrepreneurial state*. Madison: University of Wisconsin Press.

Elzinga, Aant. 1987. Foresighting Canada's emerging science and technologies. In *The spatial impact of technological change*, ed. John F. Brotchie, Peter Hall, and Peter W. Newton, 343-56. New York: Croom Helm.

Engstrom, Therese. 1987. Little Silicon Valleys. *High Technology* (January): 24-32.

Ettlie, John E. 1980. Manpower flows and the innovation process. *Management Science* 26: 1086-95.

Evan, William M., and Paul Olk. 1990. R&D consortia: A new U.S. organizational form. *Sloan Management Review* (Spring):37-46.

Evans, Chris, and Linda D. Triplett. 1989. Measuring the immeasurable. *State Legislatures* 15 (March): 19-21.

Fairburn, Carolyn. 1988. Sun, sea and science. *Business* (November): 110-14.

Falk, William W. and Thomas A. Lyson. 1988. *High tech, low tech, no tech: Recent industrial and occupational change in the South*. Albany: State University of New York Press.

Feller, Irwin. 1988. Evaluating state advanced technology programs. *Evaluation Review* 12: 232-52.

Ferguson, Ronald F., and Helen F. Ladd. 1988. Massachusetts. In *The new economic role of American states: Strategies in a competitive world economy*, ed. R. Scott Fosler, 9-87. New York: Oxford University Press.

Finkelstein, Joseph (ed.). 1989. *Windows on a new world: The third industrial revolution*. Westport, Conn.: Greenwood Press.

Fisher, Peter. 1988. Product development corporations and state economic development. *Economic Development Quarterly* 2: 113-29.

_____. 1989. Response to "Product development corporations and state economic development: The importance of R&D spillovers," by Timothy J. Bartik. *Economic Development Quarterly* 3: 329-30.

Fitz Simon, Jane. 1989. Job chill on 128. *Boston Globe* (April 30): A1.

Florida, Richard L., and Martin Kenney. 1988. Venture capital-financed innovation and technological change in the USA. *Research Policy* 17: 119-37.

_____. 1990a. High technology restructuring in the USA and Japan. *Environment and Planning A* 22: 233-52.

_____. 1990b. *The breakthrough illusion: Corporate America's failure to move from innovation to mass production*. New York: Basic Books.

Flynn, Patricia M. 1988. *Facilitating technological change: The human resource challenge*. Cambridge, Mass.: Ballinger Publishing Co.

Fong, Chan Onn. 1986. *Technological leap: Malaysian industry in transition*. New York: Oxford University Press.

Forester, Tom. 1989. The myth of the electronic cottage. *Computers and Society* 19: 4-19.

Fosler, R. Scott. 1988. The state economic role in perspective. In *The new economic role of American states: Strategies in a competitive world economy*, ed. R. Scott Fosler, 8-20. New York: Oxford University Press.

Frieden, Bernard J. 1990. American business still wants to go downtown. *Wall Street Journal* (January 16): A16.

Frieden, Bernard J., and Lynne Sagalyn. 1989. *Downtown, Inc.: How America rebuilds cities*. Cambridge, Mass.: MIT Press.

Friedman, John. 1966. *Regional development policy: A case study of Venezuela*. Cambridge, Mass.: MIT Press.

Friedman, Joseph, Simon Hakim, and J. Weinblatt. 1989. Casino gambling as a "growth pole" strategy and its effect on crime. *Journal of Regional Science* 29: 615-23.

Friedmann, John F. 1986. The world city hypothesis. *Development and Change* (17): 69-83.

Friedmann, John F., and Goetz Wolff. 1982. World city formation: An agenda for research and action. *International Journal of Urban and Regional Research* 6: 309-44.

Fujita, Kuniko. 1988. The technopolis: High technology and regional development in Japan. *International Journal of Urban and Regional Research* 12: 566-94.

Fulman, Diane. 1990. Economic adversity sows seeds of future business opportunity. *Boston Globe* (March 20): 40.

Fusi, Deborah S. 1989. States, provinces step up high-tech incentives. *Site Selection* (June): 716-17.

Galbraith, John Kenneth. 1966. *The new industrial state*. Boston: Houghton Mifflin.

Gallese, Liz Roman. 1990. The most entrepreneurial place on earth. *Inc.* (March): 60-61.

Garfinkle, Steven M. 1989. New twists on high-tech highway. *Boston Business Journal* (July 3): 18.

Garnick, Daniel H. 1990. Accounting for regional differences in per capita personal income growth: An update. *Survey of Current Business*. U.S. Department of Commerce 70, no. 1 (January): 29-40.

Gendron, Marie, and David Callaway. 1989. Spontaneous generation? *Boston Herald* (June 13): 23, 28.

Gentile, Ralph, and Keith Stave. 1988. Highly-trained workers and the resurgence of New England: Inter-regional flows of scientists, engineers, and technicians, 1975-80. *New England Economic Indicators* (second quarter): iv-ix.

Giese, Ernst. 1987. The demand for innovation-oriented regional policy in the Federal Republic of Germany: Origins, aims, policy tools and prospects of realisation. In *The spatial impact of technological change*, ed. John F. Brotchie, Peter Hall, and Peter W. Newton, 240-53. New York: Croom Helm.

Gilder, George. 1989. *Micro-cosm: The quantum revolution in economics and technology*. New York: Simon and Schuster.

Gillespie, A., and H. Williams. 1988. Telecommunications and the reconstruction of regional comparative advantage. *Environment and Planning A* 20: 1311-21.

Glasmeier, Amy K. 1988. The Japanese technopolis programme: High technology development strategy or industrial policy in disguise? *International Journal of Urban and Regional Research* 12: 268-83.

Goddard, John B. 1989. The city in the global information economy. In *The rise and fall of great cities*, ed. Richard Lawton, 154-67. London: Belhaven Press.

Gold, Allan R. 1989. Computer changes jolt Route 128. *New York Times* (August 11): D1, D3.

Goldstein, Carl. 1988. Planting high-tech ideas: Hong Kong sows the seeds of interventionist industrial policy. *Far Eastern Economic Review* 139 (March 17): 68.

Goldstein, Harvey A., and Michael I. Luger. 1989. Research parks: Do they stimulate regional economic development? *Economic Development Commentary* 13: 3-9.

———. 1990. Science/technology parks and regional development theory. *Economic Development Quarterly* 4: 64-78.

Goldstein, Harvey A., and Emil E. Malizia. 1985. Microelectronics and economic development in North Carolina. In *High hopes for high tech: Microelectronics policy in North Carolina*, ed. Dale Whittington, 225-55. Chapel Hill. University of North Carolina Press.

Gottmann, Jean. 1961. *Megalopolis: The urbanized northeastern seaboard of the United States*. New York: Twentieth Century Fund.

Graham, Julie, and Robert J. S. Ross. 1989. From manufacturing-based industrial policy to service-based employment policy?: Industrial interests, class politics and the 'Massachusetts miracle.' *International Journal of Urban and Regional Research* 4: 121-36.

Grassmuck, Karen. 1990. Wariness dampens 1980's craze for building university-sponsored technology parks. *Chronicle of Higher Education* (June 27): A29-A30.

Graves, Philip E. 1980. Migration and climate. *Journal of Regional Science* 20: 227-37.

Grove, Andrew. 1987. Executive forum: The future of Silicon Valley. *California Management Review* 29: 154-60.

Gupta, Udayan. 1990. Science parks fall victim to overly high expectations. *Wall Street Journal* Eastern edition (April 17): B2.

_____. 1991. How big companies are joining forces with little ones for mutual advantages. *Wall Street Journal* (February 25): B1, B2.

Hall, Peter. 1962. *The industries of London*. London: Hutchinson.

_____. 1985. The geography of the fifth Kondratieff. In *Silicon landscapes,* ed. Peter Hall and Ann Markusen, 1-19. Boston: Allen and Unwin.

_____. 1987. The geography of the post-industrial economy. In *The spatial impact of technological change*, ed. John F. Brotchie, Peter Hall, and Peter W. Newton, 3-17. New York: Croom Helm.

_____. 1988. Urban growth and decline in Western Europe. In *The metropolis era:* Vol. 1, *A world of giant cities*. ed. Mattei Dogan and John D. Kasarda, 111-27. Newbury Park, Calif.: Sage Publications.

_____. 1989. *London 2001*. London: Unwin Hyman.

Hall, Peter, Michael Breheny, Ronald McQuaid and Douglas Hart. 1987. *Western sunrise: The genesis and growth of Britain's major high technology corridor*. London: Allen and Unwin.

Hall, Peter, and Ann Markusen. 1985. Preface. In *Silicon landscapes,* ed. Peter Hall and Ann Markusen, vii-ix. Boston: Allen and Unwin.

Hall, Peter, and P. Preston. 1988. *The carrier wave: New information technology and the geography of innovation, 1846-2003*. London: Unwin Hyman.

Hammond, John Winthrop. 1941. *Men and volts: The story of General Electric*. Philadelphia: J. B. Lippincott Co.

Hansen, Niles M. 1978. *Location preferences, migration, and regional growth: A study of the South and Southwest United States*. New York: Praeger.

Hanson, Dirk. 1982. *The new alchemists: Silicon Valley and the microelectronics revolution*. Boston: Little Brown and Co.

Harbison, Frederick, and Charles A. Meyers. 1964. *Education, manpower and economic growth*. New York: McGraw-Hill.

Harding, Charles F. 1989. Location choices for research labs: A case study approach. *Economic Development Quarterly* 3: 223-34.

Harrison, Bennett. 1984. Regional restructuring and "good business climates": Economic transformation of New England since World War II. In *Sunbelt/snowbelt: Urban development and regional restructuring*, ed. Larry Sawers and William K. Tabb, 48-96. New York: Oxford University Press.

Harrison, Bennett, and Barry Bluestone. 1988. *The great U-turn: Corporate restructuring and the polarization of America*. New York: Basic Books.

Harrison, Bennett, and J. Kluver. 1989. Reassessing the 'Massachusetts miracle': Reindustrialization and balanced growth, or convergence to 'Manhattanization'? *Environment and Planning A* 21: 771-801.

Hart, Jeffrey. 1989. The origins of the U.S.-Japan semiconductor dispute. In *Pacific dynamics: The international politics of industrial change*, ed. Stephan Haggard and Chung-in Moon, 129-53. Boulder, Colo.: Westview.

Hekman, John S. 1980a. Can New England hold onto its high technology industry? *New England Economic Review* (March/April): 35-44.

_____. 1980b. The future of high technology industry in New England: A case study of computers. *New England Economic Review* (January/February): 5-17.

Hekman, John S., and John S. Strong. 1981. The evolution of New England industry. *New England Economic Review* (March/April): 35-46.

Henderson, Jeffrey W., and Allen J. Scott. 1987. The growth and internationalization of the American semiconductor industry: Labor process and the changing spatial organization of production. In *High technology industry: An international survey*, ed. Michael J. Breheny and Ronald McQuaid, 37-79. London: Croom Helm.

Henderson, Yolanda K. 1989. The emergence of the venture capital industry. *New England Economic Review* (July/August): 64-79.

_____. 1990. Defense cutbacks and the New England economy. *New England Economic Review* (July/August): 3-24.

Henry, David K., and Richard P. Oliver. 1987. The defense build-up, 1977-85: Effects on production and employment. *Monthly Labor Review* (August): 3-11.

Henton, Douglas C., and Steven A. Waldhorn. 1988. California. In *The new economic role of American states: Strategies in a competitive world economy*, ed. R. Scott Fosler. 203-47. New York: Oxford University Press.

Hepworth, Mark E. 1986. The geography of technological change in the information economy. *Regional Studies* 20: 407-24.

_____. 1987. Information technology as spatial systems. *Progress in Human Geography* 11: 157-80.

Hepworth, Mark E., and Michael Waterson. 1988. Information technology and the spatial dynamics of capital. *Information Economics and Policy* 3: 143-63.

Higgins, Benjamin. 1988. François Perroux. In *Regional economic development: Essays in honour of François Perroux*, ed. Benjamin Higgins and Donald J. Savoie, 31-47. Boston: Unwin Hyman.

Higgins, Benjamin, and Donald J. Savoie. 1988. Introduction: The economics and politics of regional development. In *Regional economic development: Essays in honour of François Perroux*, ed. Benjamin Higgins and Donald J. Savoie, 1-27. Boston: Unwin Hyman.

Hirschman, Albert O. 1958. *The strategy of economic development*. New Haven: Yale University Press.

Hobson, John. 1938. *Imperialism: A study*. London: Allen and Unwin.

Hock, Tan Lee. 1988. Hi-tech vision turns industry wheels. *Asian Finance* 14 (September): 92-95.

Hooper, Laurence. 1991. Big Blue cultivates new markets by thinking small. *Wall Street Journal* (February 27): B-2.

Hoover, Edgar M. 1948. *The location of economic activity*. New York: McGraw-Hill.

Hoover, Edgar M., and Raymond Vernon. 1959. *Anatomy of a metropolis*. Cambridge, Mass.: Harvard University Press.

Howells, Jeremy. 1988. *Economic, technological and locational trends in European services*. Aldershot: Avebury.

Howells, Jeremy, and A. Green. 1988. *Technological innovation, structural change and location in UK services*. Aldershot: Avebury.

Hoy, John C. 1988. Higher skills and the New England economy. In *The Massachusetts miracle: High technology and economic revitalization*, ed. David Lampe, 331-47. Cambridge, Mass.: MIT Press.

Hymer, Stephen. 1975. The multinational corporation and the law of uneven development. In *International firms and modern imperialism*, ed. Hugo Radice, 37-62. Baltimore: Penguin Books.

Jacobs, Jane. 1969. *The economy of cities*. New York: Random House.

Jefferson, David J. 1990. Enterprise: Incubators could use some help themselves. *Wall Street Journal* Eastern edition (April 24): B1.

Jingyuan, Yu, Song Yuhe, and Zhou Zheng. 1988. A new research institute in China. In *Creating the technopolis: Linking technology commercialization and economic development*, ed. Raymond W. Smilor, George Kozmetsky and David V. Gibson, 69-80. Cambridge, Mass.: Ballinger Publishing Co.

Johnson, Chalmers A. 1982. *MITI and the Japanese miracle: The growth of industrial policy, 1925-1975*. Stanford: Stanford University Press.

Johnstone, Bob. 1988. Diverting the brain drain. *Far Eastern Economic Review* 139 (January 28): 70-71.

Joseph, R. A. 1989. Technology parks and their contribution to the development of technology-oriented complexes in Australia. *Environment and Planning C: Government and Policy* 7: 173-92.

Kaplan, Marshall. 1990. Infrastructure policy: Repetitive studies, uneven response, next steps. *Urban Affairs Quarterly* 25: 371-88.

Kasarda, John D. 1988. Economic restructuring and America's urban dilemma. In *The metropolis era: Vol. 1. A world of giant cities*. ed. Mattei Dogan and John D. Kasarda, 56-84. Newbury Park, Calif.: Sage Publications.

Kawashima, T. and Walter Stöhr. 1988. Decentralized technology policy: The case of Japan. *Environment and Planning C: Government and Policy* 6: 427-39.

Kaye, Lincoln. 1989. Problem programme. *Far Eastern Economic Review* 143 (March 2): 87.

Keeble, David. 1976. *Industrial location and planning in the United Kingdom*. London: Methuen.

_____. 1988. High-technology industry and local environments in the United Kingdom. In *High technology industry and innovative environments: The European experience*, ed. Philippe Aydalot and David Keeble, 65-98. London: Routledge.

Keeble, David, and Egbert Wever (eds.) 1986. *New firms and regional development in Europe*. London: Croom Helm.

Ken-ichi Imai. 1986. Japan's industrial policy for high technology industry. In *Japan's high technology industries*, ed. Hugh Patrick, 137-69. Seattle: University of Washington Press.

Kidder, Tracy. 1981. *The soul of a new machine*. New York: Avon Books.

Killian, James R., Jr. 1985. *The education of a college president: A memoir*. Cambridge, Mass.: MIT Press.

Kirn, Thomas J. 1987. Growth and change in the service sector of the U.S.: A spatial perspective. *Annals of the Association of American Geographers* 77: 353-72.

Klak, Thomas. 1989. Does high technology polarize the work force? *Environment and Planning C: Government and Policy* 7: 223-41.

Kobu, Bulent, and David Bryer. 1989. Skill and entrance requirements for production jobs in high-tech and non-high-tech manufacturing industries. *The Northeast Journal of Business and Economics* 15: 45-59.

Kohut, Andrew, and Linda DeStefano. 1989. Cities enjoy new popularity. *The Gallup Report* (October): 24-31.

Kondratieff, Nicolai D. 1935. The long waves of economic life. *Review of Economic Statistics* 17: 105-15.

Kotkin, Joel, and Paul Grabowicz. 1982. *California, Inc.* New York: Rawson, Wade Publishers.

Kuhn, Sarah. 1982. *The computer industry of New England*. Cambridge, Mass.: Joint Center for Urban Studies.

Kunzmann, Klaus R. 1988. Military production and regional development in the Federal Republic of Germany. In *Defence expenditure and regional development*, ed. Michael J. Breheny, 49-66. London: Mansell Publishing.

Kutay, A. 1988a. Technological change and spatial transformation in an information economy: 1. A structural model of transition in the urban system. *Environment and Planning A* 20: 569-93.

_____. 1988b. Technological change and spatial transformation in an information economy: 2. The influence of new information technology on the urban system. *Environment and Planning A* 20: 707-18.

Kuznets, Simon. 1930. *Secular movements in production and prices*. New York: A. M. Kelley.

Ladinsky, Jack. 1967. The geographic mobility of professional and technical manpower. *Journal of Human Resources* 2: 477-94.

Laffitte, Pierre. 1988. Sophia-Antipolis and the movement south in Europe. In *Creating the technopolis: Linking technology commercialization and economic development*, ed. Raymond W. Smilor, George Kozmetsky, and David V. Gibson, 91-95. Cambridge, Mass: Ballinger Publishing Co.

Lampe, David. 1988. Introduction: The making of a miracle. In *The Massachusetts miracle: High technology and economic revitalization*, ed. David Lampe, 1-18. Cambridge, Mass.: MIT Press.

Larsen, Judith K., and Everett Rogers. 1988. The rise and falling off of entrepreneurial fever. In *Creating the technopolis: Linking technology commercialization and economic development*, ed. Raymond W. Smilor, George Kozmetsky, and David V. Gibson, 99-115. Cambridge, Mass: Ballinger Publishing Co.

Leborgne, D., and Alain Lipietz, A. 1988. New technologies, new modes of regulation: Some spatial implications. *Environment and Planning D: Society and Space* 6: 263-80.

Lenin, Vladimir Ilich. 1970. Imperialism: The highest stage of capitalism. Moscow: Progress Publishers.

Lichtenberg, Frank R. 1990. Want more productivity? Kill that conglomerate. *Wall Street Journal* (January 16): A16.

Liles, Patrick R. 1977. *Sustaining the venture capital firm*. Cambridge, Mass.: Management Analysis Center, Inc.

Lipietz, Alain. 1986. New tendencies in the international division of labor: Regimes of accumulation and modes of social regulating. In *Production, work, territory: The geographical anatomy of industrial capitalism*, eds. Allen J. Scott and Michael Storper, 16-40. Boston: Allen and Unwin.

Livingston, Amy. 1989. State capital. *Venture* (May): 57-63.

Lösch, August. 1954. *The economics of location*. New Haven: Yale University Press.

Loth, Renee. 1991. A jobless pool that's different: This time we're all getting wet. *Boston Globe* (March 24): A17.

Lovering, John. 1988. Islands of prosperity: The spatial impact of high-technology defence industry in Britain. In *Defence expenditure and regional development*, ed. Michael J. Breheny, 29-48. London: Mansell Publishing.

Lowe, Julian. 1985. Science parks in the UK. *Lloyds Bank Review* (April): 31-42.

Lozano, Beverly. 1989. *The invisible work force: Transforming American business with outside and home-based workers*. New York: The Free Press.

Luger, Michael I. 1984. Does North Carolina's high technology development program work? *Journal of the American Planning Association* 50: 280-89.

McCrackin, Bobbie H. 1985. Why are business and professional services growing so rapidly? *Economic Review* 70: 14-28.

Macdonald, Stuart. 1987a. British science parks: Reflections on the politics of high technology. *R&D Management* 17: 25-37.

_____. 1987b. Towards higher high technology policy. In *The spatial impact of technological change*, ed. John F. Brotchie, Peter Hall, and Peter W. Newton, 357-74. New York: Croom Helm.

Machlup, Fritz. 1962. *The production and distribution of knowledge in the United States*. Princeton, N.J.: Princeton University Press.

McKee, David L. 1987. On services and growth poles in advanced economies. *Service Industries Journal* 7 (April): 165-75.

McLoughlin, P. 1984. A note on job creation in high technology industries and local economic development planning. *Prometheus* 2: 258-66.

Mager, Nathan H. 1987. *The Kondratieff waves*. New York: Praeger.

Malecki, Edward J. 1980. Corporate organization of R&D and the location of technological activities. *Regional Studies* 13: 269-80.

_____. 1983. Technology and regional development: A survey. *International Regional Science Review* 8: 89-125.

_____. 1986. Research and development and the geography of high technology complexes. In *Technology, regions and policy*, ed. John Rees, 51-74. Totowa, N.J.: Rowman and Littlefield.

_____. 1987. The R&D location decision of the firm and "creative" regions—a survey. *Technovation* 6: 205-22.

_____. 1989. What about people in high technology? Some research and policy considerations. *Growth and Change* 20: 67-79.

Malecki, Edward J., and Peter Nijkamp. 1988. Technology and regional development: Some thoughts on policy. *Environment and Planning C: Government and Policy* 6: 383-99.

Malecki, Edward J. and Lois M. Stark. 1988. Regional and industrial variation in defence spending: Some American evidence. In *Defence expenditure and regional development*, ed. Michael J. Breheny, 67-101. London: Mansell Publishing.

Malecki, Edward J. and P. Varaiya. 1986. Innovation and changes in regional structure. In *Handbook of regional and urban economics*, Vol. 1, ed. Peter Nijkamp, 629-45. Amsterdam: Elsevier Science Publishers.

Malone, Michael S. 1985. *The big score: The billion dollar story of Silicon Valley*. Garden City, N.Y.: Doubleday & Co.

_____. 1989. In Silicon Valley, it's mostly sunny. *Boston Globe* (April 30): A1.

Marcuse, Peter. 1989. "Dual city": A muddy metaphor for a quartered city. *International Journal of Urban and Regional Research* 13: 697-708.

Markoff, John. 1990. Silicon Valley is changing programs. *The New York Times* (January 14) Section 4: 24.

_____. 1991. An aging dancer fights to keep up. *The New York Times* (February 10): III, 1.

Markusen, Ann R. 1985. *Profit cycles, oligopoly and regional development*. Cambridge, Mass.: MIT Press.

_____. 1986. Defense spending and the geography of high-tech industries. In *Technology, regions and policy*, ed. John Rees, 94-119. Totowa, N.J.: Rowman and Littlefield.

_____. 1988. The military remapping of the United States. In *Defence expenditure and regional development*, ed. Michael J. Breheny, 17-28. London: Mansell Publishing.

Markusen, Ann R., and Virginia Carlson. 1989. Deindustrialization in the American Midwest: causes and responses. In *Deindustrialization and regional economic transformation: The experience of the United States*, ed. Lloyd Rodwin and Hidehiko Sazanami, 29-59. Boston: Unwin Hyman.

Markusen, Ann R., Peter Hall, and Amy Glasmeier. 1986. *High-tech America: The what, how, where and why of the sunrise industries.* Boston: Allen and Unwin.

Markusen, Ann R. and Karen McCurdy. 1989. Chicago's defense-based high technology: A case study of the "seedbeds of innovation" hypothesis. *Economic Development Quarterly* 3: 15-31.

Marshall, Michael. 1987. *Long waves of regional development.* New York: St. Martin's Press.

Martin, John E. 1966. *Greater London: An industrial geography.* Chicago: University of Chicago Press.

Martin, Ron, and Bob Rowthorn. 1986. Editor's preface. In *The geography of de-industrialization,* ed. Ron Martin and Bob Rowthorn, xv-xxiii. London: MacMillan Education Ltd.

Massachusetts Institute of Technology. 1958. *Economic impact study of Massachusetts Route 128.* Cambridge, Mass.

Masser, Ian. 1990. Technology and regional development policy: A review of Japan's technopolis programme. *Regional Studies* 24: 41-53.

Massey, Doreen. 1984. *Spatial divisions of labor: Social structures and the geography of production.* New York: Methuen.

_____. 1986. The legacy lingers on: The impact of Britain's international role on its internal geography. In *The geography of de-industrialization,* ed. Ron Martin and Bob Rowthorn, 31-52. London: MacMillan Education Ltd.

Massey, Doreen, and John Allen (eds.). 1988. *Uneven re-development: Cities and regions in transition.* London: Hodder and Stoughton.

Massey, Doreen, and Richard Meegan. 1982. *The anatomy of job loss: The how, why and where of employment decline.* London: Methuen.

Mead, Arthur C., and Glenworth A. Ramsay. 1985. Regional responses to business cycles: The New England experience. *Northeast Journal of Business and Economics* 11: 27-35.

Michalski, Wolfgang. 1989. Advanced information technologies: Challenges and opportunities. In *Information technology and global interdependence,* ed. Meheroo Jussawalla, Tadayuki Okuma, and Toshihiro Araki, 9-18. Westport, Conn.: Greenwood Press.

Miller, Roger and Marcel Côté. 1987. *Growing the next Silicon Valley: a guide for successful regional planning.* Lexington, Mass: Lexington Books.

Milward, H. Brinton, and Heidi Hosbach Newman. 1989. State incentive packages and the industrial location decision. *Economic Development Quarterly* 3: 203-22.

Minshall, Charles W. 1984. An overview of science parks and settings for high technology activities. *Economic Development Review* 2: 17-26.

Moomaw, Ronald L. 1988. Agglomeration economies: Localization or urbanization. *Urban Studies* 25:150-61.

Morgan, Kevin, and Andrew Sayer. 1988. *Microcircuits of capital.* Boulder, Colo.: Westview.

Moriarty, Barry M. 1986. Productivity, restructuring and the deglomeration of American manufacturing. In *Technology, regions and policy,* ed. John Rees, 141-70. Totowa, N.J.: Rowman and Littlefield.

Morita, Keisuke, and Hiroshi Hiraoka. 1988. Technopolis Osaka: Integrating urban functions and science. In *Creating the technopolis: Linking technology commercialization and economic development,* ed. Raymond W. Smilor, George Kozmetsky, and David V. Gibson, 23-49. Cambridge, Mass: Ballinger Publishing Co.

Moscovitch, Edward. 1990. The downturn in the New England economy: What lies behind it. *New England Economic Review* (July/August): 53-65.

Moulaert, Frank, and Eric A. Swyngedouw. 1989. A regulation approach to the geography of flexible production systems. *Environment and Planning D: Society and Space* 7: 327-45.

Mullin, John R., Jeanne H. Armstrong, and Jean S. Kavanagh. 1986. From mill town to mill town: The transition of a New England town from a textile to a high-technology economy. *Journal of the American Planning Association* 52: 47-59.

Munnell, Alicia H. 1990. Why has productivity growth declined? Productivity and public investment. *New England Economic Review* (January/February): 3-22.

Myrdal, Gunnar. 1957. *Economic theory and underdeveloped regions.* New York: Harper and Row.

Nason, Robert W., Nikhilesh Dholakia, and Dennis W. McLeavey. 1987. A strategic perspective on regional redevelopment. *Journal of Macromarketing* 7: 34-48.

National Council on Public Works Improvement. 1988. *Fragile foundations: A report on America's public works.* Washington, D.C.: U.S. Government Printing Office.

National Governors' Association. 1986. Using high tech to encourage economic growth. *Governors' Weekly Bulletin* 39 (October 3): 1-3.

Nelson, Richard R. 1984. *High-technology policies: A five nation comparison.* Washington: American Enterprise Institute for Public Policy Research.

Nicol, Lionel. 1985. Communications technology: Economic and spatial impacts. In *High technology, space, and society,* ed. Manuel Castells, 191-209. Beverly Hills: Sage Publications.

Nijkamp, Peter, and Arnoud Mouwen. 1987. Knowledge centres, information diffusion and regional development. In *The spatial impact of technological change*, ed. John F. Brotchie, Peter Hall, and Peter W. Newton, 254-70. New York: Croom Helm.

Nijkamp, Peter, and Walter B. Stöhr. 1988. Technology policy at the crossroads of economic policy and physical planning. *Environment and Planning C: Government and Policy* 6: 371-74.

Nishioka, Hisao, and Atsuhiko Takeuchi. 1987. The development of high technology industry in Japan. In *The development of high technology industries: An international survey*, ed. Michael J. Breheny and Ronald W. McQuaid, 262-95. London: Croom Helm.

Norton, R. D. 1987. The role of services and manufacturing in New England's economic resurgence. *New England Economic Indicators.* (second quarter): i-viii.

Norton, R.D., and John Rees. 1979. The product cycle and the spatial decentralization of American manufacturing. *Regional Studies* 13: 141-51.

Noyelle, Thierry J. 1987. Services, urban economic development and industrial policy: Some critical linkages. In *The state and local industrial policy question*, ed. Harvey A. Goldstein, 73-84. Chicago: American Planning Association.

Oakey, Ray P. 1984. *High technology small firms: Regional development in Britain and the United States.* New York: St. Martin's Press.

Oakey, Ray P., and Sarah Cooper. 1989. High technology industry, agglomeration and the potential for peripherally sited small firms. *Regional Studies* 23: 347-60.

Oakey, Ray P., Roy Rothwell, and Sarah Cooper. 1988. *The management of innovation in high technology small firms.* Westport, Conn.: Quorum Books.

O'Brien, Peter, and Melissa Tullis. 1989. Strategic alliances: The shifting boundaries between collaboration and competition. *Multinational Business* 4: 10-17.

OECD Observer. 1987. The science park as a regional development stimulus. (August-September): 21-22.

Office of Economic Development. 1987. *Creating the future: Opportunity, innovation and growth in the Massachusetts economy.* Boston: Commonwealth of Massachusetts.

Office of Technology Assessment. 1984. *Technology, innovation and regional economic development: Encouraging high-technology development*. Background paper no. 2. Washington: U.S. Congress Office of Technology Assessment.

OhUllacháin, Breandán. 1987. Regional and technological implications of the recent buildup in American defense spending. *Annals of the Association of American Geographers* 77: 208-23.

_____. 1989. Agglomeration of services in American metropolitan areas. *Growth and Change* 20: 35-49.

Olshaker, Mark. 1978. *The Polaroid story: Edwin Land and the Polaroid experience*. New York: Stein and Day.

Onda, Masahiko. 1988. Tsukuba Science City complex and Japanese strategy. In *Creating the technopolis: Linking technology commercialization and economic development*, ed. Raymond W. Smilor, George Kozmetsky, and David V. Gibson, 51-68. Cambridge, Mass: Ballinger Publishing   Co.

Organisation for Economic Co-operation and Development. 1978. *Regional policies and the services sector*. Washington, D.C.: OECD Publications Center.

Osborne, David E. 1988. *Laboratories of democracy*. Boston: Harvard Business School Press.

Passer, Harold C. 1972. *The electrical manufacturers 1875-1900: A study in competition, entrepreneurship, technical change and economic growth*. Cambridge, Mass.: Harvard University Press.

Perrin, Jean C. 1988. A deconcentrated technology policy—lessons from the Sophia-Antipolis experience. *Environment and Planning C: Government and Policy* 7: 415-25.

Perroux, François. 1950. Economic spaces: Theory and applications. *Quarterly Journal of Economics* 64: 90-97.

_____. 1955. Note sur la notion de pole de croissance. Translated in *Economic policy for   development*, ed. Ian Livingstone, 278-89. Baltimore: Penguin Books, 1971.

_____. 1961. *The economy of the twentieth century*. Paris: PUF.

_____. 1973. Multinational investments and the analysis of development and integration poles. *Economies et Societes* 24: 831-68.

Personick, Valerie A. 1989. Industry output and employment: A slower trend for the 90s. *Monthly Labor Review*.   U.S. Department of Labor, 112, no. 11 (November): 25-41.

Peterson, George E. 1987. Infrastructure support for industrial policy. In *The state and local industrial policy question*, ed. Harvey A. Goldstein, 95-104. Chicago: American Planning Association.

Piore, Michael, and Charles Sabel. 1984. *The second industrial divide*. New York: Basic Books.

Poe, Robert. 1986. Japan fosters technology strongholds. *High Technology* 6 (June): 64-65.

Porrell, Frank W. 1982. Intermetropolitan migration and quality of life. *Journal of Regional Science* 22: 137-58.

Porter, Michael E. 1990. *The competitive advantage of nations*. New York: The Free Press.

_____. 1991. *The competitive advantage of Massachusetts*. Boston: Monitor Company.

Pottier, Claude. 1987. The location of high technology industries in France. In *The development of high technology industries: An international survey*, ed. Michael J. Breheny and Ronald W. McQuaid, 192-222. London: Croom Helm.

Premus, Robert. 1982. *Location of high technology firms and regional economic development*. Joint Economic Committee. Washington, D.C.: U.S. Government Printing Office.

_____. 1988. US technology policies and their regional effects. *Environment and Planning C: Government and Policy* 6: 441-48.

Prescott, Samuel C. 1954. *When MIT was "Boston Tech": 1861-1916*. Cambridge, Mass.: The Technology Press.

Putka, Gary. 1989. Fading miracle: Massachusetts suffers as its revenues lag and Route 128 falters. *Wall Street Journal* Eastern edition (February 8): A1.

Quinn, James Brian. 1987. The impacts of technology in the services sector. In *Technology and global industry: Companies and nations in the world economy*, ed. Bruce R. Guile and Harvey Brooks, 119-59. Washington, D.C.: National Academy Press.

Rand, Christopher. 1964. *Cambridge USA: Hub of a new world*. New York: Oxford University Press.

Rees, John. 1979. Regional industrial shifts in the U.S. and the internal generation of manufacturing in growth centers of the Southwest. In *Interregional move-ments and regional growth*, ed. W. Wheaton. Washington, D.C.: Urban Institute.

_____. 1981. The impact of defense spending on regional industrial change in the United States. In *Federal and regional development*, ed. G. W. Hoffman, 193-222. Austin, Texas: University of Texas Press.

_____. 1989. Regional development and policy. *Progress in Human Geography* 13: 576-88.

Rees, John, and R. Bradley. 1988. State science policy and economic development in the United States: A critical perspective. *Environment and Planning A* 20: 999-1012.

Rees, John, and Howard Stafford. 1984. High-technology location and regional economic development: The theoretical base. In *Technology, innovation and regional economic development*, U.S. Congress, Appendix A, 97-107. Washington, D.C.: Office of Technology Assessment.

Reich, Leonard S. 1985. *The making of American industrial research: Science and business at G.E. and Bell, 1876-1926*. Cambridge, England: Cambridge University Press.

Rietveld, Piet. 1989. Infrastructure and regional development: A survey of multi-regional economic models. *Annals of Regional Science* 23: 255-74.

Rifkin, Glenn, and George Harrar. 1988. *The ultimate entrepreneur: The story of Ken Olsen and Digital Equipment Corporation*. Chicago: Contemporary Books.

Robinson, Sue. 1985. WA switches from tonnages to technology mentality. *Business Review Weekly* 58: 74-77.

Rogers, Everett M., and Judith K. Larsen. 1984. *Silicon Valley fever: Growth of high-technology culture*. New York: Basic Books.

Ronayne, Jarlath. 1987. Technology, the market and government intervention. In *The spatial impact of technological change*, ed. John F. Brotchie, Peter Hall, and Peter W. Newton, 331-342. New York: Croom Helm.

Rosenberg, Nathan C. 1972. *Technology and American economic growth*. New York: Harper and Row.

_____. 1982. *Inside the black box: Technology and economics*. Cambridge, England: Cambridge University Press.

Rosenberg, Ronald. 1991. The red ink never stopped flowing. *Boston Globe* (June 11): 76.

Rosenfeld, Stuart A. 1987. Education, training and industrial policy. In *The state and local industrial policy question*, ed. Harvey A. Goldstein, 85-94. Chicago: American Planning Association.

Rosengren, Eric S. 1990. How diversified is New England? *New England Economic Review* (November/December): 4-16.

Rothwell, Roy, and W. Zegveld. 1982. *Innovation and the small and medium-sized firm.* London: Frances Pinter.

Rubin, Michael Rogers, and Mary Taylor Huber. 1986. *The knowledge industry in the United States, 1960-1980.* Princeton, N.J.: Princeton University Press.

Ryans, John K., Jr., and William Shanklin. 1988. Implementing a high tech center strategy: The marketing program. In *Creating the technopolis: Linking technology commercialization and economic development,* ed. Raymond W. Smilor, George Kozmetsky, and David V. Gibson, 209-19. Cambridge, Mass: Ballinger Publishing Co.

Saxenian, AnnaLee. 1984. The urban contradictions of Silicon Valley: Regional growth and the restructuring of the semiconductor industry. In *Sunbelt/ snowbelt: Urban development and regional restructuring,* ed. Larry Sawers and Willliam K. Tabb, 163-97, New York: Oxford University Press.

———. 1985a. The genesis of Silicon Valley. In *Silicon landscapes,* ed. Peter Hall and Ann Markusen, 20-34. Boston: Allen and Unwin.

———. 1985b. Silicon Valley and Route 128: Regional prototypes or historic exceptions. In *High technology, space and society,* ed. Manuel Castells, 81-105. Beverly Hills: Sage Publications.

———. 1988. The Cheshire cat's grin: Innovation and regional development in England. *Technology Review* 91: 66-75.

———. 1990. Regional networks and the resurgence of Silicon Valley. *California Management Review* 33: 89-112.

Sayer, Andrew. 1989. Post-Fordism in question. *International Journal of Urban and Regional Research* 13: 666-95.

Sayer, Andrew, and K. Morgan. 1986. The electronics industry and regional development in Britain. In *Technological change, industrial restructuring and regional development,* ed. Ash Amin and John Goddard, 157-87. London: Allen and Unwin.

Schamp, Eike W. 1987. Technology parks and interregional competition in the Federal Republic of Germany. In *New technology and regional development,* ed. Bert van der Knapp and Egbert Wever, 119-36. London: Croom Helm.

Schares, Gail. 1988. 'Silicon Bavaria': The continent's high-tech hot spot. *Business Week* (February 29): 75-76.

Schell, Douglas W. 1983. Entrepreneurial activity: A comparison of three North Carolina communities. In *Frontiers of entrepreneurship research: Proceedings of the annual Babson College Entrepreneurship Research Conference,* 495-518. Wellesley, Mass.: Babson College Center for Entrepreneurial Studies.

Schmandt, Jurgen, Frederick Williams, and Robert H. Wilson (eds.). 1989. *Telecommunications policy and economic development: The new state role.* New York: Praeger.

Schmandt, Jurgen, and Robert Wilson. 1987. *Promoting high-technology industry: Initiatives and policies for state governments.* Boulder, Colo.: Westview.

Schoenberger, Erica. 1986. Competition, competitive strategy, and industrial change: The case of electronic components. *Economic Geography* 62: 321-33.

———. 1988. From Fordism to flexible accumulation: Technology, competitive strategies, and international location. *Environment and Planning D: Society and Space* 6: 245-62.

———. 1989. Some dilemmas of automation: Strategic and operational aspects of technological change in production. *Economic Geography* 65: 232-47.

Schultz, Theodore. 1981. *Investing in people: The economics of population quality.* Berkeley: University of California Press.

Schumpeter, Joseph A. 1934. *The theory of economic development.* Cambridge, Mass.: Harvard University Press.

_____. 1950. *Capitalism, socialism and democracy.* New York: Harper and Row.

_____. 1982. *Business cycles: A theoretical, historical and statistical account of the capitalist process.* New York: McGraw-Hill.

Sciacca, Joe. 1989. Flynn gets technical with budget. *Boston Herald* (July 20): 7.

Scott, Allen J. 1988a. Flexible production systems and regional development: The rise of new industrial spaces in North America and western Europe. *International Journal of Urban and Regional Research* 12: 171-86.

_____. 1988b. *Metropolis: From the division of labor to urban form.* Berkeley: University of California Press.

_____. 1988c. *New industrial spaces: Flexible production organization and regional development in North America and Western Europe.* London: Pion.

Scott, Allen J., and D. P. Angel. 1987. The U.S. semiconductor industry: A locational analysis. *Environment and Planning A* 19: 875-912.

Scott, Allen J., and P. Cooke. 1988. Guest editorial: The new geography and sociology of production. *Environment and Planning D: Society and Space* 6: 241-44.

Scott, Allen J., and E. C. Kwok. 1989. Inter-firm subcontracting and locational agglomeration: A case study of the printed circuits industry in Southern California. *Regional Studies* 23: 405-16.

Scott, Allen J., and Michael Storper. 1987. High technology industry and regional development: A theoretical critique and reconstruction. *International Social Science Journal* 39:215-32.

Scott, Otto J. 1974. *The creative ordeal: The story of Raytheon.* New York: Atheneum.

Sculley, John. 1987. *Odyssey: Pepsi to Apple . . . a journey of adventure, ideas and the future.* New York: Harper & Row.

Segal, Nick S. 1988. The Cambridge phenomenon: Universities, research and local economic development in Great Britain. In *Creating the technopolis: Linking technology commercialization and economic development*, ed. Raymond W. Smilor, George Kozmetsky, and David V. Gibson, 81-90. Cambridge, Mass: Ballinger Publishing Co.

Shapero, Albert. 1985. *Managing professional people.* New York: The Free Press.

Sharp, Margaret. 1990. David, Goliath and the biotechnology business. *OECD Observer* 164: 22-24.

Sheets, Robert G., Stephen Nord, and John J. Phelps. 1987. *The impact of service industries on underemployment in metropolitan economies.* Lexington, Mass.: Lexington Books.

Shimshoni, Daniel. 1971. Regional development and science-based industry. In *Essays in Regional Economics*, ed. John F. Kain and John R. Meyer. Cambridge, Mass.: Harvard University Press.

Silvestri, George, and John Lukasiewicz. 1989. Projections of occupation employment, 1988-2000. *Monthly Labor Review.* U.S. Department of Labor. 112, no. 11 (November): 42-65.

Simon, Jane. 1985. Route 128: How it developed and why it's not likely to be duplicated. *New England Business* (July 1): 15-20.

Simons, Katerina. 1990. New England banks and the Texas experience. *New England Economic Review* (September/October): 55-62.

Singlemann, Joachim. 1978. *From agriculture to services: The transformation of industrial employment.* Beverly Hills: Sage Publications.

Sirbu, Marvin A., Jr., Robert Treitel, Walter Yorsz, and Edward Roberts. 1976. *The formation of a technology oriented complex: Lessons from North American and European experience.* Cambridge, Mass.: MIT Center for Policy Alternatives.

Smilor, Raymond W., David V. Gibson, and George Kozmetsky. 1989. Creating the technopolis: High-technology development in Austin, Texas. *Journal of Business Venturing* 4: 49-67.

Smilor, Raymond W., George Kozmetsky, and David V. Gibson (eds.). 1988a. *Creating the technopolis: Linking technology commercialization and economic development.* Cambridge, Mass: Ballinger Publishing Co.

_____. 1988b. Introduction. In *Creating the technopolis: Linking technology commercialization and economic development,* ed. Raymond W. Smilor, George Kozmetsky, and David V. Gibson, xvii-xxi. Cambridge, Mass.: Ballinger Publishing Co.

_____. 1988c. The Austin/San Antonio Corridor: The dynamics of a developing technopolis. In *Creating the technopolis: Linking technology commercialization and economic development,* ed. Raymond W. Smilor, George Kozmetsky, and David V. Gibson, 145-83. Cambridge, Mass: Ballinger Publishing Co.

Solomon, Julie. 1990. Corporate elite leaving home towns for headquarters in faraway places. *The Wall Street Journal,* Eastern edition (February 21): B1.

Solow, Robert M. 1957. Technical change and the aggregate production function. *Review of Economics and Statistics* 39: 312-20.

Stanback, Thomas M. 1985. The changing fortunes of metropolitan economies. In *High technology, space, and society,* ed. Manuel Castells, 122-42. Beverly Hills: Sage Publications.

_____. 1987. *Computerization and the transformation of employment: Technology and growth in the U.S. economy.* Boulder, Colo.: Westview.

Steed, G. P. F. 1986. Technology policy and entrepreneurial spinoffs. *Journal of Small Business and Entrepreneurship* 4: 26-33.

Stein, Charles. 1991. High technology's promising new wave. *Boston Globe* (June 11): 41, 44.

Stöhr, Walter B. 1986a. Regional innovation complexes. *Papers of the Regional Science Association* 59: 29-44.

_____. 1986b. Towards a framework for evaluating the effects of technology complexes and science parks. *Economia Internazionale* 39: 299-311.

Storper, Michael. 1985. Oligopoly and the product cycle: Essentialism in economic geography. *Economic Geography* 61: 260-82.

Storper, Michael, and Allen J. Scott. 1989. The geographical foundations and social regulation of production complexes. In *The power of geography,* ed. J. Welch and M. Dear, 34-69. Boston: Unwin Hyman.

Storper, Michael, and Richard Walker. 1989. *The capitalist imperative: Territory, technology and industrial growth.* New York: Basil Blackwell.

Sunman, Hilary. 1987. Science parks, technopoles and innovation centres: The European experience. *International Journal of Technology Management* 2: 142-44.

Sweeney, Gerry P. 1985. Innovation is entrepreneur-led. In *Innovation policies: An international perspective,* ed. Gerry P. Sweeney, 80-113, London: Frances Pinter.

_____. 1987. *Innovation, entrepreneurs and regional development.* New York: St. Martin's Press.

Tarcy, Brian. 1991. Where eagles dare. *Boston Business* (January/February): 20-26.

Tarr, Joel A., and Gabriel Dubuy (eds.) 1988. *Technology and the rise of the networked city in Europe and America.* Philadelphia: Temple University Press.

Tatsuno, Sheridan. 1986. *The technopolis strategy: Japan, high technology and the control of the twenty-first century.* New York: Prentice Hall Press.

_____. 1988. Building a Japanese technostate: MITI's technopolis program. In *Creating the technopolis: Linking technology commercialization and economic development,* ed. Raymond W. Smilor, George Kozmetsky and David V. Gibson, 3-21. Cambridge, Mass: Ballinger Publishing Co.

Taylor, Tony. 1985. High technology industry and the development of science parks. In *Silicon Landscapes,* ed. Peter Hall and Ann Markusen, 134-43. Boston: Allen and Unwin.

Thomas, Morgan D. 1975. Growth pole theory, technological change, and regional economic growth. *Papers of the Regional Science Association* 34: 3-25.

Thompson, C. 1987. Definitions of 'high technology' used by state programs in the USA: A study of variation in industrial policy under a federal system. *Environment and Planning C: Government and Policy* 5: 417-31.

_____. 1988. High-technology development and recession: The local experience in the United States, 1980-82. *Economic Development Quarterly* 2: 153-67.

_____. 1989. High-technology theories and public policy. *Environment and Planning C: Government and Policy* 7:121-52.

Thompson, Wilbur R. 1965. *A preface to urban economics.* Baltimore: Johns Hopkins University Press.

Thurow, Lester C. 1970. *Investment in human capital.* Belmont, Calif.: Wadsworth.

_____. 1988. Foreword. In *The Massachusetts miracle: High technology and economic revitalization,* ed. David Lampe, xi-xii. Cambridge, Mass.: MIT Press.

_____. 1990. The end of the post-industrial era. *Business in the Contemporary World* 2: 21-26.

Toda, T. Tsunekazu. 1987. The location of high-technology industry and the technopolis plan in Japan. In *The spatial impact of technological change,* ed. John F. Brotchie, Peter Hall, and Peter W. Newton, 271-83. New York: Croom Helm.

Tyson, Laura D'Andrea, and John Zysman. 1989. Developmental strategy and production innovation in Japan. In *Politics and productivity: The real story of why Japan works,* 59-140. Cambridge, Mass.: Ballinger.

U.S. Congress. 1984. Industrial Competitiveness Act. Committee on Banking, Finance and Urban Affairs. 98th Congress, second session.

Vernon, Raymond. 1966. International investment and international trade in the product cycle. *Quarterly Journal of Economics* 80: 190-207.

_____. 1977. *Storm over multinationals: The real issues.* Cambridge, Mass.: Harvard University Press.

_____. 1979. The product life cycle hypothesis in a new international environment. *Oxford Bulletin of Economics and Statistics* 41: 255-67.

von Thünen, Johann Heinrich. 1966. *Isolated state,* ed. Peter Hall, translated by Carla M. Wartenberg. New York: Pergamon Press.

Walker, Richard A. 1985. Technological determination and determinism: Industrial growth and location. In *High technology, space, and society,* ed. Manuel Castells, 226-64. Beverly Hills: Sage Publications.

Wang, An. 1986. *Lessons: An autobiography.* Reading, Mass.: Addison-Wesley.

Warsh, David. 1988. Decade of slow growth seen for Mass. economy. *Boston Globe* (June 23): 1.

_____. 1989. Some miracles never cease. *Boston Globe Magazine* (May 7): 20-21, 54-55, 67-83.

_____. 1990. The ailing SIC: On rebuilding federal statistics. *Boston Globe* (February 4): A1.

Warshofsky, Fred. 1989. *The chip wars: The battle for the world of tomorow*. New York: Charles Scribner's Sons.

Watanabe, Teresa. 1989. Science park key to Taiwan's growth. *Los Angeles Times* (December 29): D1, D5.

Weber, Alfred. 1929. *Theory of the location of industry*, translated by C. J. Friedrich. Chicago: University of Chicago Press.

Weil, Ulric. 1982. *Information systems in the 80's Products, markets, and vendors*. Englewood Cliffs, N.J.: Prentice-Hall.

Weinstein, Bernard L., and Robert Firestine. 1978. *Regional growth and decline in the United States*. New York: Praeger.

Welter, Therese R. 1988. Pooling in the park: Collaboration works in North Carolina. *Industry Week* 246 (April 4): 26-28.

Westmeyer, Paul. 1985. *A history of American higher education*. Springfield, Ill.: Charles C. Thomas.

Wheaton, William C. (ed.). 1979. *Interregional movements and regional growth*. Washington D.C.: Urban Institute.

Whittington, Dale (ed.). 1985a. *High hopes for high tech: Microelectronics policy in North Carolina*. Chapel Hill: University of North Carolina Press.

_____. 1985b. Preface. In *High hopes for high tech: Microelectronics policy in North Carolina*, ed. Dale Whittington, vii-xvi. Chapel Hill: University of North Carolina Press.

_____. 1985c. Microelectronics policy in North Carolina: An introduction. In *High hopes for high tech: Microelectronics policy in North Carolina*, ed. Dale Whittington, 3-31. Chapel Hill: University of North Carolina Press.

Wigand, Rolf T. 1988. High technology development in the Phoenix area: Taming the desert. In *Creating the technopolis: Linking technology commercialization and economic development*, ed. Raymond W. Smilor, George Kozmetsky, and David V. Gibson, 185-202. Cambridge, Mass: Ballinger Publishing Co.

Wildes, Karl L., and Nilo A. Lindgren. 1985. *A century of electrical engineering and computer science at MIT, 1882-1982*. Cambridge, Mass.: MIT Press.

Williams, Allan M. 1987. *The Western European economy*. London: Hutchinson.

Wilson, John W. 1985. The slumpbusters of Silicon Valley. *Business Week* (October 21): 116D, 116H.

Wilson, Robert H., and Paul E. Teske. 1990. Telecommunications and economic development: The state and local role. *Economic Development Quarterly* 4: 158-74.

Winkler, Matthew, and William Power. 1990. Merrill Lynch, in a new cutback, will slash 3,000 jobs. *Wall Street Journal* Eastern edition (January 15): C1.

Wright, Karen. 1990. The road to the global village. *Scientific American* 262 (March): 83-94.

Wrubel, Robert. 1990. Silicon Valley squirms. *Financial World* (March 20): 58-61.

Wylie, Francis E. 1975. *MIT in perspective*. Toronto: Little Brown.

Zegveld, Walter. 1988. Technology policy under changing socioeconomic conditions. *Environment and Planning C: Government and Policy* 6: 375-81.

Zuboff, Soshana, 1988. *In the age of the smart machine: The future of work and power*. New York: Basic Books.

Index

ABOUT THE AUTHOR

ROBERT W. PREER is a professional journalist who has also served as the director of the Special Committee on Long-range Policy Planning of the Massachusetts state senate. He holds a bachelor's degree from Oberlin College and a master's and doctoral degree from Boston University.